◆ SAIS Papers in Latin American Studies ◆
Sponsored by the Central American and Caribbean Program

Contadora and the Diplomacy of Peace in Central America

Volume I: The United States, Central America, and Contadora

♦ *SAIS Papers in Latin American Studies* ♦

Sponsored by the Central American and Caribbean Program

♦ *Bruce M. Bagley, Series Editor* ♦

Contadora and the Diplomacy of Peace in Central America. Vol. 1: The United States, Central America, and Contadora, edited by Bruce M. Bagley

Contadora and the Diplomacy of Peace in Central America. Vol. 2: The Contadora Process, edited by Bruce M. Bagley

Development Postponed: The Political Economy of Central America in the 1980s, Richard E. Feinberg and Bruce M. Bagley

State and Society in Contemporary Colombia: Beyond the National Front, edited by Bruce M. Bagley, Francisco E. Thoumi, and Juan G. Tokatlian

◆ About the Book and Editor ◆

Contadora—the Central American peace negotiations launched on Contadora Island by Mexico, Venezuela, Colombia, and Panama in 1983—has been the focus of heated polemics in the United States and abroad. Contadora's supporters contend that it represents the only viable alternative to deepening conflict in Central America, which could ultimately produce a direct U.S. military intervention in Nicaragua. Critics of Contadora view the initiative as a collection of unverifiable and unenforceable proposals that could pave the way for the consolidation of a Soviet-Cuban presence and legitimize a Communist regime on the mainland of the Americas, thus irreparably damaging U.S. security interests.

The first of these two volumes examines the evolution of U.S. policy toward Central America and Contadora during the first half of the 1980s in an effort to clarify the nature of the debate over the Contadora process and its potential contributions to regional peace. The contributors define U.S. security interests in Central America and analyze the internal dynamics of the Contadora negotiations as well as Contadora's "fit" with U.S. interests and policies in the region.

Bruce M. Bagley is associate professor of comparative politics and Latin American Studies at the Johns Hopkins University School of Advanced International Studies. He is the co-editor of *Development Postponed: The Political Economy of Central America in the 1980s* (Westview, 1986).

*Published in cooperation with the
Central American and Caribbean Program,
the School of Advanced International Studies,
The Johns Hopkins University*

Contadora and the Diplomacy of Peace in Central America

Volume 1: The United States, Central America, and Contadora

edited by
Bruce M. Bagley

Westview Press / Boulder and London

SAIS Papers in Latin American Studies   CLSI

This Westview softcover edition is printed on acid-free paper and bound in softcovers that carry the highest rating of the National Association of State Textbook Administrators, in consultation with the Association of American Publishers and the Book Manufacturers' Institute.

Published in 1987 in the United States of America by Westview Press, Inc.; Frederick A. Praeger, Publisher; 5500 Central Avenue, Boulder, Colorado 80301

Library of Congress Cataloging-in-Publication Data
Contadora and the diplomacy of peace in Central
   America.
   (SAIS papers in Latin American studies)
   Includes index.
   Contents: v. 1. The United States, Central America,
and Contadora — v. 2. The Contadora process.
   1. Central America—Foreign relations—United
States. 2. United States—Foreign relations—Central
America. 3. Grupo de Contadora. 4. United States—
Foreign relations—1981- . 5. Geopolitics—Central
America. I. Bagley, Bruce Michael. II. Series.
F1436.8.U6C666 1987   327.730728   86-33967
ISBN 0-8133-7335-2 (v. 1)
ISBN 0-8133-7345-X (v. 2)

Composition for this book originated with conversion of the author's word-processor disks. This book was produced without formal editing by the publisher.

Printed and bound in the United States of America

The paper used in this publication meets the requirements of the American National Standard for Permanence of Paper for Printed Library Materials Z39.48-1984.

6   5   4   3   2   1

Contents

Foreword

The Central American and Caribbean Program at the Johns Hopkins University School of Advanced International Studies held a two-day international conference in February 1986 on "The United States, Central America, and Contadora." The purpose of the conference, which drew participants from the United States, Latin America, Western Europe, and Canada, was to "take the pulse" of the negotiating process which began in January 1983 as an effort to find a peaceful solution to the conflicts in Central America.

Colombia, Mexico, Panama, and Venezuela initiated the Contadora process (so-called for the location of the first meeting of the foreign ministers of the four countries—an island off the coast of Panama) in 1983 as a regional peace-searching alternative to halt the escalation of violence in Central America. As the process moved ahead, the original four were joined by a "Support Group" in July 1985 comprised of Argentina, Brazil, Peru, and Uruguay.

As the excellent collection of essays contained in this book will verify, the Contadora process has raised a number of significant issues in U.S. foreign policy in the Western Hemisphere and in the formulation of that policy in Washington. It has brought the United States face-to-face with the major nations of Latin America in a conflict highlighted by sharply different perceptions of U.S. security interests in the region. Contadora has exposed the complexity and difficulty of regional peace-keeping efforts in the hemisphere, particularly when the positions of the United States and Nicaragua seem irreconcilable. Meanwhile, the debate within the Reagan administration over an appropriate U.S. response to Contadora and the issue of Nicaragua has brought the executive branch into direct conflict with Congress.

Initiated on January 8–9, 1983, the obituary for Contadora has been written a number of times; all efforts to kill the peace process have been failures. The process gained increasing coherence, and credibility, throughout 1983 as it produced a series of statements and documents aimed at establishing peace in Central America. In September 1983, a twenty-one point "Document of Objectives" was signed by the four Contadora countries and the five states of Central America. That was followed in January 1984 with the "Norms for Implementation of the Commitments Undertaken in the Document of Objectives." In late 1984, the group promulgated a revised draft of the "Act of Contadora for Peace and Cooperation in Central America." A "Statute of the Verification and Control Mechanisms for Security" emerged in April 1985. Later, at the inauguration of President Alan García in Lima, Peru, in July, the four South American states added their diplomatic weight to the process.

The U.S. reaction to the Contadora process has been ambivalent. That ambivalence is based in the deeply rooted belief of the president and his chief political advisors that a negotiated, verifiable and enforceable peace in Central America is impossible. According to the Reagan administration, the Sandinista regime is not interested in accommodation. Supported by the Soviet Union, ultimately, its goal is to export revolution throughout the region, posing a dire threat to the security interests of the United States in the region. Thus, the United States reluctantly agreed to discussions with the Nicaraguans in 1984 in Manzanillo, Mexico. Simultaneously, Washington participated in the mining of Nicaraguan harbors in blatant violation of international law and sought to increase lethal support for the *contras*. Intermittent meetings between Secretary of State Shultz and President Daniel Ortega have produced little of substance. The efforts of the President's special representatives, Ambassador Harry Shlaudeman (appointed in mid-1984) and Ambassador Phillip Habib (appointed in 1986) have yielded nothing. The appointment of Elliot Abrams as Assistant Secretary of State for Inter-American Affairs in early 1985 confirmed the view of many observers that the administration's half-hearted efforts at negotiations were, at best, a smoke screen to maintain public support for its policy.

To be successful, the Reagan administration's efforts in Central America have required the active participation of the U.S. Congress. Contadora has emerged as part of a complex and often contentious exchange between the executive and legislative branches of the U.S. government. A vote in 1982 to provide support for covert operations for the *contras* ended with another vote in July 1983 to terminate such assistance. Democrats, and a majority of Republicans, were fearful that the escalation of violence in Central America would increasingly require greater U.S. involvement and, ultimately, the use of American troops. Throughout 1984, the Congress wavered. Finally, in July 1985, the House voted in favor of $14 million of non-lethal aid for the *contra* forces. The vote represented the belief by a number of congressmen that the administration has succeeded in winning popular support for aid for the *contra* forces.

Indeed, the actions of the Sandinista regime—such as the visit to Moscow of President Daniel Ortega soon after the positive House vote—made it easier for President Reagan and his advisors to argue that aid was needed to pressure the regime in Managua to democratize, or at least to contain the revolutionary regime within the borders of Nicaragua.

1986 has seen a continuation of the debate. Contadora has remained a vital element in the search for peace. The United States has remained uncommitted, if not increasingly distant from the possibility of a negotiated, political settlement. Indeed, in February 1986, the foreign ministers of Contadora as well as of the Support Group met with Secretary of State Shultz to press for further negotiations. They were unsuccessful.

The conflict in Central America continues. The issue of funding for the *contras* remained one of the most contentious issues in foreign policy since the Vietnam War. Those who opposed aid for the *contras* were branded sympathizers of Marxism or, at best, naive about the destructive goals of revolutionary regimes. Those who supported aid believed it was the only mechanism available to force the Sandinista regime to moderate its course of action—or to eliminate it entirely. A shifting group of legislators sits uneasily in the middle. The votes in the House and the Senate in mid-1986 in favor of $100 million for the *contras* clearly contribute to the constraints of the Contadora process and the escalation of violence in the region.

The essays in this volume seek to sharpen the terms of the debate. The crisis in Central America does not lend itself to simple or simplistic policy responses. While no one denies that vital U.S. security interests are involved, there remain legitimate differences of opinion as to whether only the United States has interests to be protected. The wariness with which the Contadora process is viewed by the Reagan administration indicates that the efforts of Latin America, while crucial to a resolution of the crisis, will not be met with reciprocal efforts by the United States. While a wide variety of opinions are expressed in these essays, all of them stress the importance of a negotiated settlement that respects the national interests of all actors in the effort to restore peace to the region. Moreover, the authors emphasize the importance to the future of the United States in the hemisphere of a nonconflictual resolution of the current standoff. In seeking that ultimate outcome, the Central American and Caribbean Program hopes that the conference results will provide useful background material and policy prescriptions for those responsible for U.S. policy in the region.

Riordan Roett,
Director, Latin American Studies Program
School of Advanced International Studies
The Johns Hopkins University

Introduction

During 1985 and 1986 the debate in the United States over Central America grew to a fevered pitch. The key questions underlying all the sound and the fury concerned the nature of U.S. security interests in the region and the extent of the threats to them, the shape of U.S. policy towards Central America, and the viability of the Contadora peace negotiations as an alternative to unilateral U.S. military action, either covert or overt.

Unfortunately, the heat generated by the public debate in Washington on Central America prevented these questions from being answered with clarity. In an effort to come to grips with these basic issues in a more systematic fashion, the Central American and Caribbean Program (CACP) of The Johns Hopkins University School of Advanced International Studies sponsored a two-day conference on "The United States, Central America, and Contadora," on February 3–4, 1986.

The essays compiled in this volume, along with those contained in a companion volume to be published shortly, were presented at the SAIS Conference. The first volume focuses specifically on the debate in the United States over Central America and Contadora. The second volume explores the views and concerns of the Contadora Four, the Support Group, the Central American nations, other hemispheric actors such as Cuba and Canada, and extra-hemispheric powers such as the Soviet Union and Western Europe.

The present volume is divided into four parts. Part 1 seeks to clarify U.S. security interests in Central America. Margaret Daly Hayes' contribution sets out a general framework for conceptualizing U.S. national security in the context of Central America. Alan L. Sternberger discusses the military dimensions of U.S. security in the region and concludes that a strong U.S. military posture is necessary, although not sufficient, to protect U.S. interests in Central America. Jack Child analyzes Contadora as a confidence-building regime and concludes that U.S. interests in the area could be protected by a verifiable Contadora treaty. Wayne S. Smith rounds out this section with a liberal critique of the Reagan administration's emphasis on military responses to perceived threats to U.S. security in Central America and proposes, instead, a return to Contadora-style diplomacy and negotiations as the best way of safeguarding U.S. interests in the region.

Part 2 reviews the evolution of U.S. foreign policy towards Central America since the triumph of the Sandinista Revolution in Nicaragua in July 1979. William M. Leogrande provides a critical overview of U.S. policy from the Carter through the Reagan administrations. He concludes that Reagan has sought, from the outset, to roll back the Nicaraguan revolution. Richard A. Nuccio examines the difficulties that the Reagan administration has encountered in the U.S. Congress in its efforts to generate a consensus around its approach to Central America. Cynthia Arnson provides a detailed study of the divisions over U.S. policy towards Central America that have erupted in Congress in the 1980s. Roy Gutman analyzes the problems and contradictions inherent in the process of consensus decision making in both Washington and Contadora. In Part 3, Susan Kaufman Purcell provides a review and critique of Contadora from the perspective of the United States.

In Part 4, the concluding section, Bruce M. Bagley summarizes the evolution of the Contadora process and U.S. attitudes towards the peace talks in Central America. He argues that as of mid-1986 Contadora had failed to produce a diplomatic solution acceptable to both the United States and Nicaragua because the Reagan administration has sought not only guarantees that U.S. security interests in the region would be protected but also the recomposition of U.S. hegemony in Central America, including the right to dictate the nature of the political regime in Nicaragua. Because the Sandinista revolutionaries would not accept this latter condition, no Contadora-style accord was possible. He concludes that the impasse in the Contadora negotiating process made an escalation of armed conflict in the region virtually inevitable.

This book is the result of the combined efforts of a number of individuals and institutions. The Central American and Caribbean Program at SAIS is especially grateful to colleagues from co-sponsoring institutions for their financial and intellectual support: Dr. Fernando Cepeda Ulloa of the Centro de Estudios Internacionales (CEI), Universidad de los Andes, Bogota, Colombia; Dr. Wolf Grabendorff from the Instituto de Relaciones Europeo-Latinoamericanas (IRELA), Madrid, Spain; and Dr. Richard A. Nuccio from the Roosevelt Center for American Policy Studies, Washington, D.C. The financial support provided by the Andrew W. Mellon Foundation to the Central American and Caribbean Program that made this project possible is also gratefully acknowledged.

The CACP staff at SAIS deserves our sincere thanks. Mr. Juan G. Tokatlian and Ms. Lilia Ferro-Clérico were involved in the planning of both the conference and the book. Their help was invaluable. Ms. Diane Monash coordinated the entire process with her customary efficiency and aplomb. Ms. Vanessa Cano undertook the tasks of copy editing with professional dispatch and good humor. The opinions expressed in these essays are, of course, those of the individual authors and not of the CACP or SAIS.

Bruce Michael Bagley
Associate Professor of Comparative
Politics and Latin American Studies
School of Advanced International Studies
The Johns Hopkins University
Washington, D.C.
September 1986

Part 1
U.S. Security Interests
in Central America

1

U.S. Security Interests in Central America

Margaret Daly Hayes

DEFINING U.S. SECURITY INTERESTS

Security is a dimension of the United States relations with Latin America that is little understood and frequently maligned. Different studies of U.S. security interests yield many different understandings of what security is with no agreed upon definition of security, of security interest, or of what might constitute threats to security. Dictionary definitions of security include concepts such as "free from fear, care, doubt, anxiety, or danger," or "safe, sure, certain, confident, or undisturbed." The international relations literature is replete with studies of perceptions of threat to security, but does not define what constitutes a state of security.

In Hans Morgenthau's writings, security is mentioned only in the context of "collective security," "disarmament," or "policing."[1] A recent text entitled *American National Security* suggests that:

> clearly (national security) signifies protection of the nation's people and territories against physical assault and in that narrow sense, is roughly equivalent to the traditionally used term, *defense*. National security, however, has a more extensive meaning than protection from physical harm; it also implies protection, through a variety of means, of vital economic and political interests, the loss of which could threaten fundamental values and the vitality of the state.[2]

Former Secretary of Defense Harold Brown defines national security as "the ability to preserve the nation's physical integrity and territory; to maintain its economic relations with the rest of the world on reasonable terms; to protect its nature, institutions and governance from disruption from outside and to control its borders." In Brown's view, the Soviet

Union's pursuit of its national security goals poses the greatest threat to the United States, but domestic international economic problems, regional instability, and terrorism also figure prominently.[3]

Security is not an absolute, but a matter of degree, and national security is defined only in its most simplistic form as freedom from physical, i.e., military threat. National security also entails defense of economic interests, and promotion of a world order that is compatible with national interests and goals and that is accepting of national values and ideology. Security implies confidence, opportunity and capability in dealing with events. It is the end result of a nation's successful coping with its political, economic and geographic environment. Threats, challenges, crises and routine change all influence the degree of security that a nation perceives itself to enjoy. The more supportive a nation's environment is, the more secure the nation is. The more the environment challenges the nation's physical or managerial capabilities, or is hostile to national goals and interests, the more insecure the nation is. Except in situations of direct military threat, security is a state of mind.

U.S. SECURITY INTERESTS IN CENTRAL AMERICA

In defining U.S. security interests in Latin America, a broad definition of national interest is appropriate. Such a focus gives greater emphasis to the nonmilitary dimensions of security—to the things that contribute to security in the long term rather than those that threaten security.

The United States has a special interest in Latin America as a whole and in Central America and the Caribbean Basin in particular. The special interest derives from geographic proximity, from shared histories and from common ambitions. While the relationships that derive from that special interest are different from the special relationships that the United States has with its European allies or with Japan, the United States also has a special relationship with Latin America.

Given the U.S. special interest in the region, a broad definition of the U.S. national interest in Latin America must include the following considerations:

> It is in the United States national interest that there exist in the hemisphere friendly, prosperous states, with stable responsive governments that permit the free movement of goods and services through the region, that respect the political integrity of their neighbors and that offer no support to the United States global political rivals.[4]

It is in the U.S. interest that these conditions exist in the hemisphere and it is the goal of U.S. policy to see that they are obtained. U.S. security is enhanced to the extent that these goals are achieved.

In establishing policy by which one can pursue the national interest, it is necessary to establish priorities. Any nation's most fundamental interest is to secure its borders against hostile enemies. No Latin American country is likely to attack the United States. However, it has been the United States' historical concern to prevent powers from outside the hemisphere from establishing a base of power or influence within the region. The Monroe Doctrine, the Spanish–American War, contingency planning for defense of the Panama Canal and the development of the inter-American security system in the post World War II climate were all predicated on the goal of preventing powers from outside the hemisphere from establishing a base of power or influence. In the forty years since World War II, concern that revolutionary Marxism associated with the Soviet Union (or Marxism–Leninism) might establish a hostile, ideological foothold in the region has been the key factor influencing U.S. policy in the hemisphere.

Increasingly, it is recognized that preventing what is politically and militarily unacceptable—the hostile foreign ideological base—may well depend on the success with which the United States identifies and pursues policies that strengthen the capabilities of other nations to prevent those unacceptable outcomes. The challenge, as Kissinger noted in 1969, is that the United States is:

> no longer in a position to operate programs globally. It has to encourage them. It can no longer impose its preferred solution; it must seek to evoke it. . . . Our designs can be meaningful only if they generate willing cooperation. We can continue to contribute to defense and positive programs, but we must seek to encourage and not stifle a sense of local responsibility. Our contribution should not be the sole or principal effort, but it should make the difference between success and failure.[5]

U.S. INTEREST IN STABLE, RESPONSIBLE GOVERNMENTS

Political instability anywhere in the world is of concern to the United States for a variety of reasons. Because of the U.S. global commitments, instability in the regions proximate to our own borders, particularly when that instability has ideological overtones, is especially worrisome to the U.S. government. The United States is accustomed to managing its relations with the hemisphere with minimum resources and not worrying about the security of its southern flank. For these and other reasons it is in the United States' interest that Latin American countries be able to manage their own affairs, to cope with and to accommodate change, and to deal more responsibly with their domestic political problems.

In the past, in part because of the limited interest in the region, the United States has focused almost exclusively on the stability of regional governments, forgetting that stability may be a temporary thing if governments do not serve the needs of their societies in some minimal way. Governments must be judged by their accomplishments for their societies. These must include respecting human rights, planning for the political and economic well-being of the population and responding to the demands of a variety of groups. Many, if not most, Latin American governments have been wanting on these essential dimensions of responsibility. Increasingly, the United states recognizes that these failures of government responsibility have contributed to the endemic political instability of the region.

Stability as used here does not mean status quo right-wing dictatorships. It means, again, effective, efficient, responsive governments that are able to cope with the demands of their own populations. It also means political systems that can conduct elections and absorb changes of political leadership through constitutional means and not just by coup or revolution. It means political systems and practices that serve to incorporate all elements of society into the political process. It means in effect, "good government."

U.S. INTEREST IN FRIENDLY RELATIONS
IN THE AMERICAS

It is in the United States' national interest that relations among the nations of the hemisphere and with the United States be friendly. Friendly relations mean cordial relations that facilitate accomplishing mutual goals. They presume a level of confidence and trust among leaders. Having friendly relations does not mean that there are no differences between countries. Too often it is assumed that the United States demands that its Latin American neighbors acquiesce to the U.S. desires. This should not be the case. The United States has friendly relations with its allies in Europe and Japan and yet has important differences with those countries as well. Having friendly relations means keeping differences in perspective.

Friendly relations need have nothing to do with alignment or non-alignment. Factors other than mere labels define the quality of relations between nations. Having friendly relations does mean using normal diplomatic channels to accomplish the business of the bilateral relationship. It means avoiding purposely irritating uses of high rhetoric. Latin American politicians sometimes fail to appreciate how their own use of rhetoric asserting their national independence from the dominant regional power complicates the quality of U.S.-Latin American relations.

U.S. INTEREST IN REGIONAL ECONOMIC PROSPERITY

It is in the United States' national interest that all countries of the Western Hemisphere be prosperous. Latin America's poverty and deprivation are a human tragedy that has direct consequences for the United States. Poverty and income inequality in Latin America and especially in Central America, the Caribbean and Mexico have resulted in large scale, uncontrolled migrations from the region. Regional poverty and income inequality have created fertile ground for the development of political instability, for exploitation by hostile ideologues, and for the emergence of militant opposition groups. The political factors that cause migrations complicate U.S. domestic and foreign policy.

Latin America's economic recession of the early 1980s resulted in hundreds of thousands of dollars of lost income and employment in the United States as purchases from Mexico, Brazil and other large market countries were cut back.

It should be stressed that prosperity does not mean economic activity dominated by U.S. multinational corporations. Latin American governments long ago learned to regulate and control foreign investors for their own purposes.[6] Nor does economic prosperity mean just growth measured by an expanding gross domestic product. It also means distribution of the benefits of growth across the populations and the involvement of that population in the development process. Stable economic growth requires not only access to external markets and sources of hard currency, but also broad-based domestic consumption.

We now recognize that fundamental changes in the domestic economic policies of our neighbors must be undertaken in order to end the cyclical and structural causes of the severe economic problems that they face. Latin American leaders and mainstream economists in those countries and in the multilateral lending institutions also have recognized the limits of import-substituting industrialization. All now have begun to look for ways to develop export markets and to encourage domestic and foreign capital investment in their economies.

U.S. INTEREST IN THE FREE MOVEMENT OF GOODS AND SERVICES

In describing U.S. security interests in the Caribbean Basin, U.S. government spokesmen and academicians like to exhibit a large map of the region with fat arrows pointing out U.S. strategic military and commercial sea lanes. These sea lanes are vital to the United States in the event of global conflict and must be defended. However, even the most pessimistic of future conflict scenarios grants low probability to sustained global conflict. A much more immediate requirement for U.S. security in the region is regional prosperity and growth. Prosperity must be associated with increased commerce throughout the hemisphere. The economies of the Caribbean Basin countries and of many of the South American countries are too small to support the diversity of economic activity necessary to achieve prosperity and competitiveness in the world. Even the larger economies—Mexico, Brazil, Argentina—must trade today as an integral part of efforts to recover economic development momentum.

Finally, the United States has a budgetary interest in Latin American and particularly Caribbean Basin prosperity. The region's dependence on U.S. foreign assistance is a source of both domestic and bilateral contention. Over the past several years the region has taken an increasing share of the diminishing U.S. foreign assistance pie. The countries' dependence on the U.S. dole is a blemish to national pride. Both the United States and countries of the region would benefit from a less dependent relationship.

U.S. INTEREST IN RESPECT FOR POLITICAL INTEGRITY OF BORDERS

On a more political dimension, it is in the United States national interest that the countries of the region respect each others' sovereignty and the political integrity of each other's borders. For the most part, Latin American countries have managed disagreements over border definitions and other classic international disputes well and peacefully. The record for managing subversion is less clear.

The Latin American tradition is one of nonintervention by governments in the affairs of neighbors. Often this posture seems to be extended to cover studied ignorance of the efforts of organized groups to undermine and destabilize governments of the region. From the U.S. perspective, Latin America's broad tolerance for cross-border movements of political organizers of the radical left is a source of concern. U.S. concerns are justified to the extent that the instability caused by such movements affects U.S. domestic and foreign affairs. The effects are often quite direct. When there is instability in the region, the United States is called upon to take sides. The example of El Salvador is illustrative. At the height of the recent Salvadoran crisis, representatives of the Salvadoran center, right and left all came to the United States seeking to establish and exploit constituencies in this country. The U.S. public was ineluctably drawn into and made part of the domestic conflict in El Salvador and that country's domestic political contest became an issue in U.S. domestic politics.

Yet, there is very little that we as a nation can do to resolve the domestic political problems of other countries. As Henry Kissinger argued in the essay cited above:

> The United States is no longer in a position to operate programs globally; it has to encourage them. It can no longer impose its preferred solution; it must seek to evoke it. . . . (Our role is) to contribute to a structure that will foster the initiative of others . . . to encourage and not stifle a sense of local responsibility.[7]

The political problems of Latin American countries must be resolved by the people of those countries themselves. Nevertheless, we are drawn into the political instability of the region. We are drawn into the conflict between countries when the political institutions of those countries are threatened. For these reasons it is in the U.S. interest and in the interest of every country of the region that those institutions be strengthened.

U.S. INTEREST IN THE POLITICAL ALIGNMENT OF ITS NEIGHBORS

Finally, it is in the U.S. national interest that the countries of the region not provide support for or align themselves with the U.S. global political rivals. This, of course, is the key to our current problems with Cuba and Nicaragua in the hemisphere.

The United States is a global power and the global power balance is of vital interest to us. In this sense, the U.S. supports the world status quo. I use that term as it was used by political realists like Hans J. Morgenthau, for whom the "status quo" referred to the distribution of power among nations at any given moment in time. But, I hasten to add, as Morgenthau himself added, the status quo does not refer to the distribution of power within nations. That is to say, the political makeup of individual nations, other things being equal, does not need to concern us.[8] But the political support and alliances that nations might establish with our major rivals, especially hostile rivals, is important and vitally so.

In the context of the global power balance, and from the U.S. perspective, Latin America is a part of East-West competition. A cornerstone of U.S. policy toward the hemisphere has always been that the ideological balance shall not shift against it in this hemisphere. It is useful to reflect on John F. Kennedy's pronouncements in this regard after the 1962 missile crisis. The public record states that Kennedy's understanding of the "agreement" reached with the Soviet Union was that the Soviet Union would withdraw its missiles from Cuba in exchange for a U.S. commitment not to threaten Cuba. The United States in turn would understand that Cuba would not interfere in the politics of the countries of the region. That is, Cuba would not seek to export its revolution, or to aid "brothers in revolution" in the Western Hemisphere.

Of course, most of these understandings were not joined by either the Soviets or the Cubans. Neither was eager to limit its future options in that way. Nevertheless, the principles established in Kennedy's statements—U.S. acceptance of a Marxist Cuba and Cuban nonintervention outside its borders—have remained a cornerstone of U.S. policy toward the region. Critics of recent policy in Central America often have failed to appreciate the singularity and consistency with which those principles have persisted over time and have guided the formulation of attitudes at the highest levels of U.S. government and in the public at large.

A second anecdote of the Kennedy period underscores this posture, and also illustrates the dilemma the United States confronts in dealing with ideology in the hemisphere. The anecdote concerns Kennedy's reflection on possible U.S. policy position following the death of the dictator Trujillo in the Dominican Republic. Arthur M. Schlesinger, Jr., reports in his book on the Kennedy period the Kennedy inner staff's discussions of what might emerge in the untested political system of the Dominican Republic following Trujillo's death. Kennedy noted:

> There are three possibilities . . . in descending order of preference: a decent democratic regime, a continuation of the Trujillo regime, or a Castro regime. We ought to aim at the first, but we really can't renounce the second until we are sure that we can avoid the third.[9]

The foremost issue is that of alignment in foreign policy. Internal political dynamics can be secondary in the U.S. assessment of countries' attitudes toward the global political rivals of the United States. Foreign policy is the element on which a country is judged most strictly. However, it is difficult to envisage a Communist government that does not have an aggressive and pro-Soviet foreign policy. Certainly recent experience provides little encouragement. In 1979 the United States and many other countries wished the Nicaraguan Sandinistas well in their efforts to bring a better quality of life in Nicaragua. As the Sandinistas have moved more toward Cuba, the Soviet Union and its Eastern bloc allies, increasingly U.S. government policy and U.S. public opinion have turned against the Nicaraguan regime. In Grenada, in spite of Maurice Bishop's possible desire for a warming of relations with the United States, other colleagues were uncomfortable with the proposition and ultimately disposed of him to have their way. Even while Bishop was asking for more lenience on the part of the United States, Grenada was voting in the United Nations in support of the Soviet invasion of Afghanistan, an issue on which only the hardest line Soviet bloc countries cast their votes with the Soviet Union. Captured papers of the Bishop government show a strong commitment to establishing a Marxist-Leninist regime in Grenada.[10]

PROMOTING U.S. INTERESTS IN CENTRAL AMERICA

Over the past five years, the United States has followed a policy in Central America that dovetails neatly with the framework presented above. The key goals of U.S. policy have been to prevent the occurrence of a Marxist-Leninist regime on the isthmus; to constrain the efforts of elements in Nicaragua to export their ideology elsewhere in the region; to promote the emergence of more responsible and stable governments so that they may better resist insurgents and to foster economic recovery in the region. The record of policy success in most countries is good. El Salvador and Guatemala have both survived serious threats from insurgencies as well as the temptations of military leaders to preempt democratic process—each in taking the first steps in implementing a more effective democratic process. Honduras has been spared an insurgency, but it has successfully managed its own political transition, solidifying, to date, civilian control over its political system. All three countries have taken important steps to restart economic activity in the region.

U.S. policy towards Nicaragua has been less successful. While Sandinista activities in support of cross-border insurgencies may have diminished, their apparent ideological commitments have not waned. Internal controls are tighter than ever and a very substantial segment of moderate political leaders has left the country. The options for turning the course of the Sandinista revolution seem significantly reduced today. At the same time, the Sandinistas have exhausted the majority of support they enjoyed in the international community which today recognizes them as being committed to the Marxist-Leninist road. The Sandinistas' options are also reduced.

The Contadora peace process began in 1983 as an effort to forestall an imagined U.S. invasion of the Central American mainland. Fears of invasions were, at the time, a misreading of U.S. high rhetoric which was intended to "worry" the Sandinistas. The Contadora process became bogged down by a number of factors: the complexities of Central American countries' concerns for their own security; the political aspirations of one and another of the Contadora countries themselves; the intransigence of various parties affected by the process (including the United States);

the essential timidity of the countries involved; and the countries' own early ignorance of the complexity of the Central American conflict.

Early on, the Contadora countries recognized that the Central American conflict was rooted in political, economic and military circumstances. In its document of objectives, Contadora recognized that the political roots of the crisis lay in the weakness of political institutions, lack of access to the political process for the majority of peoples, and the need for reconciliation among parties disaffected by the recent struggles. The formulas recommended were democratic processes and elections. The document of objectives also recognized that the long-term problem of Central America was economic and urged the revitalization of the region's economy, the reemergence of institutions for regional integration, and domestic policies that would promote better distribution of incomes.

On the military side, the document recognized that the escalation of arms within the region presented threats to neighbors, that insurgents trained or given hospitality in one country were threatening the political being of nations in the region, and so forth. Public attention has focused on the military dimensions of the problem and the recommended solutions have focused on removing trainers and advisors, policing borders, etc. But the key to regional peace remains political—the permanence in frontier countries of armed insurgents determined to overthrow existing governments in the region. Honduras is the unwilling host to insurgent forces from both El Salvador and Nicaragua. Costa Rica cannot remove Nicaraguan *contras* from its territory. Until some form of political reconciliation permits the majority of insurgents to return home to practice a normal political life, there cannot be peace in Central America. The difficult task that Contadora must achieve is to alter the domestic policies of the Central American governments and then to reconcile the fears each has of the others. Everyone, including the United States and the Sandinistas, will ultimately have to compromise.

The objectives of Contadora, as outlined in several documents, are not inconsistent with U.S. interests. Those objectives, interpreted and implemented strictly, would be sufficient to support U.S. security concerns. That is to say, a strictly interpreted position by Contadora that required pluralism, rejected support for subversives and insurgencies, and that was committed to taking action in the event of contrary trends, would be consistent with U.S. interests. The chief U.S. concern in Contadora has been that a less than strict interpretation would ensue, leaving the countries of the region vulnerable and the United States no better off than if there were no Contadora process.

NOTES

1. Morgenthau, Hans J., *Politics Among Nations: The Struggle for Power and Peace* (Fifth Edition, New York: Alfred A. Knopf, 1973).

2. Jordan, Amos A., and Taylor, William J., Jr., *American National Security Policy and Process* (Baltimore, MD: Johns Hopkins University Press, 1981).

3. Brown, Harold, *Thinking About National Security: Defense and Foreign Policy in a Dangerous World* (Boulder, CO: Westview Press, 1983).

4. Hayes, Margaret Daly, "United States Policy Toward Latin America: A Prospectus," in Jack Child ed., *Conflict in Central America: Approaches to Peace and Security* (London: C. Hurst and Company for the International Peace Academy, 1986).

5. Kissinger, Henry A. "On the National Interest," in *American Foreign Policy* (Expanded edition, New York: W. W. Norton, 1973).

6. Latin American governments have been so successful in regulating the activities of multinationals that the region has ceased to be an especially desirable place for investment. See Council of the Americas, "Debt, Economic Crisis and United States Corporations in Latin America," (mimeo, 1984).

7. Kissinger, *op. cit.*

8. Morgenthau, *op. cit.*

9. Schlesinger, Arthur M., *A Thousand Days* (Boston: Houghton Mifflin, 1968).

10. Valenta, Jiri, and Ellison, H. J., *Grenada and Soviet Cuban Policy: Internal Crisis and U.S./OECS Intervention* (Boulder, CO: Westview, 1985) and Valenta, Jiri and Virginia, "Leninism in Grenada," in *Problems in Communism* (July-August 1984), pp. 1–23.

2

U.S. Security and Central America: Why Be So Concerned?

Alan L. Sternberger

The course of U.S. involvement in Central America over the last century has frequently been steered toward military intervention based on loosely described security interests and vague threats. Although the current Central American imbroglio appears to have no easily discernable political solutions, it is possible to establish a fairly clear idea of the security interests involved and the forces threatening to those interests. Focusing this discussion on the questions of U.S. security interests in Central America, the capabilities of regional militaries to control a regional threat, and the proper level of U.S. military response will provide a better understanding of the limits of the security-threat argument.

U.S. SECURITY INTERESTS

U.S. strategic interests in Central America revolve around the security of the strategic southern flank—the Caribbean Basin. Soviet behavior in the region indicates the Soviet Union is seeking targets of opportunity within this area, and if this pattern continues, adverse regional developments could erode the security posture of the United States. Consequently, U.S. security is linked to preventing a consolidation of hostile regimes in Central America that could threaten maintenance of secure lines of communication through the Caribbean Basin and free access to strategic raw resources—primarily oil and natural gas.

The Secretary of Defense has made U.S. vital interests very clear in formulating security policy guidance. In his annual report before Congress,

Secretary Weinberger stressed the strategic importance of Central America and the Caribbean Basin:

> In this area, the primary U.S. objective is to maintain the security of the North American continent and the contiguous Caribbean Basin, and to create a security environment conducive to Democracy. The proximity of Central America and the Caribbean, and our close ties of culture, kinship and trade make the security of this area of paramount importance not only to our own territorial security but also to U.S. interests in other regions. . . . Our task is to help our neighbors address their underlying problems, while countering and ultimately reversing Soviet and Cuban expansion. U.S. policy supports the growth of democratic institutions, economic development, the achievement of regional solutions to problems through diplomatic negotiation, and the enhancement of security assistance so that the democratic and democratically inclined nations of this region can help themselves to survive.[1]

His emphasis is on the protection of the U.S. security interests by a policy of ensuring free access to the Panama Canal, ensuring free access to sea lanes, air corridors and trade routes, reversing the trend of Soviet and Cuban expansion in the region, neutralizing the destabilizing effect of a disproportionately militarized Nicaragua, supporting democratic and economic development in the region, achieving regional solutions to problems through diplomatic negotiations, and increasing security assistance where needed.

Why is U.S. policy so concerned with ensuring the security of the Caribbean Basin? The following points illustrate the strategic importance of this area:

- Two-thirds of the crude oil imported by the United States and many strategic minerals pass through the Panama Canal and/or the Caribbean;
- The oil refineries and tanker port facilities in the region are among the largest in the world;
- The Panama Canal and pipeline transport 45 percent of Alaskan crude oil to those refineries;
- U.S. gulf ports and Caribbean shipping lanes handle almost half of the foreign trade tonnage entering and leaving the United States;
- The countries and islands of the Caribbean Basin occupy strategic locations due to their proximity to the sea and air lines of communications;
- All the nations of this hemisphere make constant use of these sea and air lines.[2]

The traditional security of the southern perimeter of the United States has allowed U.S. policymakers, particularly in the postwar period, the flexibility to respond to crises worldwide. This proliferation of U.S. interests makes it a strategic imperative that the United States prevent threats from arising in Central America that would require the diversion of military and other resources, to the detriment of U.S. strength and flexibility elsewhere.[3]

The classic example used to explain the vulnerability of United States security to developments in the Caribbean is the case of NATO reenforcement and resupply during a conventional conflict. In this situation, more than half of the U.S. effort would use the Caribbean sea lines of communications. These shipments would include food, fuel, and troops and would all be vulnerable to attack from submarine, cruise missile patrol boats, and attack aircraft operating from Cuban or other Caribbean bases. To counter this threat, an increased number of valuable naval, air, and ground assets must be dedicated to securing free transit through the Caribbean.

The conventional war example has its greatest utility in describing the vulnerabilities of U.S. security policy in the region by providing a baseline for quickly assessing the nuances of that policy; a much more immediate example with similar impact on U.S. security interest/policy is the spread of low-intensity conflict in the region. Many of the strategies outlined by the Secretary of Defense are aimed at countering this threat:

- Reverse Soviet, Cuban, and Nicaraguan gains in the hemisphere and counter Soviet-, Cuban-, and Nicaraguan-supported insurgency, terrorism, and military and political influence and destabilization efforts in the region.
- Maintain access to, and acquire as needed, upgraded base and support facilities and operating transit and overflight rights for defense of Caribbean and South Atlantic lines of communication and U.S. security efforts in Central America. Continue to provide and improve command and control facility infrastructure throughout the hemisphere.
- Initiate actions with governments in the region to strengthen bilateral security links, including new status arrangements as needed.
- Urge key allies to contribute to the security of the Caribbean Basin by providing military and economic assistance to less-developed countries and threatened states in the region.
- Maintain access to strategic raw materials, including energy sources and processing facilities.
- Support collective actions through U.S. government encouragement of interregional cooperation, rationalization, standardization, and

interoperability to include appropriate development of low technology defense industries.[4]

In defense planning terms, an increased focus of finite resources toward defense of the perimeter of the United States means fewer resources are available to defend the established interests of the United States and her allies worldwide.

The armed forces of Cuba and Nicaragua are disproportionate in manning and equipment when compared to the other Central American nations (Tables 1-6) and consequently represent a threat to the stability of the region.[5] Critics of the strategic southern flank argument point out that the large military establishments of Cuba and Nicaragua would soon collapse if these countries were cut off from the support of their Soviet sponsor. This argument assumes the dedication of assets to blockade these countries and the initiation of offensive operations within the region and says nothing about the impact of this redirection of assets on the U.S. ability to support actions in defense of established interests worldwide.

REGIONAL THREAT ASSESSMENT

Debate over an appropriate Central American policy has become polarized over differing perceptions of the roots of the current crisis. Some say the causes are indigenous, others claim they were imposed from the outside. What makes development of a successful Central American/ Caribbean Basin policy complex is that both positions are correct. As Castro found out during the Cuban regional adventurism of the 1960s, revolutions cannot be exported. The current crisis has its roots in a regional pattern of poverty, exploitation, repression, and an increasing disparity in the distribution of land and income. These are the objective factors that exist in Central America and fuel the hate and fear which lead to political polarization and radicalization. These factors must be dealt with in any effective policy to stabilize the region and secure the strategic southern flank—the strategic backyard of the United States. It is equally important to understand that the Soviets and Cubans also recognize the root issues fueling instability in Central America and have a vested interest in both exploiting that instability and increasing the intensity of that instability to the detriment of U.S. security interests.

Three related sources of serious threat to U.S. security interests are developing in Central America and the Caribbean Basin: first, Moscow's perception of the geopolitical/geoeconomic advantages of weakening the U.S. position of primacy in the Caribbean Basin; secondly, development of a hostile military alignment between Nicaragua and Cuba that further

TABLE 1
MILITARY FORCES AND EQUIPMENT

CUBA
Total Strength: 297,000
Military Service: Conscription

GROUND FORCES
Total Strength: 265,000

Units
10 Active Divisions (1 armor/9 mech infantry)
13 Reserve Divisions (6 mech infantry/7 infantry)
14 Independent Brigades/Regiments (tank/field
    artillery/assault/air defense)

Equipment
900 Mortars: 81 mm, 82mm, 120mm, 160mm
3000 RPG-2/RPG-7
120 Recoilless Rifles 75mm/82mm
450 Antitank Guided Missiles
1400 Air Defense Artillery Pieces
340+ Air Defense Missile Launchers
1450 Field Artillery Pieces
900 Medium Tanks: T-34, T-54/55, T-62
80   Light Amphibious Tanks: PT-76
20   Heavy Tanks: JS-2/3
800 Armored Personnel Carriers
Various Surface to Surface Rocket and Missile Systems

NAVY
Total Strength: 18,500

Equipment
3   Foxtrot Diesel Attack Submarines
2   Koni Frigates
2   Medium Amphibious Landing Ships
6   Amphibious Assault Craft
22   Missile Attack Patrol Boats

Table 1 (Continued)

75   Coastal Patrol Craft
13   Mine Warfare Craft
4   ASW Helicopters

AIR FORCE
Total Strength: 13,500

Units
6   All Weather Fighter Squadrons
3   Day Fighter Squadrons
1   Reconnaissance/Fighter Squadron
5   Helicopter Squadrons
2   Transport Squadrons

Equipment
39   MiG-23 Fighter aircraft
184 MiG-21 Fighter aircraft
12   Mi-24 Attack helicopters
55   Mi-8   Assault helicopters
24   An-26 Transport aircraft

Paramilitary Forces
Militarized Security Forces: 83,000

Source: Janes Defense Weekly

TABLE 2
MILITARY FORCES AND EQUIPMENT

NICARAGUA
Total Armed Forces: 61,800
Military Service: Conscription

ARMY
Total Strength: 60,000
(including 12,000 reserves)

Units
1 motorized infantry brigade
5 armored battalions
10 infantry battalions
3 counterinsurgency battalions
1 field artillery battalion
1 engineer battalion
1 antiaircraft artillery group

Equipment

3	M-4A3, 110+ T-54/55 main battle tanks
30	PT-76 light tanks
20	BRDM-2, 20 Staghound armored cars
200+	BTR-40/60/152 APC's
30	M-1942 76mm guns
3	105mm, 48 122mm howitzers
24	152mm howitzers
24	BM-21 122mm rocket launchers
24	120mm mortars
	73mm recoilless launchers
48	ZIS-2 57mm antiaircraft guns
300+	SA-7 SAM's

NAVY
Total Strength: 1,000

Table 2 (Continued)

Equipment
4   Dabur Class, 2 French
1   Seward, 8 other patrol craft
3   Soviet Zhuk, 2 N Korean Kimjin,
      2 N Korean Sinhung Patrol boats
2   Soviet Yevgenya inshore minesweepers
4   Polish K-8 minesweepers
1   ex-U.S. LCM-6 class

AIR FORCE
Total Strength: 2,000

Units
1 counterinsurgency squadron
1 transport squadron
1 helicopter squadron

Equipment
3   TA-33A, 3 T-28D#
4   SF-260 Warriors
1   C-212 A
1   Arava
4   C-47 Skymasters
2   AN-26 medium transports
8   AN-2 transports
1   Falcon 20
2   OH-6 A, 2 Allouette III
6   MI-24 Hind D, 12+ Mi-8 Hip helicopters

Paramilitary Force
Border Guard: 4,000
Civilian Militia: 40,000

Source: Journal of Defense and Diplomacy/
November-December 85

TABLE 3
MILITARY FORCES AND EQUIPMENT

EL SALVADOR
Total Strength: 41,650
Military Service: Conscription

ARMY
Total Strength: 39,000

Units
4 infantry brigades
1 mechanized calvary regiment
1 artillery brigade
14 independent infantry battalions
1 engineer battalion
1 antiaircraft battalion
1 parachute battalion
3 special forces battalions

Equipment
12   AMX-13 light tanks
18   AML 90 armored cars
10   M 113 armored personnel carriers
20   UR-416 personnel carriers
30   M 110
6   105mm field howitzers
6   155mm howitzers
81   mm mortar
8   120 mm mortars
M-18 57mm, M-20 75mm recoilless launchers
LAW Rocket launchers
20mm, 40mm antiaircraft guns

NAVY
Total Strength: 300

Equipment
4   Patrol boats: 3 Camcraft, 1 Sewart

Table 3 (Continued)

AIR FORCE
Total Strength: 2,350

Units
2 fighter/ground attack squadrons
1 light counterinsurgency squadron
1 reconnaissance unit
1 transport squadron
2 helicopter squadrons

Equipment
11	Ouragan
18	Super Mystere B-2
7	Magister
17	A-37
6	O-2
5	C-47 Skymasters
2	DC-6 B
5	Arava
2	C-123K Providers
9	UH-1H Iroquois
3	SA-315 Lama
2	Allouette III
3	T-34, 8 T-6, 6 T-41
3	CM-170 Magister

Source: Journal of Defense and Diplomacy/
November-December 85

TABLE 4
MILITARY FORCES AND EQUIPMENT

GUATEMALA
Total Strength: 40,000
Military Service: Conscription

ARMY
Total Strength: 38,000

Units
4 regional brigade headquarters
1 armored battalion
17 infantry battalions
4 field artillery groups
1 antiaircraft group
1 engineer battalion
4 reconnaissance squadrons
1 presidential guard brigade
1 special forces brigade

Equipment
25   light tanks
24   armored cars
22   armored personnel carriers
12   75mm pack howitzers
36   105mm mortars
81   mm mortars
12   105mm howitzers
12   120mm mortars
12   40mm antiaircraft guns

NAVY
Total Strength: 1,000

Equipment
2   Broadsword coastal patrol craft
5   U.S. Cutlass coastal patrol craft
3   other coastal patrol craft

Table 4 (Continued)

1	ex-U.S. LCM-6 type
2	Machete class troop carrier
30	river patrol craft

AIR FORCE
Total Strength: 1,000

Units
1 counterinsurgency squadron
1 transport squadron
1 communication squadron
1 helicopter squadron

Equipment

10	A-37 B
6	PC-7 Turbotrainers
1	DC-6 B
10	C-47 Skymasters
8	Arava
2	U-206 C
9	UH-1D Iroquois
9	light helicopters
41	light aircraft

Source: Journal of Defense and Diplomacy/
November-December 85

TABLE 5
MILITARY FORCES AND EQUIPMENT

HONDURAS
Total Strength: 17,200
Military Service: Conscription

ARMY
Total Strength: 15,500

Units
1 infantry brigade
1 presidential guard
3 infantry battalions
3 artillery battalions
1 engineer battalion
1 special forces battalion

Equipment
16   Scorpion light tanks
12   reconnaissance vehicles
75   mm pack howitzers
24   105mm howitzers
30   120mm mortars
106 mm recoilless launchers

NAVY
Total Strength: 500

Equipment
3   Swift class fast patrol craft
5   Swift class coastal patrol craft
1   ex-Holylock class
1   hydrographic launch

Table 5 (Continued)

AIR FORCE
Total Strength: 1,200

Units
1 fighter/ground attack squadron
1 counterinsurgency squadron
1 transport squadron
1 support squadron
1 helicopter squadron

Equipment

1	Super Mystere B2
12	F-86E Sabres
10	A-37B
4	Tucano
10	C-47 Skymasters
2	Arava, 1 Electra
1	Westwind
18	helicopters
19	light aircraft

Source: Journal of Defense and Diplomacy/
November-December 85

TABLE 6
MILITARY FORCES AND EQUIPMENT

BELIZE AND COSTA RICA

BELIZE

ARMY
Total Strength: 750

Unit
1 infantry battalion

NAVY
Total Strength: 50

Equipment:
1 coastal patrol craft

BRITISH CONTINGENT

ARMY
Total Strength: 1,200

Units
1 infantry battalion
1 armed reconnaissance troop
1 field artillery battery
1 light air defense troop
1 engineer squadron
1 helicopter flight

NAVY

Equipment
1 destroyer/frigate

Table 6 (Continued)

AIR FORCE
Total Strength: 200

Unit
1 flight
1 air defense detachment

Equipment
4   Harrier
4   Puma helicopters
Rapier missiles

COSTA RICA

Paramilitary Forces
Total Strength: 8,000

Equipment
1   armored car
3   helicopters
6   81mm mortars
5   patrol craft
1   armed tug

Source: Journal of Defense and Diplomacy/
November-December 85

complicates U.S. defense planning; and finally, the spread of low-intensity conflict within the region by means of guerrilla warfare, terrorism, government repression, and border conflict.

GEOPOLITICAL AND GEOECONOMIC MOTIVATION

A recent article attempts to explain Moscow's motivation to become involved in the developments in the Caribbean Basin in terms of geopolitical analysis. The Mackinder-Spykman geopolitical model[6] is used in this explanation. Accordingly, the Soviet Union is described as the landlocked "Heartland" power in competition with the United States as the "Insular" power for global conflict. "Global control" equates here to a primacy of influence within the "World-Island" which Mackinder describes in the U.S./Soviet example as the Eurasian-African landmasses.[7] Several "Rimlands" (Europe, the Middle East, the Indian Ocean littoral, East and Southeast Asia) lie between the Heartland and the "Outer Crescent"—the latter being comprised of the Insular power of the "New World" and other offshore continents and islands.[8] The competition for global control is therefore a competition between the Soviet Union (Heartland power) and the U.S. (Insular power) for control of these Rimlands.

Within this competition the Insular power (the U.S.) has three tasks: to ensure that the Heartland power (the Soviet Union) does not manipulate itself into a position from which it can exercise control over the Eurasian-African World-Island, to maintain the requisite balance of power to ensure the defensibility of the Rimland dike, and to ensure that the lines of communication linking itself to these dikes are perpetually kept open for political, economic, and military reasons. The objective of the Heartland power (Soviet Union) is to control the Eurasian World-Island by establishing primacy over the Rimlands, thus isolating the Insular power (U.S.) and the Outer Crescent as a whole from access to influence and natural resources within the World-Island. If World-Island hegemony were to be achieved, the inherent advantages of the Heartland power (Soviet Union)—geographic location, manpower, and natural resources— could be used to develop effective political and economic weapons that would eventually force the Outer Crescent to come to an accommodation with the Heartland power (Soviet Union) for access to World-Island markets and resources and eventually result in Heartland power (Soviet Union) global domination. End game.

Within this model, the Rimlands of Europe and the Middle East are of particular importance since these are areas where the U.S. has considerable political and economic investment and would provide a secure bridgehead into Africa for Soviet political, economic, and military expansion. In both geopolitical and geoeconomic terms the loss of U.S. access to either the markets, natural resources, or military basing rights within either of these areas would seriously affect the global balance in favor of the Soviet Union. Establishing Soviet primacy in these areas, whether by a process of gradual diplomatic and economic initiatives or through the graduated support of low-intensity conflicts thus becomes a Soviet strategic priority.[9] U.S. political, economic, and security commitments in these areas are closely linked to the use of seapower. Securing lines of communication linked to seapower is of necessity dependent upon secure logistic capabilities for resupply and reenforcement. The ability to deny that logistic capability and therefore threaten those lines of communication would put into question U.S. capabilities to meet its political, economic, and security commitments to these Rimland areas: that is, the nation's ability to defend the established interests of the United States and its allies worldwide. It is in this context that Central America takes on particular importance.

RISING SOVIET INTEREST

The Soviets have been and remain reluctant to become overtly involved in the politics of Central America and the Caribbean Basin. Although they presided over the creation of some seventeen Communist parties throughout Latin America between 1918 and 1950,[10] Soviet foreign policy logically appears to have been much more absorbed with developing Soviet interests within Europe and the Middle East and controlling China than with expanding Soviet influence into an area accurately understood to be the "strategic backyard" of the United States.[11] Soviet interest in the Caribbean Basin (and in Latin America as a whole) has traditionally recognized the limits of their involvement based upon:

- the complexity of relationships within the region between diverse structures including moderate regimes (such as Mexico and Venezuela), leftist regimes (like Cuba and Nicaragua), local Communist parties, Trotskyite and Maoist groups, radical and moderate military dictatorships, and leftist guerrillas who may or may not be amenable to communization, and
- the tacit implications of the doctrine of "geographic fatalism" which implied that the U.S. would react strongly to any overt Soviet-Cuban incursion into the "proximate area of (U.S.) geographic influence."[12]

The Soviet perception of these limitations moderated their actions in this region through the period of Cuban adventurism (exportation of revolution) in the 1960s and into the 1970s. During this period the Soviets saw limited advantage to be gained from encouraging armed revolution of the Castro, Guevara, or Debray genre in an area perceived to be neither capitalist nor particularly ripe for wars of national liberation. An established U.S. economic, corporate, and military presence in Central America and the Caribbean Basin supported by ongoing aid, development, and military assistance programs combined with the increasing faction-alization of regional interests convinced Soviet planners that the Cuban initiatives were inappropriate at that time.[13] Strong U.S. response to regional crises—Guatemala (1954, 1963), Cuban Missile Crisis (1962), Dominican Republic (1965), as well as increased U.S. military support to counterinsurgency operations throughout the region—tended to sup-port the Soviet perception of "geographic fatalism" during this period. From the Soviet point of view, any Soviet-Cuban successes within Central America and the Caribbean Basin would be based upon the normalization of diplomatic relations and trade, and exploitation of any resurgence of anti-American sentiment. On the other hand, Moscow recognized the advantages of continuing to support, at least rhetorically, the myriad of leftist political and guerrilla organizations evolving throughout Latin America.[14] Consequently, the Soviets tried to encourage all forces for change without committing themselves to any—a difficult balancing act even for the Soviets. If successful, however, this act had the potential for a superb payoff for Moscow in terms of providing the ability to quickly insert advisors, equipment, trade, and aid into any emerging pro-Soviet or potentially pro-Soviet regime.

U.S. policy shifted in the early to mid-1970s from a policy of activist economic, development, and military support to a policy of benign neglect.[15] This loosening of inter-American relations provided Moscow with an opportunity to exploit the potential gained from balancing normal state-to-state relations with support for more radical movements. The rise of anti-American military regimes in Peru, Panama, Ecuador, and Honduras stimulated Moscow to begin adjusting its regional policies in the early 1970s to take advantage of regimes favorably inclined toward cooperation with the Soviet Union. Latin American Communist parties were instructed to cooperate and lend support to emerging anti-American regimes and to increase their efforts to infiltrate trade unions and other parts of the political mainstream.[16] Moscow, for its part, continued to pursue normalization of diplomatic and trade relations throughout Latin America. Editorials began appearing in *Pravda* touting the ability of "progressive military regimes to aid [the progress of] socialism." Castro, having adjusted his policy on the exportation of armed revolution, began patching up shattered relations with both regional regimes and Communist parties.

The 1970 election of Salvador Allende, at the head of a leftist block, as president of Chile seemed to confirm the accuracy of the Soviet Latin American policy approach. However, after Allende was overthrown by a military coup, evidence began appearing that Moscow was reassessing its position. The same party organs that were praising Allende's peaceful assumption of power in 1970 were, by mid-1974, railing against the Chilean Communist party for not being flexible enough to recognize the need for the use of "revolutionary violence" to "repel the counterrevolutionary violence."[17]

Setbacks in Chile and Uruguay and the rise of right-wing military regimes in Bolivia and Argentina provided the impetus for Latin American leftists to agree with Castro that Latin American socialism could only be achieved through revolutionary war and the adoption of a policy of immediate economic and social transformation. Ruben Darío Souza, secretary-general of the Peoples Party of Panama, expressed this in a January 1975 article in the CPSU organ Kommunist, when he spoke of reaching a turning point in the "liberation" struggle in Latin America and claimed that Latin America had become a "socio-political volcano." That Moscow was leaning toward the support of armed struggle in the region is suggested by the appearance of this article in a prominent CPSU journal.

The Sandinista victory in Nicaragua provided the final proof that convinced the Soviet theoreticians and planners of the viability of armed revolution as an instrument of socioeconomic transformation—at least in the Caribbean Basin. Soviet theoreticians—previously critical of the Castro, Guevara, Debray concept of the efficacy of armed struggle—began to pay deference to Castro-style logic. Latinskaya Amerika and the World Marxist Review commission report on the "Problems in Latin America and the Continent" mirror the shift in Soviet policy in articles that contend that "far from impeding armed struggle, as some petty bourgeois theorists contend with reference to the experience of the 1960's, the present international situation largely predetermines its favorable outcome."[18] This quote effectively summarizes the evolution of Soviet policy from an emphasis on the normalization of relations and trade to an emphasis on the support of radical movements and regimes in an effort to further destabilize the region and weaken U.S. ability to project military and economic power worldwide.

Continued reluctance to become overtly involved in the support of radical revolutionary movements so close to the U.S. strategic backyard has prompted Moscow to move cautiously. Apart from support for loyal Communist parties, expansion of economic aid and trade, insertion of military advisors and equipment to support radical regimes, and occasional KGB attempts at subversion,[19] the Soviets have, in the past decade, relied heavily upon a network of associates and surrogates including East Germany, Czechoslovakia, North Korea, Libya, the PLO, and, of course, Cuba. A variety of services are provided through this network including technical and economic assistance to "progressive" regimes, shipment or transshipment of arms to progressive regimes and to leftist insurgents and terrorists, as well as unconventional warfare, psychological operations, and political training in camps in Czechoslovakia, East Germany, Libya, and Cuba.[20] As a consequence, Moscow now finds itself in an advantaged position with regard to both promoting instability in Central America and the Caribbean Basin and reaping the advantages of that instability.

CUBA AND NICARAGUA: ANOTHER PIECE TO THE PUZZLE

The primary Soviet-Cuban success in the region to date is the Sandinista National Liberation Front's (FSLN) rise to power in Nicaragua. Nicaragua's extensive military buildup, supported by an intricate network of Cuban—and to a lesser extent Soviet and Warsaw Pact—advisors, threatens U.S. regional security interests. Nicaragua provides Moscow with a continental beachhead from which the Cubans and their Sandinista allies can work to erode U.S. military and political influence in the region and weaken U.S. power projection capabilities worldwide. Nicaragua's growing military capability serves to intimidate its neighbors while providing a military shield behind which support can be funnelled to leftist insurgents and subversives operating in El Salvador, Guatemala, Honduras, and Costa Rica. The growing militarization of Cuba and Nicaragua with Soviet and Warsaw Pact arms represents a serious developing threat to U.S. attempts to promote regional stability and inter-American security.

Soviet arms transfers to Cuba in the post-1975 period of Soviet policy adjustment have included an impressive array of modern offensive weaponry including (Table 1 applies) MiG-21 and MiG-23 combat aircraft, T-62 tanks, BM-21 multiple rocket launchers, BMP armored (combat) personnel carriers, ZSU-23-4 SP anti-aircraft guns, MI-24 assault helicopters, SA-2 and SA-6 surface-to-air missiles, Turya missile and torpedo fast attack craft and Zhuk patrol boats, Foxtrot class submarines, Osa/Komar class missile patrol boats, Koni class frigates, and two amphibious landing ships and associated amphibious assault craft capable of landing 1,000 combat troops with tanks or artillery support on regional beaches.[21] Since 1981, Moscow has transferred a record 66,000 tons of military stores annually to Cuba.

The Soviets currently maintain 2,800 military advisors and a ground force brigade of 2,800 troops on the island. In addition, 2,000 Soviet personnel monitor the United States from the intelligence collection site at Lourdes, near Havana. This site is the largest Soviet communications and electronic monitoring site outside the Soviet Union. Soviet access to basing facilities at Cienfuegos provides them with protective submarine pens, advanced surface-to-air missiles, sophisticated electronic intelligence and electronic warfare systems and the protection of MiG-21 and MiG-23 fighter aircraft. The Soviet naval ships visit program—initiated in 1969—has hosted a variety of Soviet naval vessels including cruisers, frigates, destroyers, and nuclear and conventional submarines. The regular presence of Ugra class submarine tenders, with their associated support barges, has prompted U.S. analysts to speculate on the future use of this facility for Soviet SSN replenishment.[22]

The core issue is not the armament of Cuba, but the nature and quality of the weapons used in that armament and the type of military facilities established for Soviet and Cuban use. The bulk of Soviet arms generosity to date has fallen into the realm of high quality power projection and assault weaponry: weaponry more useful in projecting Soviet-Cuban interests over the Caribbean sea lines of communication and supporting regional destabilization than protecting the Cuban island from any perceived regional threat.

The rise of the FSLN in Nicaragua marked a watershed in the developing regional instability. From 1976 onward, Fidel Castro became increasingly involved in supporting the FSLN. By the spring of 1979 Cuba had replaced Venezuela and Panama as the Sandinistas' principal arms supplier and logistic supporter.[23] Castro used his leverage and prestige with the various Sandinista leaders—many of whom he knew personally from the 1960s and 1970s—to forge a United Sandinista National Liberation Front Directorate in March of 1979. Shortly after Somoza's ouster in 1979 more Cuban advisors arrived, joining those who had been covertly supporting the Sandinistas. By late 1981 approximately 600 Cuban military/security advisors had been invited into Nicaragua. Today there are an estimated 3,500 to 4,000 of them.[24] These advisors are essential to the operation of the Nicaraguan military and appear to be essential to the ability of the Nicaraguan military to quickly absorb extensive military hardware transfers.[25] In addition, some 3,000 Cuban civilian advisors assist in efforts to consolidate the Sandinista bureaucracy along Marxist-Leninist lines.[26] The importance of these civilian advisors should not be underestimated for it is these bureaucrats, teachers, technical advisors, police, security, and intelligence personnel who will provide at least the support, if not the design for the future Nicaraguan governmental infrastructure, and Cuba's privileged (and leveraged) position within that infrastructure in the future.

Since 1979, the Sandinistas have embarked on an extensive military buildup. (See Table 2 for Nicaraguan forces and equipment.) This buildup has been supported by arms agreements worth nearly $500 million with

Warsaw Pact countries—primarily the USSR and Bulgaria—and Cuba accounting for 90% of the total. The extent of this military assistance exceeds that provided to any other Central American country including combined U.S. assistance to El Salvador and Honduras. This buildup reflects the Sandinistas' public pronouncements that they will build a military organization capable of defending Nicaragua from any regional threat, while deterring any possible U.S. intervention. The continuing buildup, although defensive in nature, has provided Managua significant capabilities to offensively threaten its neighbors and add a new force to other serious problems facing the region. Additionally, the presence of some 4,000-plus Communist military advisors (primarily Cuban) provides further evidence of a developing Nicaraguan-Cuban "militarized hostile alignment."

Although Moscow has proven the availability of weapons and Havana is providing the support and training infrastructure, a credible "militarized hostile alignment" between Cuba and Nicaragua as described by Gonzalez, Jenkins, Ronfeldt, and Sereseres would take years to fully develop. This kind of an alignment would require the arming of Nicaragua with weapons similar in power projection capability to those of Cuba, as well as providing basing rights and/or basing facilities to the Cubans and Soviets.[27] However, if this alignment were to take place it would threaten U.S. security interests throughout the region. At the very least, such a development would undermine the U.S. economy-of-force principle for the Caribbean Basin, complicate U.S. defense planning for response to incidents elsewhere, and damage perceptions of U.S. power around the world.

The stationing of Soviet or Cuban offensive aircraft or naval vessels in Nicaragua would provide those countries with a capability to greatly augment their regional threat potential and further strain U.S. defense requirements. To say that this hasn't happened yet or to doubt the logic of a concern for this outcome is to deny the prudence of planning or the lessons of history. Aircraft revetments capable of handling high performance fighters have been completed at Puerto Cabezas and Bluefields on the Atlantic coast and the runway at Montlimar on the Pacific coast has been extended, providing Montlimar with the capability to host MiG-type fighters. When completed, a new airfield at Punta Huete will have the 10,000-foot runway necessary to accommodate Soviet jet fighters, Bear reconnaissance and antisubmarine warfare aircraft, heavy transport aircraft, or Backfire bombers.

The Soviets have signed agreements with the Nicaraguans to repair and use the port facilities at San Juan del Sur on the Pacific coast and to develop a major port facility at El Bluff on the Caribbean coast near Bluefields. This facility, scheduled for completion in 1986, will boast a

1,000-foot pier and be capable of handling ships up to 25,000 tons. Since the revolution the Nicaraguans have added over 36 new military installations, all built to Cuban standards.[28]

Critics of U.S. security policy suggest that these developments are a reaction to the strong U.S. anti-Sandinista policy; however, security analysts warn that this pattern of gradual Soviet and Cuban expansion into the governmental infrastructure and the security apparatus of nations weakened by internal struggle is not a new phenomenon. Similar attempts to make weakened nations dependent on Soviet and/or Cuban generosity have been successful (to differing degrees) in Angola, Mozambique, Viet Nam, North Korea, and Yemen—to name a few. If successful in Nicaragua, these developments would open the way for an expanded Soviet and Cuban military presence that effectively severs the hemisphere by potentially hostile military influences, provides a base of operations from which to exploit regional instability, puts free access to the Panama Canal into jeopardy, and threatens U.S. hemispheric and worldwide crisis response capability. Neutralizing this capability after it is established would require a major diversion of U.S. military assets.

REGIONAL STABILITY AND LOW INTENSITY CONFLICT

Low-intensity conflict continues to spread throughout the region in the form of guerrilla warfare, terrorism of the left and right, government repression, and border conflicts. Providing support and assistance to the governments of the region in order to control the spread of these conflicts has become not only a U.S. security interest but increasingly a U.S. security priority. This environment provides fertile ground for Marxist exploitation and the internationalization of local conflicts. Deliberate internationalization of local conflicts serves to bring in the support of like-minded actors—Cuba, the Soviet Union, Libya, the PLO, the Basque Nationalists, the Red Brigades, East Germany, and North Korea. Available evidence indicates that an evolving Cuban-Nicaraguan support structure exists to host the spread of these conflicts.[29]

Throughout the 1960s and 1970s Fidel Castro's success with Cuba held great fascination for young university students in Central America. Castro's mystique attracted many young people to apply for training in Cuba. In Cuba these young people would receive socialist party indoctrination and training in guerrilla warfare. Many of the current leaders of the Sandinista National Liberation Front (FSLN) and the Farabundo Martí National Liberation Front (FMLN) were trained in Cuba during this period. In this way the groundwork, contacts, linkages, and procedures were established that would provide the infrastructure for future insurgent conflicts.

Prior to the unification of El Salvador's FMLN into the Unified Revolutionary Directorate in 1980, the support structure for the Salvadoran insurgency already had been incorporated into the Nicaraguan FSLN party structure in the "Comisión Política" headed by FSLN National Coordinator Bayardo Arce, and the "Comisión Militar," composed of Cuban and Nicaraguan staff officers who worked directly with Salvadoran guerrillas. A supply network was quickly established that followed land, air, and sea routes into El Salvador. Cuba and Nicaragua quickly recognized Honduras as a critical link in that route and worked to expand their operational support network in that country. Today ammunition and logistical support continue to flow to El Salvador by sea aboard Nicaraguan fishing boats and large motorized canoes staged out of Nicaragua's Consigina peninsula, by direct air routes, and by land through supply networks that transit Honduras. Captured FMLN documentation and FMLN defectors verify that over 80% of the support required for the insurgency comes from Nicaragua and Cuba. FMLN guerrillas continue to maintain command and control, training, replenishment, and communications facilities in Nicaragua. The support structure originally established to support the Salvadoran guerrillas and insurgent operations in El Salvador has evolved into a regional structure that has supported Guatemalan insurgents and Honduran and Costa Rican subversives.[30]

El Salvador Insurgency

Prior to 1979, Cuban support to the Salvadoran guerrillas involved training, modest financial aid, and serving as a conduit between Salvadoran extremists and radical groups outside the hemisphere.[31] After the fall of Somoza, Cuba and Nicaragua stepped up support for the Salvadoran guerrillas. In 1980, in an attempt to overthrow the junta and regain its lost political appeal, the Salvadoran guerrillas shifted from terrorism to full scale guerrilla warfare. Havana's first priority and precondition for continuing support was the unification of the guerrilla leadership. This was accomplished in the creation of the Farabundo Martí National Liberation Front and its political body the Democratic Revolutionary Front (FDR).[32]

With unified tactics and operations now possible, Cuban and Nicaraguan specialists began assisting in the organization of military strategies.[33] Hopes of inciting a Nicaraguan-style popular victory were dashed in January 1981 when the FMLN "final offensive" failed to rally popular support behind the insurgents. The FMLN then shifted to a "foco theory" strategy and focused their activities on the countryside in an effort to build larger bases of support and recruitment among the peasantry to shift the military balance decisively in their favor.[34] Salvadoran military success in turning back guerrilla efforts to disrupt the national elections of 1982 deflated guerrilla morale and set the stage for a further expansion of the conflict. With U.S. military and economic assistance beginning to improve the government's capability to counter insurgent advances and realizing that they lacked the popular support to achieve a quick and decisive victory, the guerrillas settled in for a long war of attrition. The FMLN developed a strategy of attacking the economic infrastructure of the country, while negotiating power sharing with the government.[35] A major offensive was launched in the fall of 1983 that resulted in the successful attacks on the military garrison at El Paraíso and the Cuscatlan Bridge. This offensive was not enough, however, and the military was able to secure the March and May 1984 national elections that brought President José Napoleón Duarte and the Christian Democratic Party to power.

The rise of the Duarte government has seriously weakened support for the FMLN. Over the last year we have seen the support for the guerrillas weakened by Duarte's initiatives at the agricultural and credit reform and the initiation of the La Palma talks between the insurgents and the government. A valid argument can be made that, when the FMLN/FDR decided to break off these talks, it seriously weakened their legitimacy in the eyes of the world community and strengthened the position of President Duarte. This is a development that could not have escaped President Duarte's attention—even prior to the initiation of the talks.

EL SALVADOR MILITARY

The Salvadoran military active duty forces (see Table 3) have tripled in size to over 48,950 men since 1979—a development prompted by the Nicaraguan military buildup and in response to the continuing insurgent war.[36] The military has shown its increased capability by maintaining the initiative against Salvadoran insurgents since March of 1984—a development that has prompted the insurgents to return to a campaign of urban terrorism and attacks on the economic infrastructure. Development of a tough, independently capable military force in El Salvador is still several years away and will be impeded by continuing counterinsurgent war.

The final note on El Salvador is that while the FMLN insurgency appears to be reaching a controllable level, the Cuban and Nicaraguan support upon which the insurgents depend will not go away of its own accord. Denying a Salvadoran expansion of the Nicaraguan experience to Cuba and their Soviet mentor will come only with internal evolution of the Salvadoran system that provides solutions to the root causes for unrest. Until that socioeconomic evolution is accomplished, the best that can be hoped for is keeping the insurgency at "a controllable level."

GUATEMALA INSURGENCY[37]

The roots of the current Guatemalan insurgency go back to 1960 when disgruntled army officers, students, and labor groups first joined in a guerrilla warfare against the government. In the wake of the Nicaraguan experience Castro also stepped up his support of the Guatemalan insurgent factions, whom he has aided with arms and training since he has come to power. As with El Salvador, support to the Guatemalan guerrillas was contingent upon the ability of the divided extremist groups to unite and show commitment to armed struggle against the established order, as well as form a unified strategy for that armed struggle.[38] After several previous meetings, representatives of four of the six Guatemalan insurgent groups—Guerrilla Army of the Poor (EGP), Rebel Armed Forces (FAR), Organization of People in Arms (ORPA), and the dissident faction of the Guatemalan Communist Party (PGT/D)—were represented. The 13th of November Revolutionary Movement (MR13), the Revolutionary Movement of the People (MRP), and the traditional faction of the Guatemalan Communist Party (PGT) were not represented. Those in attendance met at the invitation of the Sandinista *commandantes* in Managua to discuss unification. The result of this meeting was the creation of the Guatemalan National Revolutionary Unity (URNG), with a directorate called the General Revolutionary Command. The document creating these organizations was signed in Managua in November 1980. The ceremony was attended by Manuel Piniero Losada—head of Castro's Americas Department—and Ramiro Jesus Abreu Quintana—Americas Department Director for Central America—representing Fidel Castro. After the ceremony, members of the newly formed General Revolutionary Command were flown to Havana to present the document to Castro. Although total unification of the Guatemalan groups had not been achieved, Castro seemed willing to work with what had been accomplished. To date, however, the Guatemalan National Revolutionary Unity has shown itself to be little more than a propaganda shell and strong differences plague insurgent efforts.

A military coup in March 1983 replaced the repressive regime of Lucas Garcia with General Jose Rios Montt. The new military government used offensive military action and an active civil defense program to reverse the tide of the insurgency. Combined with promises of political and economic reform and the return to civilian democratic government (elections took place on 3 November 1985), the Guatemalan regime was able to decrease the guerrillas' peasant support base. These successful efforts have given the advantage in the conflict to the government. As expected, the Guatemalan insurgent groups have also returned to patterns of increased urban terrorist attacks and stepped up attacks against the economic infrastructure to gain the public (and world) attention necessary to obtain support and financing. Reports of increased Cuban and Nicaraguan support to Guatemalan insurgents serve to remind that advantage in an insurgent war changes quickly.

GUATEMALA MILITARY[39]

The Guatemalan active duty armed forces (see Table 4) have expanded significantly over the last two years to an active duty force of 40,000 men. The army, in particular, is a tough, tactically and technically proficient organization proven in small-unit skirmishes and counterinsurgency warfare. The Guatemalans are proud that they have been able to contain their insurgency and expand their armed forces without U.S. assistance. The armed forces, however, continue to experience severe equipment and maintenance problems that limit their overall military capability. Recovering from the effects of prolonged insurgent war will limit the ability of the Guatemalan military to become a major player against any regional military threat.

HONDURAS INSURGENCY[40]

The strategic position of Honduras between Nicaragua and El Salvador has not been lost on the Cubans and Nicaraguans. Historical evidence indicates that Honduran subversive groups received limited training and logistic support from Cuban and Sandinistan sources as early as 1980 and before Nicaraguan anti-Sandinistan insurgent *contras* began their operations from Honduran soil. In late 1983 and again in 1984, some 100 guerrillas, trained in Cuba and Nicaragua, attempted to ignite a popular insurgency. Both efforts failed when many of these guerrillas turned themselves in and assisted the military in locating their former comrades. Evidence from those captured indicates that most of the forces had been trained for nine months inside Cuba at a camp called P-40 run by the Cuban Ministry of the Interior, receiving combat experience fighting *contras* alongside Sandinista units in northern Nicaragua.

While these efforts failed, other subversive groups have been successful in carrying out a number of violent actions including kidnappings of prominent individuals, seizure of the Chamber of Commerce in San Pedro Sula, and numerous bombings in and around major cities. Most of the arms for these operations were brought in from Nicaragua by El Salvador's FMLN. Cuba has consistently supported efforts by the Honduran subversives to form a united front. These efforts finally succeeded in creating the National Unity Directorate of the Revolutionary Movement (DNU-MRH) in March of 1983. Despite these efforts to destabilize Honduras, the Cubans, Nicaraguans, and Salvadoran insurgents have been remarkably unsuccessful to date.

HONDURAS MILITARY[41]

The Honduran active duty military (see Table 5), over 21,600 strong, has increased its emphasis on counterinsurgency and border defense training. The Honduran Air Force maintains local air superiority with its fleet of high-performance fighter aircraft. How long the Hondurans can sustain this advantage is in question as the fighter fleet is rapidly aging and increasingly plagued with maintenance problems that make readiness a major concern. Influenced by continued Nicaraguan incursions across their borders, the Honduran army recently decided to purchase 72 Saladin armored personnel carriers. This purchase will significantly increase the mobility and fire power of the Honduran army.[42] Honduran forces are now capable of containing a modest insurgency. However, due to continuing problems with logistics, communications, training and equipment, the Honduran military could probably defend its territory from only a limited, short-duration attack.

COSTA RICA AND BELIZE[43]

Costa Rica and Belize are not currently faced with insurgent threats. There is increased concern over the presence of anti-Sandinista insurgent forces inside Costa Rican territory along the Nicaraguan-Costa Rican border. Their presence is viewed by many in Costa Rica as representing a serious threat in that they provoke increased Nicaraguan incursions. There are also well-grounded fears that such incursions will lead to increased confrontations between Costa Rican and Nicaraguan forces, as evidenced by last summer's sortie. Costa Rica sees the continuing clashes between Honduran and Nicaraguan armed forces over *contra* staging from Honduran territory as a precursor of similar problems for itself.

Costa Rica has had no standing armed forces and has depended upon its paramilitary civil guard and rural assistance guard (see Table 6) since 1949. It has, however, remained an example of democracy in the region and is now faced with the prospect of reinstituting its armed forces due to the potential of Nicaraguan aggression. Many people in the country feel they are being pressured—particularly by the U.S.—into accepting this buildup. This dissension against the present Costa Rican government could result in political upheaval during the 1986 presidential campaign.

Guatemala still claims two-thirds of the territory of neighboring Belize. The threat is regarded seriously enough that Belize has asked for the stationing of British troops in the former colony under an agreement signed at Belizian independence. While the Belizian defense force (see Table 6) is currently being trained and equipped by the British, it will remain substantially outnumbered by the Guatemalan army. While Guatemala is faced by its own internal insurgent problems, it will probably not present a credible threat to Belize.

STRUCTURAL PROBLEMS: INTERRELATED INTERESTS

What emerges from this threat analysis is a pyramid of interrelated interests broadly based in structural problems, taxing the local governments' flexibility and providing fertile ground for the continuation of political violence. The structural problems include extreme demographic pressures, large youthful populations, weak export economies, rigid and repressive socioeconomic systems, and immoderate political systems.[44] Any viable approach to stability in the region must be keyed to regional economic growth. The resources for this growth are available in Central America but require both regional cooperation and a stable political environment to attract the degree of private investment needed to stimulate this growth. The current environment of political violence discourages this type of investment.[45]

On this base of continuing political upheaval rests the developing Cuban-Nicaraguan hostile military alliance. Left alone, the Sandinista regime would consolidate its power under a Cuban-type system that would align Nicaragua militarily with Cuba and the Soviet Union. Without U.S. support, the government of El Salvador will collapse and probably be replaced by another radical revolutionary dictatorship. Continued Cuban and Sandinista support of the forces of instability in the region will weaken interregional ties and inter-American ties and blunt attempts at encouraging regional economic growth and political stability. Whether the United States applies pressure or attempts concessions, neither Castro's Cuba nor the Sandinistas' Nicaragua is likely to abandon its ambitions as a pro-Soviet partner and revolutionary force in the region.

On top of this turbulent pyramid, as discussed earlier, rests the Soviet Union, content in its ability to supply support to Cuba and the Sandinistas and watch them stir the cauldron of regional instability. The Soviet gain from the balanced approach developed since the early 1960s is simple— restraint of the U.S. ability to project military and economic power globally with the same freedom as in the past. In the aggregate, as with the geopolitical model used earlier, restraint of the United States in this way provides the Soviet Union with more freedom to make military and economic investments in the Rimland areas. The two Rimland areas of prime interest are Europe and the Middle East. Considered from this perspective, Soviet Secretary Gorbachov's renewed interest in political, economic, and military ties with Western Europe becomes less a gesture toward détente and more a matter of realpolitik.

LEVELS OF RESPONSE

Through a balanced program of military assistance and economic aid, the United States has begun to have an impact on the immediate crisis while laying the groundwork for long-term development and stability—both military and economic.[46]

To date, U.S. efforts to address the situation in the region have met with limited success. Prior to 1982, the situation appeared to be deteriorating and Soviet-Cuban-Nicaraguan influence appeared to be in ascendancy. The efforts of the U.S. and her allies in the region have managed to blunt the dynamics of deterioration and reduce the situation to more manageable proportions. Quick projection of substantial U.S. military force and the reestablishment of a program of security assistance for the region demonstrated U.S. commitment to its allies and led to a regional consensus to restrain the spread of Marxist-Leninist initiatives. Effective use of military assistance capabilities and joint exercises in particular contributed to the improvement of Salvadoran and Honduran military capabilities. Our rapid application of additional intelligence assets to controlling the Salvadoran insurgency has brought excellent results. In summary, we have blunted the threat of bringing like-minded Marxist-Leninist cadres to power in the region and now face a stalemate.

Although they are now at a manageable level, insurgencies in the region continue to be active. The prospects for a quick solution to this problem are blunted by the region's poor economic prospects. In the face of this, the prospects for a permanent peace in El Salvador and limiting Soviet client influence in the region remain remote. Marxist-Leninist propaganda will continue to hold an appeal for a region suffering from continued economic and social disparities.

Sandinistan Nicaragua continues a military buildup that far overshadows the capabilities of potential regional adversaries. Currently, U.S. and regional allies have succeeded in only decreasing the extent and pace of this buildup. It seems logical to assume that the Sandinistas will continue this military buildup—as Cuba has done over the past 25 years—and increasingly develop the capability to threaten the critical secure lines of communication through the region.

As has been described, Soviet aims in supporting instability in Central America are much more intricate than simply promoting insecurity about the "strategic backyard" of the United States. Consequently, it becomes a strategic imperative to provide the economic and military assets necessary to promote socioeconomic transformation of the region and return Central America to stability. As was recognized by General Gorman, there is no military solution to the problems of Central America. The prime advantage to a military presence in the region is to promote a "stalemate of force" that will allow the political forces time to institutionalize new socioeconomic structures in the region. The military presence appears to be providing that "stalemate of force," in order for it to be effective against the developing hostile threats in the region the political forces must now be brought to bear.

Notes

1. Caspar W. Weinberger, *Report of the Secretary of Defense to the Congress, Fiscal 1986*, February 4, 1985, p. 30.

2. Ibid., p. 32.

3. Gonzalez, Jenkins, Sereseres, and Ronfeld, *U.S. Policy for Central America*, March 1984, p. vii. David Ronfeld, *Geopolitics, Security, and U.S. Strategy in the Caribbean Basin*, Santa Monica: Rand, 1983, also provides analysis of this question.

4. Gabriel Marcella, "Defense of the Western Hemisphere," *Journal of Inter-American Studies and World Affairs*, fall 1985, p. 6.

5. Tables 1 through 6 give a basis for comparison of military force and equipment strengths for Central American nations. These data will provide the basis for an analysis of the comparative sophistication of the military equipment. I investigated the question of comparative military strengths during interviews with Sandinista military officials in Managua (March 1986). The official Sandinista military line, explained by Captain Rosa Pasos, EPS-Sandinista Foreign Military Liaison Officer and spokesman, is that the threat to Nicaragua comes first from U.S. invasion, second from the counterrevolutionaries (*contras*), and third from their Central American neighbors. The question of a coordinated attack by an alliance of Central American nations was not a serious planning consideration. If this prioritization of the threat is accepted—and given the fact that *Comandante* Cuadra (Sandinista Chief-of-Staff) privately admits that the sophisticated military hardware will not be effective against a U.S. invasion force and, in fact, within a few days the Sandinistas will have returned to guerrilla operations from the mountains—the disproportionate manning and equipment levels cannot be explained as purely defensive in nature. A one-on-one threat analysis of the Nicaraguan military vs. either the *contra* or the other Central American nations does not support the type of build-up Nicaragua has undergone.

6. Mackinder's most useful formulations are found in A.J. Pearce, ed., *Democratic Ideals and Reality*, Westport: Greenwood Press, 1962, also see Spykman's work in *America's Strategy in World Politics: The United States and the Balance of Power*, New York: Harcourt, Brace and Co., 1942, and *The Geography of Peace*, New York: Harcourt, Brace and Co., 1944. Recent articles by Irving Kristol, "A

Transatlantic Misunderstanding," *Encounter*, March 1985, and Ashley Tellis, "The Geopolitical Stakes in Central American Crisis," in *Strategic Review*, fall 1985, provide useful updates to the utility of this approach.

7. Pearce, op. cit., p. 58.

8. Ibid., p. 62.

9. Tellis, op. cit., builds a strong case for this as it applies to Europe, p. 48.

10. Roger E. Kanet, "Soviet Attitudes Toward Developing Nations Since Stalin," in Roger E. Kanet, ed., *The Soviet Union and Developing Nations*, Baltimore: The Johns Hopkins Press, 1974, pp. 34–36.

11. Ibid., p. 36.

12. An accurate discussion of Soviet perceptions of these limits is presented in Ramet and López-Alves, "Moscow and the Revolutionary Left in Latin America," *Orbis*, vol. 28, no. 2, Summer, 1984, and "In Support of the Latin American Peoples," *Pravda* editorial, Jan. 26, 1971, in *Current Digest of the Soviet Press*, vol. xxiii, no. 4, p. 12.

13. Ramet and López-Alves, op. cit., p. 344.

14. Ibid., p. 346.

15. Jack Child, *Unequal Alliance: The Inter-American Military System 1938–1978*, Boulder: Westview Press, 1980. Also, Jack Child, *US–Latin American Strategic Relationship, 1965–1977*, Washington, 1977. These works provide an in-depth analysis of U.S. policy during this time.

16. "Latin America and the World Revolutionary Process," *Current Digest of the Soviet Press*, op. cit., pp. 30–31.

17. *Pravda*, Nov. 4, 1971; *Current Digest of the Soviet Press*, Nov. 30, 1971, p. 16.

18. "Latin America, A Continent in Struggle," *World Marxist Review*, June 1981, p. 47.

19. Brian Freemantle, *KGB*, New York: Holt, Rinehart, and Winston, 1982, p. 120, and James Theberge, *The Soviet Presence in Latin America*, 1974, p. 34.

20. Ramet and López-Alves provide a host of international sources in their article to verify the existence of these connections. In addition, the Freemantle and Theberge selections mentioned above. Dept. of State and Dept. of Defense joint document "News Briefing on Intelligence Information on External Support of the Guerrillas in El Salvador," Aug. 8, 1984, provides very useful data.

21. Department of State, "Cuban Armed Forces and the Soviet Military Presence," Special Report No. 103, August 1982, and *The Soviet-Cuban Connection in Central America and the Caribbean*, joint document of Dept. of State and Dept. of Defense, March 1985.

22. *Congressional Record—Senate*, vol. 129, no. 53.

23. U.S. Congress, House, Permanent Select Committee on Intelligence, *Report to Accompany H.R. 2760*, Report 98-122, Part 1.

24. Sánchez Nestor, "U.S. Policy in Central America," *Defense*, June 1985. Once past the rhetoric, this document contains valuable and accurate data on force structures.

25. Department of State and Department of Defense, joint document, *The Sandinista Military Buildup*, April 1985, p. 20.

26. Reported in daily *Barricada*, Managua, Nicaragua, June 11, 1984; also see Miguel Bólanos Hunter's testimony before the Senate Judiciary Committee's Subcommittee on Security and Terrorism, Oct. 19, 1983, and Bólanos' interview with the *Washington Post*, June 16-17, 1983.

27. The logic for questioning any defensive component in the Sandinista military buildup is presented in note 5. Gonzales, et. al., op. cit., p. 11, provides an excellent examination of the impact of this buildup on U.S. defense planning and the available options.

28. R. Bruce McColm, "Central America and the Caribbean: The Larger Scenario," *Strategic Review*, Summer 1983, pp. 28-42.

29. Department of State, *Revolution Beyond Our Borders: The Sandinista Intervention in Central America*, September 1985, pp. 6-9, provides a description of this support structure and supporting evidence. Also see Adriana Bosch-Lemus, *The Internationalization of Conflict and Politics in Central America*, 1984, for analysis of this model of revolutionary warfare.

30. Ibid., pp. 13-16.

31. Radu Michael, *Insurgent and Terror Groups in Latin America*, Philadelphia: Foreign Policy Research Institute, 1984, p. 359, provides an in-depth study of the development and strategies of the Central America.

32. Dept. of State, "Cuba's Renewed Support for Violence in Latin America," *Special Report No. 90*, Dec. 14, 1981, pp. 6-7.

33. Dept. of State, Report No. 132, op. cit., p. 7, and Dept. of State, Report No. 90, p. 6.

34. Tricontinental Society, *Revolutionary Strategy in El Salvador*, Tricontinental Society, January 1983, p. 44.

35. Dept. of State, Report No. 90, op. cit., p. 6, from captured guerrilla documents.

36. Several useful authorities exist for research into the composition and capabilities of the Central American military. John Waghelstein, *El Salvador: Observations and Experiences in Counterinsurgency*, U.S. Army War College, Jan. 1, 1985; Caesar Sereseres, "Central America's Low Intensity Conflict Environment," paper presented at the Conference for Security Perspectives and Prospects: Central America and the Caribbean in the 1980's, Dec. 10-11, 1984; Washington, D.C.: Lambert Publications; John Keegan, *World Armies*, Second Edition, Gale Research Co., 1983; *U.S. Army Country Study and Appraisal* (series issued by country), Dept. of the Army, Washington, D.C.; as well as periodical articles in *Janes Defense Weekly*, *Defense and Diplomacy Journal*, and regional newspapers.

37. For resources on the origins and development of Guatemala's current problems, see Radu Michael, *Insurgent and Terror Groups in Latin America* (Philadelphia: Foreign Policy Research Institute, 1984). Robert H. Trudeau, "Guatemala: The Long Term Costs of Short Term Stability," *From Gunboats To Diplomacy*, Richard Newfarmer, ed. (Johns Hopkins Press, Baltimore, 1984).

38. Dept. of State, Report No. 90, op. cit., p. 7.

39. To the list from note 36, add: Casear Sereseres, *US Military Assistance and the Guatemalan Armed Forces*, Santa Monica: Rand.

40. Radu, op. cit., pp. 440-467 and 626-630, provides a balanced look at the development and support of leftist and non-leftist groups active in Honduras.

Dept. of State, Report No. 90, op. cit., p. 9, and Dept. of State, Report No. 132, pp. 13–16, provide evidence of Cuban and Salvadoran intentions.

41. Note 36 applies; for balance add Center for Defense Information, *Into the Fray: Facts on the U.S. in Central America*, 1984. The analysis in this piece is radical but the factual data are useful.

42. *Janes Defense Weekly*, Sept. 21, 1985.

43. Note 36 applies, plus "Central American Appraisal," *The Journal of Defense and Diplomacy*, November-December 1985, provides objective data.

44. Gonzales, Jenkins, Sereseres, Ronfeld, op. cit., pp. 27–28.

45. Alan Sternberger, "Evolution of Conservative Policy Toward Central America and the Caribbean," unpublished paper, p. 22.

46. The most concise appraisal available of the U.S. military programs active in Central America and the type of balanced approach needed for the future is in General Paul F. Gorman, *Prepared Statement to the Armed Services Committee*, Feb. 27, 1985: "[The current] Inter-American military system is composed of multilateral, bilateral, and U.S. command structures as follows:

1. Multilateral Structures:
   a. The Inter-American Defense Board (founded in 1941 and the oldest multilateral military organization in which the U.S. participates).
   b. The Inter-American Treaty of Reciprocal Assistance.
   c. The Inter-American Defense College which is the highest level institution in the hemisphere where Latin American and North American military and civilian officials jointly study national security. The college is a dependency of the OAS through the Inter-American Defense Board.
   d. Biannual hemispheric conferences of service chiefs and coast guards. The first conference of American armies took place at Ft. Amador, Panama, Aug. 12, 1960. It was followed by meetings of navies and air forces.
   e. Joint maneuvers and combined exercises.
   f. An Inter-American military communications network.
2. Bilateral Structures:
   a. Security assistance programs, which allowed direct contact with military institutions through equipment transfers and training.
   b. Training programs for the Latin American militaries in Panama and the U.S. The U.S. Army School of the Americas, at Ft. Gulick, Panama was closed Sept. 19, 1984, after 38 years of operation and 45,000 Latin American graduates. The school was relocated to Ft. Benning, Georgia. Other facilities have trained army, navy, and air force personnel over the years. The closing of the School of the Americas does not affect the Inter-American Air Forces Academy or the United States Navy Small Craft Training and Technical School, also located in Panama. Latin American students also attend a wide spectrum of U.S. military schools from service academies to war colleges.
   c. Exchange programs of military personnel.
   d. Bilateral Defense Commissions with Brazil and Mexico.
   e. Sharing of intelligence.

f. A variety of bilateral military relations, the most extensive of which is with Brazil. The Central American crisis has brought close strategic relationships between the U.S. and El Salvador and Honduras. Similarly the Granadan operation has given rise to the Eastern Caribbean Regional Security System, whose members are Barbados, Dominica, Antigua, St. Lucia, St. Vincent, and St. Kitts-Nevis.

g. Cooperative efforts at narcotics control, including military and civilian agencies.

h. Various periodic bilateral defense consultations.

3. Subregional Security Systems:

    a. The Central American Defense Council.

    b. The Eastern Caribbean Regional Security Systems.

4. Commands:

    a. U.S. Southern Command.

    b. The Atlantic Command."

3

U.S. Security and the Contadora Process: Toward a CBM Regime in Central America

Jack Child

PROLOGUE: THE PANAMA CANAL SECURITY DEBATE

The security aspects of the current debate on United States interests in Central America bring to mind a somewhat analogous security debate of ten years ago: that which surrounded the negotiation and ratification of the Panama Canal Treaties of 1977. Some features of that debate provide a useful point of departure for discussions of how U.S. security interests in Central America can be best protected.

In the 1975–78 period these security arguments on how to best protect U.S. interests in Panama Canal were polarized on two radically different viewpoints[1]:

The first held that U.S. security interests in the canal were vital, and that they could best be protected by traditional military means and unquestionable and indefinite U.S. control, as if the United States were sovereign in the Canal Zone. No concessions were to be made on security issues, defense of the canal would be a unilateral U.S. responsibility, and the U.S. military was to be prepared to dig in, hold, and defend the canal by all necessary means. There would be no basic changes in the 1903 Canal Treaty as far as the sovereignty issue and security responsibilities were concerned.

The second view on U.S. security interests in the Panama Canal argued that these interests, while important, were not vital, and that the basic goal was U.S. access to a functioning canal, not possession of a zone and canal which could be rendered unusable by hostilities with a

Panama supported by large sectors of Latin America and the Third World. The 1903 Treaty was seen as anachronistic, and no longer viable. Effective U.S. access to the canal could be best achieved by sharing responsibility and control with Panama, with full control and responsibility passing to Panama gradually over an extended period of time. U.S. security interests were seen as being best protected by a verifiable treaty which included specific and detailed provisions for joint U.S.-Panamanian security responsibilities.

Today's debate on U.S. security interests in Central America can also be framed in terms of two analogous poles:

The first view holds that U.S. security interests in Central America are vital, and can best be protected by traditional military means involving a range of covert and overt measures to pressure Nicaragua and support regional allies. Instruments for protecting these security interests include heavy doses of military assistance, unprecedented maneuvers, and support for *contra* guerrillas fighting the Sandinista regime in Managua.

The second view argues that this approach is sterile and confrontational and will almost inevitably lead to incremental escalation of U.S. military commitments until the moment arrives when the U.S. is faced with the stark alternatives of pulling out or inserting combat forces. Alternatively, conflict might occur through mistakes, misperceptions, accidents or irresponsible acts by any number of parties facing each other in confrontational situations at several potential flash points on the ground in Central America. Efforts to intimidate Nicaragua, argue the proponents of this view, have only caused Nicaragua to strengthen its ties to Cuba and the Soviet bloc, and attempts to tighten the screws on Nicaragua have only led to corresponding increases in Nicaragua's military strength. Thus, the spiral of tension feeds on itself and has constantly risen in the period since 1979. Those who hold this view argue that legitimate U.S. (and Central American) security interests can best be secured by trying to bring down this tension spiral through a verifiable negotiated solution to Central American conflicts. The most promising way to achieve this, they maintain, is through the Contadora process underway since early 1983. Such a process would involve a substantial reduction in the U.S. military presence and a sharing of security responsibilities with Latin American nations (and other outside parties). To be a credible protector of U.S. security interests, any Contadora treaty would have to be verifiable and specific.

INTRODUCTION

This chapter presents the argument that U.S. security interests in Central America can indeed be protected by a verifiable Contadora treaty. The Contadora process is viewed as an innovative attempt to establish a confidence-building regime in Central America with provisions for effective verification, and consequently the treaty safeguards the security interests not only of the Central American and neighboring nations, but of the United States as well.

Confidence-building measures (CBMs) have historically been associated with high-intensity conflict situations and their avoidance between the superpowers, or in the NATO-Warsaw Pact context in Central Europe. However, basic CBM principles and certain techniques can in fact be applied to lower-level conflict situations, and specifically to insurgencies and interstate tensions in Central America. Indeed, CBMs form the philosophical and substantive basis for the majority of the proposals of the Contadora process, and are specified in the various Contadora documents. These documents include: the January 1984 "Implementation Principles," the draft *Acta* of late 1984, and the April 1985 "Statutes of the Verification and Control Mechanism for Security."

The verification process is seen by many observers (and U.S. government policy-makers) as a major problem in accepting Contadora proposals or a CBM regime. This chapter will address the verification issue and suggest that these proposals can in fact be verifiable and feasible if certain multilateral initiatives are accepted, and if the proposals are combined with negotiations, development assistance and peacekeeping.

In recent years important developments have been made in the fields of peacekeeping and peace observing. These include the use of electronic sensors and other technological advances to greatly multiply the areas which can be effectively observed by relatively small groups of neutrals in regions of high tension between states. The value of such technology has been proven in situations such as the Sinai Field Mission between Egypt and Israel; and the application to Central America will require ingenuity because of the vastly differently geographic and political environment, but the possibilities are significant and to date have not been adequately explored.[2]

In the superpower and NATO-Warsaw Pact context CBMs have focused mainly on the military aspects of increasing confidence between potential adversaries as a way of avoiding conflict through misperception or mistake. The CBM concept can also be broadened to include other measures outside of the strictly military field. These might include democratization, protection of human rights, movement to lower rhetoric and verbal vituperation, economic development, and restoration of important initiatives towards political and economic integration in Central America.

The existing literature on CBMs has, understandably, focused on Europe, NATO-Warsaw Pact tensions, and the Soviet Union/United States relationship.[3] There is some literature from the United Nations perspective, including a comprehensive study made by a "Group of

Governmental Experts on Confidence-building Measures" in 1980 and 1981.[4] The relatively small volume of CBM material on low-intensity, Third World and Latin American conflicts includes work by Falk Bomsford, Victor Millan, and by Henry Wiseman and the present author in various publications of the International Peace Academy.[5]

THE NATURE OF CONFIDENCE-BUILDING MEASURES

Confidence-building approaches are an attempt to counter the dangerous features of a competitive international environment in which potential adversaries mistrust each other and their intentions, and have inadequate information about their capabilities. If unchecked, this situation creates a strong incentive to improve one's own security capabilities and surround these capabilities with secrecy; understandably, one's adversary tends to do the same thing. This in turn contributes to a cycle of tension, suspicion, and costly arms races, and increases the possibility that one or more of the actors involved in the process will start a war through misunderstanding, misperception, uncertainty, accident, or irresponsible act.

In this environment, CBMs have a number of purposes. Fundamentally, they are intended to reduce the risk of conflict through these misunderstandings or misinterpretations. They also can lower international tensions by slowing down or reversing the spiraling interaction of suspicion, insecurity and arms purchases. If successful in these objectives, CBMs can also be a vehicle for arms control and eventual disarmament.

To be successful, CBMs should include the following features:

- Transparency and openness: the measure must be obvious and unambiguous, and there must not be any way to hide or distort the capability in question. A convincing argument against attempting to hide a military capability is that it will soon become public knowledge, so there is nothing to gain by attempting to hide it. Effective means (observation technology, third-party neutrals, etc.) must exist to insure that this does in fact happen.
- Predictability: the various parties must be convinced that any preparations for aggressive acts (their own or the adversary's) cannot be carried out secretly, and that they have predictable indicators which will give the other side adequate time to respond.
- Mutuality, balance, and symmetry: any steps taken towards a CBM must be perceived as a fair quid pro quo, with balanced and symmetrical mutual concessions on either side.
- Communication: there must be adequate channels for clarification and notification to the potential adversary of any moves which might be misperceived. These communications channels must be both

technically and perceptually adequate. That is, the transmission must be rapid and direct, and the message must be credible and logical to the recipient.
- Verification: CBMs require a verification system which the adversaries can trust. This can be based on their own national means or on the resources of a third-party neutral group which can retain the confidence of both sides.

Confidence-building measures have a number of limitations. Fundamentally, the adversaries must genuinely want to avoid conflict. If one (or both) of the adversaries believes that aggression is worthwhile, or that a military solution is possible and is a zero-sum game in his favor, or if he is motivated by ideological convictions which permit no compromise, then CBMs will either break down or merely serve to prolong the conflict. CBMs in and of themselves cannot resolve conflicts; they are instruments of "negative peace" which can help avoid a conflict. This suggests that they must be combined with measures of "positive peace" designed to attack the fundamental economic, social and political causes of the conflict. Lastly, CBMs have the limitation that while most key policy makers will publicly support them, these same individuals may have a profound distrust of this approach, especially if their background is one that has stressed secrecy (i.e., the military or intelligence agencies), or if they harbor a strong ideological bias against the adversary.

Because of these limitations, it is important not to expect too much of CMBs too fast. Dramatic and bold CBMs are unlikely to produce lasting results. The process of building confidence is a slow and cautious one in which each individual step must be tested and verified before proceeding to the next one. This suggests that it is advisable to begin CBMs at a low and modest "do-able" level where mistakes and reverses would not unduly damage the process. Successes at this modest level can then be used in an incremental process to build up to more ambitious stages.

THE CONTADORA PROCESS AS A CBM APPROACH

This section proposes that the Contadora efforts be envisioned essentially as a confidence-building process in its broadest sense and be employed as such in the search for a reduction in tensions and a peaceful resolution of Central American conflicts. From the United States policy perspective a verifiable Contadora treaty should also be conceived of as supporting U.S. security interests and as being the best chance for avoiding a regional conflict or direct U.S. military intervention.

The general steps and elements of the process would include the following:

- The Contadora nations (Mexico, Panama, Colombia, Venezuela) and the Support Group (Argentina, Brazil, Peru, Uruguay) are accepted by all concerned as the catalyst that brings the parties to agreement and overseas compliance and verification. Implicit in this understanding is that these nations must be prepared to exercise pressure and make public any violations.
- The United States accepts the legitimacy of the Sandinista regime in Nicaragua and ceases overt and covert attempts to intimidate it and bring it down.
- Nicaragua accepts the legitimacy of the elected regimes in the isthmus and ceases overt and covert support for insurgencies in these countries.
- Implicit in the latter two points is the agreement to cease the illegal trafficking of arms and other support to destabilizing groups.
- Agreement is reached on limits on arms, troop levels, and foreign military advisors; an open registry is maintained by Contadora, which verifies compliance.
- Contadora puts into place a conflict resolution mechanism by interposing contingents of third-party neutrals in areas of high tension where adversaries are in contact (peacekeeping). In zones of lower tension smaller peace-observing groups aided by technological means can verify compliance with the Contadora provisions.
- Nations with extensive United Nations peacekeeping and peace-observing experience (most notably Canada and the Nordic countries) provide technical advice and support.
- Contadora group representatives (aided by international organizations and other neutral observers) observe (and guarantee, if necessary), the free electoral process in those countries where regimes have come to power by means other than elections.
- Contadora is the vehicle for continuing negotiations to settle the various issues between the parties in conflict.
- A confidence-building regime is established in Central America to lower tensions and reduce the possibility of conflict through misunderstanding, accident, or misreading of actions. Contadora assists in the establishment of this regime (specific measures which might be considered are contained in the appendix to this chapter, as well as in the various Contadora documents). As a minimum this CBM regime would include communications links ("hot lines"), verification of limits on troops, arms and advisors, advance notification of maneuvers and exercises, and exchanges of information and personnel. Other measures might involve the establishment of demilitarized

zones, bilateral (joint) border patrols, and increased military-to-military contacts through periodic conferences, sporting events and attendance at regional military training institutions.

- A major development and economic integration effort is launched to attack the socioeconomic problems underlying much of the conflict in the area. Although most of the funding for this effort will inevitably have to be from the United States, the bulk of the financing should be channelled through multilateral agencies.

To protect the security interests of the Central American nations as well as the United States, the process must be cautious, balanced, incremental and verifiable. As an interim measure existing levels of external military assistance and advisors should be frozen while negotiations are worked out for agreed on levels and their eventual reduction. Contadora's verification measures should be credible, pressures on violators should be meaningful, and there should be an understanding that consistent violation by one side leaves the other side free to increase its own efforts.

As can be seen from the outline of the Contadora process sketched out above, peacekeeping and peace observation play an important role in the implementation and verification process. Peacekeeping is a controversial topic in the inter-American system because of the way that it has been used in the past to mask intervention, and because of a commonly held perception that this type of initiative has tended to serve U.S. interests. Thus, many Latin Americans recall the intervention in the Dominican Republic in 1965 as a case of unilateral United States action which was subsequently made more palatable by the "figleaf" of multilateral OAS support (obtained by the thinnest of margins). As a result, when the United States proposed in July 1979 that an OAS peacekeeping element be sent to Nicaragua in the final days of the Somoza regime, there was much suspicion that this masked a U.S. attempt to preserve *somocismo*. These sensitivities, and current realities in Central America, suggest that the U.S. would not be able to play much of a role in any of these Contadora peacekeeping and peace-observing initiatives, other than perhaps a logistical and technical support function outside of the area. The search for acceptable third-party neutrals willing and capable of performing this function thus may be difficult. The Contadora and Support Group nations are a logical starting point; others such as Canada and some of the European nations are possible candidates, along with some of the hemisphere states. However, the technical, logistical and administrative problems of peacekeeping should not be minimized; there exists the dismaying possibility of reaching a political agreement via Contadora and then having it break down at the practical and operational level.

In May 1984 three Central American nations (El Salvador, Honduras and Costa Rica) proposed that the Inter-American Defense Board serve as a verifier of the Contadora process in a peace-observing function; the proposal was rejected by Nicaragua.[6] The proposal, and the rejection, serve to illustrate some of the characteristics of the board and the inter-American military system of which it forms a part. Essentially, the military system's history is that it was created under U.S. aegis during the Second World War as an instrument for hemispheric defense against the Axis. This orientation shifted to anti-Communism aimed at Marxist-Leninist insurgencies during the Cold War. In the context of current American tensions the board cannot realistically play a peace-observing or peace-keeping role as long as it retains this anti-Communist orientation and the historic high U.S. profile. But if the board were to shift away from this orientation there is the intriguing possibility of an important positive role for the board in the Contadora verification process as a technical advisory organ. In this connection, it should be noted that the Nicaraguan government did not withdraw from the board in 1979, and has maintained its representation.

In the constant focus on the crisis of the moment it appears that the U.S. government may not have fully appreciated that the Contadora process has acquired a broader significance which transcends immediate Central American problems. Contadora has become to many Latin Americans a symbol of greater maturity and independence. It is also seen as an indication that solutions proposed and implemented by regional Latin American powers may be more effective than the traditional solutions advocated by the United States, either unilaterally, bilaterally through selected allies, or multilaterally through the Organization of American States. Each of the four Contadora countries (Mexico, Panama, Colombia and Venezuela) has a special significance in the regional context, and with the Support Group countries they, in effect, speak for Latin America. Contadora has thus acquired a kind of mystique and aura as an important Latin American initiative supported enthusiastically by a broad range of most of the nations of the hemisphere and Western Europe.[7] At the pragmatic level the Contadora process involves a significant number of individuals from the four countries including their presidents (who have committed personal and national prestige), their foreign ministers, and a large number of lower-level officials. In and of itself Contadora thus represents a major integrative endeavor for the region, and the contacts made in the process of working out the agreements is an important reality. Further, Contadora is consistently described as a "process" which will not end when agreement is reached on its major points; the requirements for verification and confirmation will continue to keep the players active and the integrative effect will thus be open-ended.

The significance of this integrative effort is all the more important in light of the decline of the traditional instruments of the inter-American system. Damaged by the Malvinas/Falklands crisis of 1982, and again by the intervention in Grenada in 1983, the system, and the Organization of American States as its principal institution, seem more and more irrelevant to the Central American crisis and to the hemisphere's needs. The Contadora process is thus, to some extent, a replacement for the old and now increasingly anachronistic vehicles for inter-American cooperation and security. Contadora thus presents the United States with both a challenge and an opportunity to accept a new type of Latin American initiative, a new measure of hemispheric diversity, and a new cooperative approach to problems.

The Contadora process and the proposed CBM regime thus go beyond Central America's current crises and United States security interests in the region. There are important long-range benefits and costs involved for the U.S. acceptance of the basic Contadora proposals. They imply that the United States will eventually give up significant instruments of its traditional influence and power in Central America, especially those associated with the Security Assistance Program. Carried to their fullest, the Contadora proposals mean that the U.S. military presence will be drastically curtailed in the area. Further, the symbolism and mystique of Contadora may exert considerable pressure on the United States and may force it to accept agreements that in the long run may be disadvantageous; the "cut and run" fears of U.S. conservatives may not be unfounded. There is, as suggested earlier, a certain analogy to the Panama Canal negotiating process: the United States can dig in and attempt to hold on to a situation which is becoming less and less tenable, or it can adopt a more enlightened position giving the Latin Americans a greater share of benefits and responsibility. The costs and benefits of the Contadora proposals and the ensuing CBM regime must thus be carefully weighed.

There is one final element of the Contadora process that also must be considered: the psychological and propagandistic one. Because of the importance Contadora has acquired as a symbol of a cooperative Latin American effort to solve its own problems, there will be a considerable price to pay if the effort fails and the United States is portrayed as the chief reason for this failure. As will be brought out in the next section, there is a substantial body of public and official opinion in Latin America that the United States is only paying lip service to the Contadora process, and is in fact finding ways to scuttle it quietly. If Contadora fails and this opinion prevails, there may be strong Latin American resentment and the United States may find itself even more isolated than it did during the Malvinas/Falklands and other crises in recent years.

THE RECORD TO DATE[8]

As the conflict and insurgency situation in Central America became more serious in 1980 and 1981, the first tentative efforts at finding a peaceful solution got under way in the Organization of American States and through a series of bilateral consultations. However, it soon became clear that the OAS, rent by divisions and damaged by the impact of the 1982 Malvinas/Falklands crisis, was not capable of meaningful solutions to the new series of problems in Central America; some states (most notably Nicaragua) were also adamant against allowing the OAS to become involved.

Against this background the four immediate neighbors of the Central American nations (Mexico, Panama, Colombia, Venezuela) began to coordinate their efforts towards resolving the conflict. Their first formal meeting was held on the Panamanian island of Contadora in early 1983 and produced the Contadora Declaration of 9 January. In the first months of 1983 the Contadora Four engaged the five Central American nations in a series of discussions on the broad issues involved in the conflicts: military advisors, arms sales, destabilizing efforts, economic development, democratization, and refugees. Tensions between Nicaragua and Costa Rica led the latter nation to ask for an OAS peacekeeping force to patrol the border in May 1983, but the Contadora Four asked the OAS to withhold action. The OAS and Costa Rica agreed, and in mid-May the foreign ministers of the four nations established a border observer commission made up of civilian and military personnel from each of the Contadora nations. This commission was physically present on the border for about a week. This precedent suggests that a fruitful place to start constructing the Central American CBM as a "demonstration project" might be this Nicaraguan-Costa Rican border.

In July 1983 the presidents of the four Contadora nations met in Mexico and produced (17 July) the "Cancún Declaration on Peace in Central America" which proposed that the nations of the isthmus agree to a series of commitments which would lead to a peaceful solution to tensions in the area.

The July meeting was followed up by the key September 1983 21-point "Document of Objectives," signed by all nine nations, which was the first formal agreement to address the principal concerns of all parties concerned. The "Document of Objectives" listed the following major areas of concern:

- Political: democratization; national reconciliation; respect for human rights.
- Security: steps to end support for external supervision; reduction in numbers of foreign military and security advisors; controls on troop levels and armaments; halt to illegal arms trafficking.
- Socio-economic: need for greater regional cooperation; a major development effort; aid to refugees.

The second fundamental Contadora document was signed in January 1984: the "Principles for Implementation of the Commitments Undertaken in the Document of Objectives." This document built upon the previous one in an attempt to establish specific criteria for carrying out the objectives and to build the basis for a verifiable treaty; a specific timetable for three working commissions was also outlined, with the work to be completed by the end of April 1984. The January 1984 "Principles for Implementation" document presented a number of specific ideas which were clearly confidence-building measures, especially in the security area. Among them: the establishment of a registry of troops, installations, and arms, with a view to creating ceilings, eventual reductions, and the restoration of a reasonable balance of force in the area; a census of foreign military and security advisors, with a view to their eventual departure; an end to activities of destabilizing groups; locating and ending the routes and flow of illegal weapons to these groups; and the establishment of direct communications links between nations to resolve incidents.

The April 1984 deadline for the working groups to complete these proposals was not met. Mutual recriminations (especially between Nicaragua and the United States) clouded the issue of who or what was to blame for the delay. The proposal made by El Salvador, Honduras and Costa Rica attempted to provide specific verification procedures for the touchy security issues, including the use of the Inter-American Defense Board as a verification instrument, but the Nicaraguans refused to agree and the process stalled.[9] Shortly afterwards, in a step that suggested that partial and bilateral implementation of the Contadora ideas might be possible, Costa Rica and Nicaragua signed an agreement to set up a joint supervisory and preventative commission whose tasks would be to investigate border incidents and attempt to lower tensions between the two countries;[10] the Contadora four also signed this agreement and made themselves available to assist Nicaragua and Costa Rica in their efforts.

In late 1984 the Contadora Four produced the revised draft "Act of Contadora for Peace and Cooperation in Central America."[11] With an even greater degree of specificity and detail, the act confirmed the CBMs defined previously and called for the creation of a commission to verify compliance in security matters. An appendix to the act contained detailed definitions of military terms, to include technical specifications and features of weapons, aircraft, helicopters, and military organizations and logistics.

A supplementary document,[12] the "State of the Verification and Control Mechanism for Security," released in April 1985, gave further details on the "International Corps of Inspectors" and their responsibilities, organization, reports, liaison, financing, and administration.

These increasingly detailed and specific documents suggest that the Contadora process in 1984 and 1985 was moving steadily to supplement the wide-sweeping idealistic rhetoric of 1983 with the pragmatic and even mundane considerations essential to guarantee success of its efforts in the field. In this process the Contadora nations received important technical advice from nations with a long history of peacekeeping and peace-observing operations. Chief among them was Canada.[13]

In late 1985 and early 1986 a political stalemate in the Contadora process, and increasingly strained U.S.-Nicaraguan relations, caused these promising initiatives in the security field to. be put on hold.[14] Important elections in several Central American nations in this period led Nicaragua to propose (at the December 1985 OAS General Assembly in Cartagena) a five-month suspension in the Contadora process, although there were also several attempts to revive negotiations.[15] The stalemate, and the attempt to restart Contadora seemed to involve U.S.-Nicaraguan strains more than the technical questions of verification and security, which had been spelled out in considerable detail in the documents cited above.

The record to date must also include an assessment of the United States attitude towards the Contadora process. Official U.S. policy statements[16] invariably express support for Contadora and a willingness to accept its proposals if they can be verified; the lack of a more direct and active U.S. involvement in the process is explained on the basis that this is a regional effort in which U.S. involvement would be inappropriate and counter-productive until concrete results are achieved in the form of a treaty. Despite these official expressions of support, it is hard to see much Reagan administration enthusiasm for Contadora. The major emphasis on military and covert instruments for U.S. policy in Central America runs directly counter to both the spirit and specific proposals of Contadora. As indicated previously, there is a strong current of opinion in Latin America, as well as in the United States,[17] that this country is merely paying lip service to Contadora while seeking a military victory in El Salvador and the intimidation (and possible overthrow) of the Sandinista regime in Nicaragua. Many of these same observers[18] also identify the most probable vehicle for the U.S. to use to scuttle the Contadora agreements without being blamed for it: this would involve insisting on impossible conditions and verification standards and using the regional U.S. allies (principally El Salvador, Hounduras, and Costa Rica) as the instruments for posing United States objections.

CONCLUSION

The Contadora process has evolved considerably since the first meeting in early 1983. While it is true (as of three years later) that no Central American peace treaty has yet been signed, it is also true that a regional conflict or a major U.S. military intervention has not occurred either. Contadora, for all its shortcomings, deserves much credit for its contribution to this state of affairs.

In its three years of evolution Contadora has supplemented its early rhetorical and vague statements on security matters with some very specific confidence-building and control measures to verify the provisions of the draft treaty. In effect, these provisions provide the foundations for a verifiable and viable CBM regime in Central America which can protect the legitimate security interests of the United States, Nicaragua, the other four Central American nations, and the regional neighbors.

Thus, as in the case with the Panama Canal security issue ten years ago, U.S. policy-makers have a choice: they must decide if U.S. security interests in Central America are best defended by digging in and emphasizing traditional military measures, or whether shared security responsibilities and an enlightened acceptance of a verifiable CBM regime might not better secure these U.S. interests in the long run.

NOTES

1. For several expressions of the security debate surrounding the new Panama Canal Treaties, see the author's "Military Aspects of the Panama Canal Issue," *Proceedings*, Vol. 106, No. 923, U.S. Naval Institute, January 1980; "Canal Zone Defense Worries U.S.," *Christian Science Monitor*, May 13, 1976, p. 1; "A Clash of Views Over Canal Security," *U.S. News and World Report*, Oct. 24, 1977, p. 27; "Pentagon 'Fully' Backs Canal Pact," *Washington Star*, Sept. 27–28, 1977; "Military Needs Demand Negation of Canal Pacts," *Detroit News*, Dec. 12, 1977, p. 7B; "If the U.S. Had to Defend the Panama Canal," *U.S. News and World Report*, Oct. 24, 1977, p. 26; "Is the Canal Defensible?," *Baltimore News American*, Nov. 17, 1977, p. 16.

2. See *Weapons of Peace: How Technology Can Revitalize Peace-Keeping*, International Peace Academy Report No. 8, New York, 1980; and *Peace-keeping and Technology: Concepts for the Future*, International Peace Academy Report No. 17, New York, 1983.

3. Jonathan Alford, "Confidence-building Measures," *Adelphi Papers*, No. 149 (London: International Institute for Strategic Studies, 1979). Abbot Brayton, "Confidence-building Measures in European Security," *World Today*, Vol. 36,

October 1978, pp. 382–391. Johan Jorgen Holst, "Confidence-building Measures: A Conceptual Framework," *Survival*, January/February 1983. IPRA Disarmament Study Group, "Building Confidence in Europe," *Bulletin of Peace Proposals*, No. 2, 1980. Stockholm International Peace Research Institute (SIPRI), *SIPRI Yearbook, 1981*, Stockholm, 1982, chap. 17.

4. United Nations Document A/36/474, *Report of the United Nations Study Group on Confidence-building Measures*, January 1982.

5. Falk Bomsford, "The Confidence-building Measure Offensive in the United Nations," *Aussenpolitik*, No. 4, 1982, pp. 370–390. Victor Millan, "Controlling Conflict through Confidence-building Measures" in *Controlling Latin American Conflicts: Ten approaches*, edited by Michael A. Morris and Victor Millan (Boulder, Colorado: Westview, 1983), pp. 89–97. Jack Child, "The Use of Confidence-building Measures as a Contribution to Peace in Central America" in *Towards Peace and Security in the Caribbean and Central America*, International Peace Academy Report No. 16, 1984, and *Summary Report of Regional Cooperation in Peace and Security in Central America and the Caribbean*, International Peace Academy, 1984. The use of confidence-building measures as a technique for conventional arms control was assessed by the Inter-American Dialogue in their 1983 Report, pp. 51–52.

6. *Washington Post*, May 2, 1984, p. A1. U.S. Department of State, Current Policy no. 572, "U.S. Central American Policy at a Crossroads," May 2, 1984, pp. 7–8.

7. For expressions of this support, see *Washington Post*, May 1, 1984, p. A1; May 13, 1984, p. A32. *Summary Report of Regional Cooperation in Peace and Security in Central America and the Caribbean*, International Peace Academy, 1984. *La Nación* (Costa Rica), Dec. 28, 1983, p. 2; Feb. 29, 1984, p. 4; Mar. 7, 1984, p. 1. *El País* (Madrid), May 21, 1984, p. 7; June 4, 1984, pp. 3, 11. *La Nación* (Buenos Aires), Mar. 26, 1984, p. 5; July 24, 1983, p. 1. *Excelsior* (Mexico), Sept. 22, 1983, p. 1.

8. For a chronology of the Contadora process (from the U.S. Government perspective), see Department of State Special Report no. 115, "U.S. Efforts to Achieve Peace in Central America," Mar. 15, 1984. See also United Nations Document S/16041, *The Situation in Central America*, Oct. 18, 1983. Fernando Cepeda Ulloa, *Contadora: Desafío a la Diplomacia Tradicional* (Bogota: Universidad de los Andes), 1985. International Peace Academy, *Conflict in Central America: Approaches to Peace and Security* (New York: St Martin's Press), 1986.

9. *Washington Post*, May 2, 1984, p. A16. *La Nación* (Costa Rica), May 9, 1984, p. 8.

10. *Washington Post*, May 27, 1984, p. A1. *La Nación* (Costa Rica), May 23, 1984, p. 5.

11. *Act of Contadora for Peace and Cooperation in Central America (Revised Version)*, OAS document CP/INF.2222, Oct. 24, 1984.

12. *Statutes of the Verification and Control Mechanism for Security*, OAS Document CP/INF.2271/85, Apr. 15, 1985.

13. Remarks made at the York University Conference on "Central America and Peacekeeping," Toronto, Jan. 29, 1986. Also, "Se Estudia un Sistema que

Ponga en Práctica Mecanismos de Seguridad del Acta de Contadora," *Excelsior* (Mexico), Aug. 22, 1985, p. 13.

14. *Granma* (Cuba), Nov. 18, 1985, p. 11.

15. *Washington Post*, Dec. 6, 1985, Dec. 9, 1985, Jan. 16, 1986.

16. For an official U.S. policy statement on Contadora, see Department of State Special Report No. 115, "U.S. Efforts to Achieve Peace in Central America," Mar. 15, 1984. See also Susan Kaufman Purcell, "Demystifying Contadora," *Foreign Affairs*, fall 1985, pp. 74–95. *Washington Post*, Dec. 6, 1985. *Los Angeles Times*, Nov. 5, 1985. *New York Times*, Jan. 8, 1986.

17. *Los Angeles Times*, Apr. 10, 1984, p. 11. *New York News*, Apr. 10, 1984, p. 3. *New York Times*, Apr. 1, 1984, p. A18. *La Nación* (Costa Rica), Feb. 9, 1984, p. 5.

18. *Latin American Index*, May 1, 1984, p. 32. Leiken, op. cit., p. 250. Council on Hemispheric Affairs, *Washington Report on the Hemisphere,*, Apr. 2, 1984, p. 4. *La Nación* (Costa Rica), May 7, 1984, p. 4. *Philadelphia Inquirer*, May 16, 1984, p. 6; Jan. 9, 1985, p. 12. *Washington Post*, May 13, 1984, p. 32; Oct. 15, 1984, p. A14; Oct. 21, 1984, p. A23; Nov. 6, 1984, p. A1. Letter from former president Carlos Andrés Pérez of Venezuela, May 15, 1984.

SUPPLEMENT TO CHAPTER THREE: CONFIDENCE-BUILDING MEASURES FOR CENTRAL AMERICA

(These CBMs are suggested as being applicable to the Central American states in general, although some will obviously be more appropriate for countries with close relations, and others will be more suitable for those states whose relations are tense).

1. CBMs dealing with troop movements and exercises.

- Notification of maneuvers (with different procedures and length of advance notice for different types and sizes of maneuvers).
- Notification of alert exercises and mobilization drills.
- Notification of naval activities outside of normal areas.
- Notification of aircraft operations and flights near sensitive and border areas.
- Notification of other military activities (in the "out of garrison" category) which might be misinterpreted.

2. CBMs dealing with exchanges of information, directly or through third parties, in the following categories:

- Military budgets;
- New equipment and arms;
- Unit locations;
- Significant changes in a unit's size, equipment or mission;

• The major elements of a strategic and tactical doctrine.

3. CBMs dealing with exchanges of personnel, which should be balanced in terms of numbers and duration, and could include:

- Inviting observers to maneuvers, exercises and "out of garrison" activities. (The observers could be from neighboring states, from a third party neutral nation, or from an international organization).
- Stationing permanent liaison observers at major headquarters. (As in "b" above, the observers could be from neighbors, neutrals, or international organizations).
- Exchanging personnel as students or instructors at military academies, military schools, and war colleges.
- Exchanging military attaches from all three services (land, sea, air) from and to all the Central American nations. These attache positions should be filled by highly qualified personnel, and not be used as "golden exiles" to get rid of officers who are politically undesirable.

4. CBMs dealing with the assembly, collation, and dissemination of data.

- A central registry should be set up (under Contadora or international organization auspices) to assemble, collect, analyze and publish information on armaments, organization and disposition of military units.
- Independent technical means (under national, Contadora or international organization control) should be available to verify this data. There should be agreement on the nature of these means and an understanding that there will be no interference with these means.

5. CBMs dealing with border tensions.

- Set up demilitarized zones in sensitive border areas. Depending on the sensitivity of the area and the tensions between the two countries, certain types of weapons and units (i.e., armor, artillery) could be excluded from these areas.
- Establish joint patrols in these areas (with or without the participation of Contadora or other third party neutrals).
- Establish fixed observation posts in these areas manned by neutrals and representatives from the two border nations.
- Set up sensors (ground, tower, air, tethered balloons) to supplement these patrols and observations posts.

6. CBMs dealing with actions which might be interpreted as provocative.

- Agreement should be reached on acceptable and unacceptable military activities, especially in sensitive and border areas.
- Clear limits should be placed on those military activities, such as mobilizations and calling up selected reserves, which could lead to misunderstandings. Notification procedures should be established for practice movements.

7. CBMs dealing with communications.

- Direct ("hot line") communications systems should be established between heads of state, chiefs of military forces (defense ministers), general staffs, and units in contact across a border.
- The use of coded military message traffic (on-line and off-line cryptography) should be limited.

8. CBMs dealing with weapons.

- Agreement should be reached on levels and types of weapons, with emphasis on the exclusion of high-performance and expensive weapons systems.
- Agreement should be reached on levels of military arms budgets.
- Defensive weapons (anti-aircraft artillery, anti-tank weapons, mines) should be given preference in ceilings over offensive weapons (tanks, artillary, aircraft).

9. CBMs dealing with extra-military contacts.

- Encourage visits by military athletic teams.
- Encourage social and professional contacts through the attache network and the various elements of the Inter-American military system.

10. CBMs dealing with training and education.

- Teach CBM approaches in national military academies, staff schools, and war colleges, as well as in the multinational military schools (the School of the Americas, the Inter-American Air Force Academy in Panana, and the Inter-American Defense College in Washington).
- Apply CBM techniques in command post and field exercises.

- Encourage the development of military trans-nationalism (i.e., a sense of military professionalism and mutual respect that transcends national boundaries).
- Examine primary and secondary school curricula and texts for aggressive, hostile or false information on potential adversaries.

11. CBMs dealing with the role of superpowers.

- Attempt to break the linkage between local and Central American issues from East-West superpower concerns.
- Reduce military ties between the Central American nations and the superpowers.
- Compile lists of foreign military and security advisors and trainers.
- Reach agreements on levels of these advisors and attempt to reduce the levels.

12. CBMs and the Inter-American Military System.*

- The institutions and activities of the Inter-American Military System should be examined to see how they can be used in support of a confidence-building regime. The CBM support functions can include verification, contacts, channel of communications and a forum for expressing a wide range of ideas.
- Consideration should be given to lowering the presently high U.S. profile in most of the institutions of the Inter-American Military System, and to the possibility of moving key institutions (board and college) to a Latin American country.

13. CBMS and functionalism.

Certain functional areas of military-to-military cooperation should be assessed for their possible value as confidence-builders, even between adversary nations. These include: search and rescue (SAR) missions for aircraft and shipping; disaster relief; hurricane tracking; civic action; humanitarian projects.

14. CBMs dealing with ways of expanding CBMs.

---

*The institutions of the Inter-American Military System include: Inter-American Defense Board, Inter-American Defense College, multinational military schools in Panama and the U.S., Service Chief's Conferences, military attaches, joint exercises, communications links, Inter-American Treaty or Reciprocal Assistance (1947 Rio Treaty) may also be considered part of the system. Likewise, certain subregional security arrangements may be included: the Central American Defense Council (CONDECA, created in the early 1960's), and the Eastern Caribbean Regional Security System (set up after the 1983 invasion of Grenada).

- Establish a regional or subregional mechanism, similar to the Conference on Security and Cooperation in Europe (CSCE) to study confidence-building measures and ways to improve and increase the.
- Discuss CBMs at the periodic service chief's conferences.
- Explore the possibility of extending CBMs geographically beyond the Central American area (i.e., the Caribbean and South America).

4
Bringing Diplomacy Back In: A Critique of U.S. Policy in Central America
Wayne S. Smith

THE NATURE OF THE PROBLEM: WHAT IT ISN'T

The Reagan administration would have us believe the problem we face in Central America emanates first and foremost from Moscow. As its famous White Paper put it in February of 1981, this is "a classic case of indirect armed aggression . . . by Communist powers acting through Cuba." Former Secretary of State Haig had taken that line even before the White Paper came out. "In Central America," he told a group of State Department officers in early February of 1981, "we have a case of Soviet expansionism carried out by their Cuban allies. What we must do is draw a line and stop this Soviet aggression in its tracks."[1]

That view has changed little over the past four years. In a State-Defense Department booklet issued in March of 1985, for example, "Soviet and Cuban military power and intervention in Central America and the Caribbean" are said to be: "as much a part of the region's crisis as the better known indigenous and historic factors."[2]

And in a recent article in the American Enterprise Institute's journal, *Foreign Policy and Defense Review*,[3] Carl Gersham, the President of the National Endowment for Democracy, painted an alarming picture of Soviet military buildup in the area and of Moscow's determination to communize the countries of Central America by force of arms. According to Gersham, not only have the Cubans returned to across-the-board support for guerrilla warfare, but the Soviets also have abandoned their earlier, more cautious "popular front" approach in favor of armed struggle.

But is this perception an accurate one? Do we in fact face an aggressive, high-risk Soviet thrust in Central America? Is this, as the administration says, a matter of priority for the Soviets?

Even the most cursory examination of the evidence suggests that the answer to these questions is "no." If what the administration calls Moscow's advance base of Marxism-Leninism, i.e., Nicaragua, were of great importance to the Soviets, one would expect them to be prepared to risk a good deal, in treasure if not in blood, to maintain it. But is that the case with Nicaragua? No, it is not. The Soviets have provided modest amounts of economic assistance and will doubtless continue to do so, but they have consistently refused Nicaraguan requests for the kind of financial underwriting needed to get that country's troubled economy out of the red.

And what of their military commitment? The Soviets have provided arms and other war material, to be sure, but both superpowers have almost unlimited stocks of surplus armaments they can make available to their client states at no risk or onerous cost to themselves. The fact that the Soviet Union (or the U.S.) provides such assistance to a given state does not in itself mean that the state is considered a vital acquisition, or much less than it figures in some strategic design. Commitment is a better gauge of the country's importance in the Soviet scheme of things, and by that standard, Nicaragua fails to qualify as a key country. The Soviets have made it perfectly clear that in the event of a crisis, they would provide logistical support, but would not come to Nicaragua's defense.

Former Secretary of State Alexander Haig seems to have understood that in fact Nicaragua was of no great interest to the Soviets. Despite what he said about it at the time, he also seems to have understood that we did not face a Soviet threat in Central America. In his book, *Caveat*, Haig says that based on his conversations with Ambassador Dobrynin in Washington, he concluded "that Cuban activities in the Western Hemisphere were a matter between the United States and Cuba . . . Castro had fallen between two superpowers . . . the United States could defend its interests in the Caribbean with a relatively free hand."[4]

In other words, Haig was saying, the Soviets were not really interested in Central America, and given that they were not, we could take any military measures we wished against Cuba or Nicaragua without fear of Soviet retaliation. Haig made it clear that he favored such military solutions, but he favored them not because we faced Soviet aggression in Central America but precisely because we did not—the exact opposite of what he said in 1981.

As for the alleged changes in doctrine, they simply aren't there. At the meeting of Latin American communist and revolutionary parties in

Havana which Mr. Gersham cites as having confirmed the doctrinal shift (and which he incorrectly indicates as having taken place in 1979 rather than 1982), Cuban theorists in fact only found conditions for revolution to exist in two countries—El Salvador and Guatemala. Only in those countries would it be appropriate for Marxist-Leninist groups to assist revolutionary organizations in efforts to overthrow the governments. Cuba, then, has not gone back to across-the-board support for guerrillas anywhere and everywhere. Nor has the Soviet Union abandoned popular front tactics in favor of armed struggle. The doctrinal shift, to the extent that there is any at all, has reference only to the area of conflict in Central America. And even in El Salvador and Guatemala, there has been no tangible evidence of large-scale external support since early 1981.

And what of this frightening Soviet military buildup in the region of which Gersham, Jeane Kirkpatrick, and others of their persuasion talk so much? It is mostly an illusion of their own manufacture. There are no nuclear missile submarines operating out of Cuban bases as Kirkpatrick[5] and Gersham would have us believe. None. Nor has a single Backfire bomber ever even landed in Cuba. Several Soviet "Bear" long-range reconnaissance aircraft are deployed to Cuba. They do not, however, as Dr. Kirkpatrick has so inexplicably stated, overfly American territory from Cuban bases. One can understand the indignation with which the North American Air Defense Command says that is not so. After all, if Soviet military aircraft were overflying U.S. territory with the impunity suggested by Dr. Kirkpatrick, what would that say about the competence of our air defense?

LEGITIMATE U.S. SECURITY INTERESTS

It is not, then, a classic case of Soviet armed aggression with which we have to contend in Central America. Not even Alexander Haig really thought it was. The United States does, however, have legitimate security interests dictated by the region's proximity to the United States itself and to the Panama Canal. American leaders have long understood that those interests must be protected. We certainly do not want to see any Soviet or Cuban military bases established in Central America. Just as the placement of Soviet missiles in Cuba was intolerable to the United States in 1962, so too today would be the placement of any weapons systems in Central America which could strike either the United States or the Panama Canal, or block American shipping in adjacent waters.

The above is a first level of concern. Just below it on our scale of threat perception is the possibility that Nicaragua might extend its political system to neighboring countries, either as the result of outright military aggression, or by supporting native insurgencies. And beyond these concrete concerns is the fact that there are simply more Cuban military personnel in Nicaragua and more Soviet military influence there than we can be comfortable with, given our global adversarial relationship with the Soviet Union and its allies. A few hundred (or even thousand) Cuban military advisers may pose no immediate threat to the United States, nor may a close Soviet-Nicaraguan military relationship, but the presence of those advisers and the existence of those close military ties cannot but assure continuing suspicions and tensions in U.S.-Nicaraguan relations.

U.S. OBJECTIVES GEARED TO SECURITY INTERESTS

Given the above, our security-related objectives in Central America, in order of priority, should be the following:

1. To prohibit the placement of any Soviet or Cuban weapons systems which might menace the U.S. or the Panama Canal, also the transfer of any such systems to Nicaraguan control.
2. To prohibit the establishment of any other category of Soviet or Cuban military base in Central America.
3. To bring about the drastic reduction and eventually the total withdrawal of all Soviet and Cuban military personnel from Nicaragua.
4. To place limitations on the size of the Nicaraguan armed forces and the nature of their armaments so that Nicaragua not be in a position to threaten neighboring states.
5. To halt any support Nicaragua may be giving to guerrillas in El Salvador or other neighboring countries.

FALSE PROPOSITIONS

The above are sensible objectives. Few would argue with them. Their achievement does not presuppose the ouster of the Sandinista government. The administration, however, often insinuates that that is the only way U.S. security interests in the area can be preserved. It puts forward an alleged Nicaraguan threat to the Panama Canal, for example, as a justification for funding the *contras*. But under present circumstances, Nicaragua has no means of threatening the Panama Canal even if it wished to do so. It has no navy to speak of, no missiles, no military aircraft even capable of carrying a bombload as far as the canal. Its army would have to cross Costa Rica and then fight its way across half of Panama to even reach the canal, something it could do only if the United States sat idly by and watched it happen—which would certainly not be the case. A ground attack, then, is out of the question. Indeed, Nicaragua poses no threat at all to the canal and could do so only if it acquired a more sophisticated military capability than it now has. By concentrating its efforts on making certain that that capability is not acquired, the U.S. can easily and painlessly prevent a threat from developing. It need not overthrow the Sandinistas to accomplish that objective.

The same is true of the even more far-fetched threat to the sea lanes of which the administration talks so much, but which in fact is also totally beyond Nicaragua's present capability. Again, our emphasis should be on preventing the acquisition of the capability, not on the ouster of the government, and much less on funding the *contras* which accomplishes neither.

In fact, supporting the *contras* in their war against the Sandinistas fails to advance any of our security objectives. It does not reduce Soviet-Cuban military presence or influence. Quite the contrary, it leads inexorably to their augmentation. It is certainly no way to limit the size and nature of the Nicaraguan armed forces. Again, the result is the exact opposite: those forces are more formidable now than before the *contras* launched their "secret" war, with CIA assistance, in 1981. One would expect nothing else. The Sandinistas would hardly accept arms reductions at a time when their ports are being mined by the most powerful nation in the world and that nation is also supporting a force of guerrillas determined to overthrow them. The reaction of any sensible government to such circumstances would be to strengthen its military forces. That has been the reaction of the Sandinistas as well.

The administration has presented so little evidence since 1981 that it is impossible to judge how much of a flow there really is—if there is any flow at all. But whether it is imaginary or real, what is clear is that the *contra* war has had no effect in stopping it.

Finally, supporting the *contras* will not accomplish what the administration acknowledges to be its real objective in Nicaragua: getting rid of the Sandinista government. Testifying before the Congress in 1985, General Paul Gorman, our outgoing military commander in the area, judged that the *contras* did not have and would not have in the foreseeable future the capability to defeat the government in Managua. Events during the year proved him right. If anything, the *contras* lost ground. They control not a single community of any size and have been unable to do more than harass government outposts and make it difficult to harvest crops in certain areas of the country. This they can probably continue to do. They can, in other words, fight a war of attrition.

The central question is: does a war of attrition which advances none of our security objectives, and which the *contras* cannot win, really serve

U.S. interests? Some analysts argue that it does, that it is a low-cost way of keeping pressure on the Sandinistas and preventing them from consolidating their regime. It may not get rid of them outright, these analysts contend, but perhaps if we keep it up long enough it will indirectly bring about their collapse—by encouraging public dissatisfaction and adding to their economic difficulties.

This is a long-shot gamble. There is a chance that it might work out that way, but the odds are decidedly against it. The Soviet Union and its allies in Eastern Europe, while unwilling to give large-scale financial support, will continue to provide modest economic assistance. Nicaraguan trade with Western Europe and Canada, moreover, continues. Virtually no other country has joined the U.S. in imposing economic sanctions against Nicaragua and none is likely to in the future. Nicaragua is not isolated economically. Its economy, while threadbare and mismanaged, is in no danger of collapsing.

Further, while economic difficulties and Sandinista high-handedness have caused considerable disgruntlement, most foreign observers who have spent any time in Nicaragua over the past two years have come away convinced that the Sandinistas still have and are likely to retain the support of the great majority of Nicaraguans. The Sandinistas have not made a good showing in running the economy and they have often been guilty of political insensitivity and downright authoritarianism, but they have also launched many programs which the average Nicaraguan has reason to appreciate—e.g., a massive literacy campaign, an agrarian reform, making education and health care available to all, etc.

Rather than fueling a process of alienation, moreover, the *contra* war appears to be having the opposite effect. It provides the Sandinistas with a ready-made explanation for their economic difficulties and gives them an external threat against which to rally the Nicaraguan people. The will to rally is increased, moreover, by such *contra* excesses as burning schools and clinics, thus symbolically signalling an intention to turn back even the positive gains of the revolution against Somoza. It is also strengthened by the fact that most of the military commanders of the *contras* are ex-members of the Somoza National Guard. Whatever else the Nicaraguan people may want, they do not want to return to anything reminiscent of the Somoza regime.

As one Western European diplomat put it: "Few Nicaraguans want to be drafted, but even fewer would even think of taking up arms against the government. Most in fact, with varying degrees of enthusiasm or lack thereof, continue to support the government. And that being the case, the Sandinista government is solidly entrenched, unless the United States decides to dislodge it with its own troops."

What will be the consequences if the Sandinista regime survives our war of attrition, as the chances are very high that it will? We will then have created a situation much worse than the one we originally faced. Soviet-Cuban influence will have increased. The Nicaraguan armed forces will be larger and have greater capability. And having survived through bitter years all our efforts to bring them down, the Sandinistas, inevitably, will be more intractable, more hostile and perhaps even more radical than the regime first encountered by the Reagan administration in 1981. Further, they will be unrestrained by any regional agreements such as the one the Contadora countries have been trying to work out. In sum, we ourselves will have brought about a worst-case scenario.

HOW MIGHT THE U.S. BETTER PROTECT ITS SECURITY INTERESTS

If present policy does not advance U.S. security objectives, how might they be achieved? Is it really as Assistant Secretary of State Elliot Abrams said on January 2 that we have only three options: aid the *contras*, send in our own troops, or surrender?[6] Of course not. There is also the option of getting down to serious negotiations—the kind of negotiations which we have heretofore avoided. The negotiating option is open to us. Senior Nicaraguan leaders have stated categorically that as part of a verifiable regional agreement based on reciprocity and whose provisions would be adhered to by the United States as well, Nicaragua would do the following:

Prohibit Foreign Bases. The Nicaraguans would agree not to permit any foreign (i.e., Soviet or Cuban) bases in their territory, or otherwise allow the bombers, submarines or other offensive weapons systems of those or any other countries to operate out of Nicaraguan airfields or ports. In return, they would expect the other Central American countries also to prohibit foreign bases. This would mean advance U.S. bases in Honduras would have to be dismantled.

Withdraw Foreign Military Personnel. The Nicaraguans would agree to the drastic reduction and eventually the total withdrawal of Soviet and Cuban military personnel. They insist, however, that any ceiling be fully balanced and reciprocal—meaning that if all but a limited number of bloc military advisers were withdrawn from Nicaragua, all but the same number of American advisers would have to be withdrawn from Honduras and El Salvador. Further, since the participation of U.S. troops in Central American maneuvers would imply their reintroduction, such participation would have to be excluded or severely limited.

Unless the U.S. in some way commits itself to comply with these reciprocal provisions of an agreement, there can be no agreement. In fact, the U.S. should agree since the formula would almost certainly be in our favor. There are more Soviet and other bloc-country advisers in Nicaragua than there are Americans in El Salvador and Honduras. Thus, more of their personnel than ours would have to leave, and the departure of theirs would at least partially resolve one of our concerns, thus reducing the need for American military personnel in the area. Further, with our overwhelming naval and air superiority in the area, it would be far easier for us than for them to reintroduce forces should that ever be necessary.

Halt Military Buildups. The Nicaraguans have in fact already limited the nature of their armaments. They announced in December of 1982 that they would *not* acquire MIG aircraft. Privately, they said they hoped this would improve the atmosphere for negotiations. The Reagan administration, however, never even indicated that it thought the non-acquisition statement to be a positive development. Rather than that, within four months, the *contras* had begun to bomb targets in Nicaragua with planes which it was later established were supplied by the United States.

Nicaragua would agree to ceilings on the size of its armed forces and to restrictions on the number and nature of their armaments, so long as the same formula applied to the other countries of the region, and, most importantly, provided this came about as part of a settlement in which the United States ended its support for the *contras* and the latter ended their war against the Sandinistas. Obviously, the Sandinistas cannot and will not agree to arms limitations while they are still under attack.

Halt Cross-Border Support for Guerrillas. The administration accuses Nicaragua of providing material support to the guerrillas in El Salvador, but in some four years' time it has been unable to present any substantial proof to back up these charges. The argument could easily be ended. As part of a regional agreement, the Sandinistas are prepared to commit themselves not to engage in such activities (whether or not they have done so in the past) and to submit to on-site verification procedures. The other side of the coin would be that the U.S., Honduras and Costa Rica would have to halt their support for the *contras*.

THE ADVANTAGES OF AN INTERNATIONAL AGREEMENT

In addition to the pragmatic consideration that we have a better chance of achieving our objectives through diplomacy than through supporting the *contras*, entering into a multilateral convention with the Sandinistas would have at least two other major advantages:

First, it is a legal and appropriate way to proceed. Such measures as illegally mining harbors and then refusing to accept the jurisdiction of the World Court have caused deep misgivings among our friends and allies. This is one of the principal reasons present U.S. policy enjoys very little support. It is not that our allies in Western Europe, Canada and Latin America necessarily have any great sympathy of the Sandinistas. On the contrary, most are suspicious of their intentions and understand our concerns. What they do not understand is why, without giving diplomacy a serious try, we resort to such draconian methods which so flagrantly violate international law in dealing with this tiny little country which does not possess even a single first line combat aircraft. We would have a much better chance of winning international support for our policy if we were seriously pursuing a negotiated settlement.

Second, we would be in a position to exert more effective pressure on the Sandinistas, and do so with the force of international law on our side, if they were bound by the terms of a formal convention and understood that severe penalties would be imposed against them if they failed to abide by the terms of that convention.

The *contras* can harass but they cannot exert telling pressure; they lack the capability. The Sandinistas fear direct U.S. military measures, but given the nature of our policy and its consequent lack of popular support—both at home and abroad—they count on public opinion to restrain the United States in the implementation of such measures. They have a point. Under present circumstances, a U.S. attack against Nicaragua would provoke a major international brouhaha. Sandinista awareness of this reduces the degree to which U.S. threats to use force can be translated into effective leverage.

If, on the other hand, the Sandinista government had entered a solemn international agreement (with provisions for on-site verification) to limit the size of its army, send all foreign military personnel home, and halt all support for guerrillas in third countries, the United States would then have international law and public opinion on its side in moving against Nicaragua should the latter violate the convention. We might even be able to move with the support of the OAS, something which under present circumstances we could never do. Consequently, the credibility of our threat would be enhanced rather than diminished by a negotiated settlement.

THE ADMINISTRATION'S FAILURE
TO PURSUE A NEGOTIATED SETTLEMENT

The administration of course understands that it would not be good politics to openly reject diplomacy. Hence, it insists that it has tried negotiations and that it supported the now-defunct Contadora process. The falsity of that position, however, is well illustrated by the remarks of Assistant Secretary of State Elliot Abrams last July. On one day, he ruled out a negotiated agreement with the Sandinistas. The very idea, he said, was "preposterous."[7] Only a few days later, however, he assured his listeners that support for the Contadora process was the cornerstone of our policy in Central America.[8] But how could one support the Contadora process and at the same time rule out a negotiated agreement— given that the Contadora process was supposed to produce just that: a negotiated agreement.

An examination of some of the administration's other promises is also illustrative. In a letter to the Senate on April 23, 1985, for example, President Reagan promised to resume talks with the Sandinistas. In early June of the same year, in a letter to Congressman McCurdy of Oklahoma, the president promised to pursue diplomatic rather than military solutions. Perhaps encouraged by the president's words, in July, the foreign ministers of the Contadora countries called on the U.S. and Nicaragua to resume bilateral talks; Managua immediately accepted. Despite its earlier promises to the Congress, the Reagan administration rejected the Contadora proposal. In announcing the administration's rejection on July 22, 1985, Secretary of State George P. Shultz explained that the United States was not going to resume bilateral talks "to undermine the Contadora process."

Given that Shultz was rejecting a Contadora proposal which the Sandinistas had already accepted, his contention that it was the Sandinistas who were undermining the Contadora process was hardly persuasive, especially given the fact that Nicaragua was the only Central American country to accept the draft Contadora treaties sent around for signature in September of 1984. The United States torpedoed those particular treaties and made little effort to hide it. A National Security Council memo from October of 1984, for example, states with obvious satisfaction that: "we have effectively blocked Contadora efforts to impose the second draft to the revised Contadora Act."[9]

The administration blocked signature of the Contadora treaties in September of 1984 and in July of 1985 refused to resume bilateral talks with the Nicaraguan government. Yet, only a month earlier, in June of 1985, the administration had cited its wish for a successful outcome to the Contadora process as part of its rationale for continuing aid to the *contras*. The president told Congress in June that the United States had to continue that aid in order to keep the pressure on the Sandinistas to negotiate. Unless we did so, he said, "a regional settlement based on the Contadora principles will continue to elude us."[10]

One can only be astounded by the inconsistencies in the administration's reactions. The president says we must aid the *contras* in order to force the Sandinistas to negotiate, and Mr. Elliot Abrams then says that a negotiated agreement with the Sandinistas is "preposterous."

Verbal reactions have varied widely and often been contradictory, but the administration's actions have been consistent, and they have never supported a successful culmination of the Contadora process. That is not surprising. Given that the administration's goals and those of the Contadora process are mutually exclusive, the administration would see any regional agreement which left the Sandinistas in power as intolerable. So long as it holds to the goal of ousting the Sandinista government, it is not, by definition, seeking a negotiated solution. Nor, so long as it holds to that goal, is it likely to be in a mode to give first priority to U.S. security interests in the area. What it has done to date is to ignore that latter in pursuit of the former. There is every likelihood that it will continue to do so.

NOTES

1. As related to the author by one of the officers present at the meeting.

2. Issued in March 1985, the booklet was entitled *The Soviet-Cuban Connection in Central America and the Caribbean*.

3. Carl Gersham, "Soviet Power in Central America and the Caribbean: The Growing Threat to American Security," in *Foreign Policy and Defense Review*, Vol. V, No. 1, pp. 37–46.

4. Alexander Haig, *Caveat: Realism, Reagan and Foreign Policy* (New York: Macmillan Publishing Co., 1984), p. 131.

5. Speaking to the Republican National Convention in 1984, Dr. Kirkpatrick, in referring to the Carter years, alleged that "facilities were completed in Cuba in those years that permit Soviet nuclear submarines to roam our coasts, that permit planes to fly reconnaissance missions over the eastern United States...." See the *New York Times*, Aug. 21, 1981, p. A22, for the text of Dr. Kirkpatrick's speech.

6. *New York Times*, Jan. 3, 1986, p. A4.

7. *New York Times*, Aug. 18, 1985, p. 16.

8. *New York Times*, Sept. 9, 1985, p. 6.

9. *New York Times*, Nov. 16, 1984, p. A12.

10. *New York Times*, June 12, 1985, p. 3.

Part 2
Reagan in Central America: Roll-back or Containment?

5
Roll-back or Containment? The United States, Nicaragua, and the Search for Peace in Central America
William M. LeoGrande

/

When Ronald Reagan came to office in 1981, his administration's foremost objective in Central America was the same as President Carter's had been: to prevent the Salvadoran revolutionary movement from coming to power. This objective derived from the familiar imperative of containment—not to lose any additional countries to communism (or, in its Latin American variant, not to allow "another Cuba").

Many in the Reagan administration, however, were not content with containment; instead, they were eager to try to roll-back communism in the Third World—an agenda which gained considerable impetus in the second Reagan administration and came to be known as the Reagan Doctrine.[1] As applied in Central America and the Caribbean, the roll-back doctrine was aimed at Nicaragua and Grenada, and perhaps, if fortuitous circumstances arose, at Cuba as well.

Not everyone in the administration shared this zest for "pro-insurgency." Professionals in the national security bureaucracies generally saw the new doctrine as reckless, dangerous, and ineffective. But many of Reagan's political appointees, drawn as they were from the Republican party's ideological right, were more than willing to conduct a high risk foreign

Reprinted from International Security, vol. 11, no. 2, William M. LeoGrande, "Roll-back or Containment? The United States, Nicaragua and the Search for Peace in Central America," by permission of the MIT Press, Cambridge, Massachusetts.

policy if it held out hope of rolling back the Soviets' "Evil Empire" at the periphery.

This division meant that policy toward El Salvador was easier to agree upon than policy toward Nicaragua. The objective of defeating the Salvadoran rebels was universally accepted; disagreements, though often sharp, were merely tactical. Nicaragua proved to be more contentious because it crystallized the administration's internal division: Should the "communists" in Managua be overthrown or should they simply be contained? The tension between the adherents of containment and those of roll-back has produced a policy that often appears schizophrenic and difficult to decipher because the fundamental objectives behind it are in dispute. This schism was most clearly manifested in the debate over whether to seek some sort of negotiated accord with the Sandinistas based upon international security issues or to press instead for the elimination of the Sandinista "cancer."[2]

The aim of this chapter is to chronicle the various efforts to achieve a diplomatic settlement of the conflict between Nicaragua and the United States, and of the tensions between Nicaragua and its Central American neighbors. The recurrent motif in all the diplomatic efforts, bilateral and multilateral, formal and informal, has been the unwillingness of the United States to fully support them because of its own internal disagreement over its ultimate objectives in Nicaragua.

Despite enormous changes in the regional situation over the past six years—the birth and growth of the *contras*, the escalation of the rhetorical war between Nicaragua and the United States, the creation of Contadora—the diplomatic deadlock between Nicaragua and the United States has remained fundamentally unchanged. Since at least early 1981, if not earlier, the Sandinistas have indicated a willingness to make concessions to the United States regarding their foreign policy (specifically, their support for other Central American revolutionaries and their military ties to Cuba and the Soviet Union) in exchange for Washington's acceptance of their revolution. The Carter administration implicitly accepted this bargain; the Reagan administration would not. Within the Reagan administration, the faction that the *New York Times* dubbed "the war party" has successfully blocked any diplomatic settlement that would require coexistence between Washington and Managua because that would end any hope of getting Nicaragua back from "communism."[3]

HESITANT DIPLOMACY:
THE PEZZULO AND ENDERS INITIATIVES

Initially, Reagan's policy toward Nicaragua was a function of the effort to win the war in El Salvador. Nicaraguan assistance to the Salvadoran rebels (the FDR-FMLN, or Revolutionary Democratic Front-Farabundo Martí Front for National Liberation) had expanded during the months prior to their "final offensive" of January 1981 and was seen within the administration as an essential element in the war. Secretary of State Alexander Haig, in particular, firmly believed that the key lesson of Vietnam was the need to "go to the source" to defeat a guerrilla insurgency—i.e., to cutoff the guerrillas' logistics.

Initially, U.S. policy focused on how to halt Nicaragua's aid to the FDR-FMLN. U.S. Ambassador Lawrence Pezzullo was able to convince the new administration that it could restore the understanding Washington had with the Sandinistas before Reagan's election—that U.S. economic aid was contingent upon Nicaraguan restraint in El Salvador. Though the Sandinistas responded positively to Pezzullo's effort by reducing their aid to the FDR-FMLN, hardliners within the Reagan administration were determined to win Nicaragua's acquiescence not with the carrot of economic aid but with the stick of threatened military action. On April 1, 1981, U.S. economic aid was cut off.[4] Shortly thereafter, Pezzullo left his post as ambassador and retired from the foreign service.

In August 1981, Assistant Secretary of State for Inter-American Affairs Thomas O. Enders initiated a second effort to restore the earlier understandings with Nicaragua. The United States set forth two basic conditions for improving relations. Nicaragua had to cease its support for the guerrillas in El Salvador and halt its military buildup. Washington also proposed that Nicaragua join with the other Central American nations in an agreement to ban the importation of sophisticated weapons. In exchange, the United States offered to sign a nonaggression pact with Nicaragua under the terms of the Rio Treaty, make an effort to close the paramilitary training camps for Nicaraguan exiles that had sprung up in the United States, and ask Congress to restore economic assistance to Nicaragua.[5]

No agreement was reached on any of these issues. The Nicaraguans denied that they were providing material assistance to the Salvadoran rebels and rejected the U.S. demand that they limit their military buildup as a violation of their sovereignty. Moreover, the Nicaraguans did not trust the U.S. to meet its commitments. The Rio Treaty already prohibited the United States from resorting to force or the threat of force in its relations with Nicaragua, and the U.S. Neutrality Act already prohibited exile training camps of the sort operating in Florida and California. If the United States was not living up to existing commitments, of what value was its pledge to abide by them in the future?

Finally, the administration promised only to make an effort to close the training camps and to win a resumption of economic aid from Congress; it did not obligate the United States to actually close the camps or resume aid. In fairness, the administration could not guarantee that U.S. courts would interpret the Neutrality Act in a way that would allow closing the camps, or that Congress would agree to resume aid. But after the diplomatic fiasco of March, when the Nicaraguans made concessions only to have the administration cutoff aid anyway, the Sandinistas had no trust whatever in Washington's good faith.

The only agreement produced by the talks was for a cessation of acrimonious rhetoric in public exchanges between the two nations. In October, however, the United States conducted a joint amphibious assault exercise (Halcon Vista) with Honduras. Nicaragua denounced the exercise in the United Nations as a threat to its security. Washington interpreted this as a violation of the agreement to end the war of words, and broke off the diplomatic exchange initiated in August.[6]

There were, of course, deeper reasons for the failure of the Enders initiative. The hardliners in the Reagan administration were no more interested in reaching an agreement with Nicaragua than they had been in March when they blocked Pezzullo's efforts. They were able to cast the U.S. proposal in such imperial language that it would be sure to enflame the nationalism of the Sandinistas (which it did), and they were able to exploit Nicaragua's complaint over Halcon Vista as an excuse to terminate the dialogue.[7]

But perhaps the most important reason for the change in U.S. policy was the sudden resurgence of the guerrilla movement in El Salvador. After failing to depose the Salvadoran regime in January 1981, the Salvadoran rebels reduced operations during a six month period of reassessment. Washington mistook the guerrillas' quiescence during the spring and summer as a sign of military weakness. When the rebels launched a major offensive in October, the Reagan administration was thrown into a panic. A full-scale review of policy toward the whole region was initiated, including serious debate about the direct use of U.S. military forces in El Salvador, Nicaragua, or Cuba.[8] In the frantic efforts to stabilize the regime in El Salvador, the attractiveness of slow and difficult negotiations with Nicaragua disappeared.

MEXICO INTERCEDES:
PRESIDENT LÓPEZ PORTILLO'S INITIATIVES

In November, public warnings by various U.S. officials that the administration was considering direct military action against Nicaragua prompted Mexico to intercede in an effort to cool the crisis. In Mexico City, President José López Portillo warned Secretary of State Haig that an attack on Nicaragua would be "a gigantic historical error" and he called on the United States to halt its "escalation of verbal terrorism" against the Sandinistas.[9]

Mexico agreed to assume the role of mediator and the Nicaraguans, fearing that the threats of military action might be portentous, were eager to resume the bilateral talks broken off in October. Mexico's efforts led to a meeting between Haig and Nicaraguan Foreign Minister Miguel D'Escoto in St. Lucia just prior to the December 1981 OAS General Assembly meeting. Haig again raised the issues of Nicaraguan support for the Salvadoran rebels and the Sandinistas' military buildup, but this time he added a third issue: Washington's concern over the decline of political freedom inside Nicaragua.[10]

The addition of this issue to the bilateral agenda marked the beginning of a significant shift in U.S. policy. Heretofore, Washington had only insisted that Nicaragua behave peaceably toward its neighbors; now the United States was presuming to negotiate the nature of Nicaragua's internal political system. No issue was more certain to elicit summary rejection by the Sandinistas on grounds of national sovereignty. By adding it to the bilateral agenda, Washington was raising a preemptive demand that was, by its nature, almost certain to prevent any diplomatic agreement. It was no surprise, therefore, that the St. Lucia meeting between Haig and D'Escoto produced no improvement in relations.

Although the administration's November policy review ruled out direct military action in Central America, Washington did adopt a much more aggressively hostile policy toward Nicaragua. A series of major covert political and paramilitary operations were launched, and diplomatic efforts were begun to isolate Nicaragua economically and politically. Washington pressed international financial institutions and U.S. allies in Western Europe to cutoff loans to Nicaragua. Washington organized the Central American Democratic Community (composed of El Salvador, Costa Rica, and Honduras) as an instrument of regional cooperation to meet the Nicaraguan "threat." Despite Mexico's plea, Reagan administration officials intensified their rhetorical attacks on the Sandinistas, referring to them as "totalitarian" and "genocidal."

The Nicaraguans continued to express their interest in resuming bilateral talks with Washington during the early months of 1982, but to no avail. In an effort to address Washington's concern about arms aid flowing to the Salvadoran rebels and to constrain paramilitary attacks by Nicaraguan exiles operating out of bases in Honduras, Nicaragua proposed to Honduras the establishment of joint border patrols to halt both arms smuggling and infiltration. Honduras refused. When counterrevolutionary exiles (*contras*) blew up two northern bridges in March, the Sandinistas imposed a state of emergency that further restricted the political rights of the internal opposition.

In March, Mexican President López Portillo offered a peace initiative addressed to the "three knots of tension" in Central America: the war in El Salvador, the conflict between Nicaragua and the United States, and relations between the United States and Cuba.[11] He offered Mexico's good offices to get negotiations underway in each of these arenas. In El Salvador, the FDR-FMLN accepted the López Portillo initiative but the government, in the midst of its 1982 constituent assembly election campaign, rejected it.

Cuba also accepted the Mexican offer, even though Vice-President Carlos Raphael Rodríguez of Cuba had met secretly with Secretary of State Haig during his December 1981 trip to Mexico City, and nothing had come of it. In early 1982, Reagan sent Ambassador-at-Large Vernon Walters to Havana for a preliminary meeting with Fidel Castro, but never followed up on the initial exchange, claiming that the Cubans were unreceptive. In fact, it was the administration that was uninterested in any diplomatic effort with Cuba, and subsequent Cuban initiatives were studiously ignored.[12]

Regarding Washington's relations with Nicaragua, Mexico proposed a three-point plan for reducing tensions: (1) an end to U.S. threats of military action against Nicaragua; (2) a mutual reduction of military posturing; and (3) a nonaggression pact between the two countries. Nicaragua accepted the plan immediately. The initial U.S. response was silence. Reagan gave a major address to the OAS the week after the López Portillo initiative was announced and made no mention of the Mexican plan. Privately, administration spokesmen stated that no improvement in U.S. relations with Nicaragua was possible until the Sandinistas halted their aid to the Salvadoran rebels.

The U.S. Congress, however, responded very positively to the López Portillo initiative. Over a hundred members of the House of Representatives sent Reagan a letter urging him to accept the Mexican proposal. Thus, when Mexico explicitly asked for a meeting with U.S. officials in order to discuss the initiative, the administration felt politically compelled to accept. In meetings with Haig, the Mexicans proposed a more detailed plan: The United States would agree to disavow the threat or use of force against Nicaragua, to disarm and disperse the *contra* army in Honduras, and to close the *contra* paramilitary training camps in the United States. Nicaragua would agree to renounce the acquisition of sophisticated weapons and would sign nonaggression pacts with its neighbors and the United States. Haig responded that the Mexican plan was inadequate because it made no mention of the Sandinistas' support for the rebels in El Salvador, and that a halt to such aid remained a prerequisite for any improvement in U.S. relations with Nicaragua.[13]

This deadlock appeared to be broken in mid-March when the United States agreed to let Mexico act as an intermediary for the purposes of conveying the U.S. position to Nicaragua, and subsequently agreed to direct talks with the Sandinistas.[14] Washington set forth an agenda of issues similar to what had been discussed during the Enders initiative the previous year, and Nicaragua responded that it was prepared to begin talks immediately.[15] But no sooner had the Sandinistas accepted Washington's proposal than the administration began to delay the opening of the dialogue. Washington, as it turned out, was not really interested in talking after all; it had simply been interested in mollifying Mexico. The administration's strategy regarding Nicaragua was to increase the economic and military pressure in order to "soften the Sandinistas up," as one official phrased it.[16] For months, the administration refused to schedule negotiations, insisting instead that the dialogue remain at the level of the exchange of diplomatic notes. In August, even this pretense was abandoned; Nicaragua's August note never received a reply.

The U.S. response to the López Portillo initiative was never more than an exercise in public relations. As one U.S. official explained, "We were cool to the initiative from the beginning, but we were effectively ambushed by Congress and public opinion. We had to agree to negotiate or appear unreasonable."[17] A National Security Council summary of U.S. policy toward Central America prepared during this period speaks of the need to "coopt the negotiations issue," and to isolate Mexico internationally because its attitude was an obstacle to U.S. policy. No other mention was made of the López Portillo initiative or negotiations with Nicaragua.[18]

THE MEXICAN-VENEZUELAN INITIATIVE

In the summer of 1982, the *contras* launched a series of major attacks against Nicaragua from their Honduran bases. As rumors of war between Nicaragua and Honduras swept the region, Presidents Luis Herrera Campins of Venezuela and López Portillo of Mexico appealed to Honduran President Roberto Suazo Córdoba, Nicaraguan junta leader Daniel Ortega, and President Reagan to take swift diplomatic action to avert the outbreak of regional war. The initiative marked a shift in Venezuelan policy, which had previously been supportive of Washington.

Mexico and Venezuela suggested measures to reduce border tensions between Nicaragua and Honduras, offered to mediate between the two, and urged Washington to upgrade its diplomatic exchanges with Nicaragua to face-to-face negotiations. Once again, support for the proposal from the U.S. Congress was substantial, and the administration's response was noncommittal. In his reply to Herrera Campins and López Portillo, Reagan merely reiterated existing U.S. policy, asserting that Washington wanted only to promote democracy and halt support for "terrorist and insurgent groups."[19] It was shortly after the Mexican-Venezuelan initiative that the United States broke off even the exchange of diplomatic notes with Nicaragua. Honduras, taking its cue from Washington, also rejected the Mexican-Venezuelan proposal, insisting that any talks with Nicaragua had to take place within the framework of the Central American Forum for Peace and Democracy, a U.S.-sponsored regional organization that held only one meeting in October 1982 before Costa Rica's withdrawal led to its demise. The forum was a successor to the U.S.-sponsored Central American Democratic Community, and like the CADC, the aim of the forum was to build a regional alliance against Nicaragua.[20]

Although the initiative by Herrera Campins and López Portillo produced no tangible result in the short term, this joint diplomatic effort by Venezuela and Mexico set the stage for the convening of the "Contadora" group in January 1983, and with it the beginning of the most sustained and comprehensive search for a regional peace accord.

CONTADORA: AGREEING ON OBJECTIVES

In January, the foreign ministers of Mexico, Venezuela, Colombia, and Panama met on the Panamanian island of Contadora to discuss a joint peace initiative for Central America. Each of the four brought to the meeting a different set of interests and policy preferences for the region, but all were united by their fear of regional war and direct U.S. military intervention.[21] The communique from the January meeting called for an end to foreign involvement in the Central American crisis, a suspension of all outside military assistance to the region, a negotiated settlement of the war in El Salvador, and a halt to attacks against Nicaragua by Honduran-based *contras*.[22]

The first problem the Contadora nations encountered as they began their efforts to broker a peaceful settlement of the regional crisis was that the Central Americans disagreed on the most basic procedural issues. The Nicaraguans wanted to negotiate bilateral nonaggression pacts with the other nations and to set up joint border patrols with Honduras and Costa Rica. The Sandinistas also hoped to reopen bilateral negotiations with the United States. These proposals were basically a distillation of Mexico's 1982 initiatives. Honduras, reflecting the position of the Reagan administration, opposed bilateral negotiations, insisting instead that all regional issues be negotiated simultaneously and multilaterally—a formula that promised to be so complex and difficult that some observers took this demand as a veiled effort to block any negotiated settlement whatever.[23] The Honduran position was basically a restatement of recommendations that emerged from the October 1982 meeting of the Central American Forum for Peace and Democracy.

The initial attitude of the United States toward the Contadora process was ambivalent. Publicly, the administration kept a low profile, endorsing in principle the idea of negotiations among the Central Americans as offering "the best possibility to resolve the problems of the area."[24] It could hardly do otherwise without seriously damaging its chances of winning sustained congressional support for its Central America policy. Behind the scenes, the administration pressed for broad multi-issue, multilateral negotiations in which its regional allies—especially Honduras—could block any agreement regarded by Washington as unfavorable. Indeed, a negotiating process in which the United States could exercise an effective veto (albeit by proxy) over the outcome was in some ways superior to a continuation of the independent diplomatic initiatives Mexico had been making—initiatives that were invariably embarrassing for the U.S. policy. Moreover, the Contadora nations understood from the outset that no regional peace plan could succeed unless the United States supported it—a recognition that gave the Reagan administration enormous influence over the Contadora process even though it had neither formal participation in nor responsibility in it.[25]

The first major breakthrough in negotiations for a regional settlement came in July when, after a flurry of meetings, the Contadora heads of state presented a much more precisely defined negotiating agenda for security issues and Nicaragua, worried that the whole process might collapse otherwise, agreed to accept the multilateral negotiating framework demanded by Honduras.[26] A few days later, in response to a call by the Contadora heads of state for both the United States and Cuba to support negotiations for a regional peace, Fidel Castro announced his support of the Contadora process. Castro's only caveat was that a negotiated settlement could not bring peace to the region unless it included a solution to the conflict in El Salvador—an issue which was gradually slipping off the agenda as tensions between Nicaragua and the United States escalated, monopolizing the Contadora group's attention.[27]

The United States continued to insist upon its support for the Contadora process as well, although shortly after the Contadora heads of state appealed to Havana and Washington not to do anything that would raise the level of regional tensions, Reagan announced that the United States would hold the largest naval manuevers in the history of the Caribbean Basin just off Nicaragua's coasts.[28]

Washington's response to Cuba's endorsement of a negotiated settlement of the region's problems was also negative. In addition to expressing support for Contadora, Castro offered to end all Cuban military involvement in Central America if the United States and other powers outside

the region would do the same. The proposal stirred some interest in
the U.S. Congress, since it appeared to address the central issue of
concern to the United States: the danger that revolutionary regimes in
Central America would become military allies of Cuba and the Soviet
Union, thereby threatening the security of the U.S. and its allies. Secretary
of State Shultz promised Congress that the administration would review
the Cuban proposal seriously.[29]

But within days of that promise, a "high official" of the Reagan
administration advised the press that Washington had decided the Cuban
offer was "not serious," and there would be no discussions with the
Cubans about it. There was nothing to talk to Castro about, the official
continued, until the Cubans "stop doing what they're doing in Nicaragua,"
referring to Cuban military assistance to the Sandinistas.[30]

Such a demand was obviously pre-emptory—designed to avoid any
discussion with the Cubans rather than stimulate it since it demanded
that Cuba stop doing something it had every right to do as a sovereign
nation—give aid to an ally. Halting aid to Cuba's friends in Central
America was precisely what Castro had offered to do if the United States
reciprocated. It was, therefore, the issue around which negotiations would
center. For Washington to insist on it as a pre-condition made negotiations
irrelevant.

One reason the administration was so quick to disparage the Cuban
offer was that its terms were not advantageous to the United States.
Cuba's friends in Central America were much less dependent upon
outside assistance than Washington's and were therefore more likely to
prevail if all outside military aid were halted. Without U.S. assistance,
it seemed likely that the guerrilla forces of FDR-FMLN in El Salvador
would defeat the government. In Nicaragua, the *contra* army was totally
dependent upon the United States for its existence. A U.S. withdrawal
would have meant their eventual disappearance. This unfavorable balance
of forces was, of course, precisely the reason that the Reagan administration
had so escalated its military role in the region to begin with. Its strategy
for military victory in Central America rested upon the premise that it
could escalate faster and more effectively than Cuba or the Soviet Union
could respond. Cuba's willingness to propose a ban on all outside military
involvement in the region was read by the administration as proof that
its strategy was working.[31]

On September 9, 1983, the Contadora process produced its first
agreement when the Central American states signed a Document of
Objectives, formalizing the agenda for negotiations toward a binding
treaty. The document set out 21 points of agreement covering political,
economic, and security issues. The points of agreement on the security
issues, which were the most controversial, included: (1) a reduction of

military forces region-wide to produce a "reasonable balance"; (2) the elimination of foreign military advisors; (3) a halt to all forms of support, encouragement, or tolerance of insurgent groups operating against other Central American governments; (4) the eradication of such groups from the territory of neighboring states; (5) the elimination of arms smuggling; (6) the establishment of direct communications between states to reduce the danger of incidents between them.[32]

The political provisions called for the promotion of national reconciliation through dialogue, respect for human rights, and the creation of democratic electoral processes. The precise meaning of these requirements, however, was open to various interpretations. The economic provisions were uncontroversial, calling for greater regional integration and cooperation.

In some ways, the political and security provisions represented a surprising success for the United States, for they paralleled quite closely the points Washington had advanced at the October 1982 meeting of the Central American Forum for Peace and Democracy. That gathering of Washington's Central American allies adopted the U.S. proposal for a comprehensive regional accord providing for the withdrawal of all foreign troops and military advisors from Central America, the banning of heavy weapons, an end to support for insurgencies, and the establishment democratic institutions.[33] Contadora's Twenty-one Points were not substantially different.

In October 1983, Nicaragua presented to the Contadora nations and the United States four draft treaties for implementation of the Document of Objectives: a multilateral treaty for all the Central American nations; a bilateral treaty between Nicaragua; and a treaty regarding the civil war in El Salvador. The Nicaraguans, who had agreed to the multilateral approach only reluctantly, now sought to supplement the region-wide negotiations by opening bilateral talks with the two nations who were most active supporters of the *contras*.[34] Within 24 hours, Washington rejected the draft treaties, refusing to enter any bilateral negotiations with Nicaragua. Instead, the administration insisted that a peace accord could only be achieved through the Contadora process.[35]

Shortly after Nicaragua submitted the draft treaties, the crisis in Central America was overshadowed by the U.S. invasion of Grenada. The willingness of the Reagan administration to send U.S. forces into combat and the broad public support for the invasion in the United States clearly worried Nicaragua's Sandinista leadership. Equally disconcerting was the administration's claim that the Grenada invasion was justified because the island had been transformed into a Cuban-Soviet bastion that threatened the security of its neighbors—exactly the accusation against Nicaragua that the administration had been making for nearly two years. The administration, in turn, sought to exacerbate Nicaragua's fear of invasion by naming a new series of military exercises with Honduras *Granadero*.

In the wake of the invasion of Grenada, the Sandinistas took a series of unilateral steps addressing the security issues which the United States had complained about most bitterly. They asked a large number of Salvadoran revolutionary leaders who had been living in Nicaragua to leave the country, and they sent home approximately a thousand Cubans, most of them civilians. Internally, the Sandinistas eased press censorship, opened a new dialogue with the Church hierarchy, released some 300 Miskito Indians who had been imprisoned for political reasons, and offered an amnesty to the *contras* including all but their leadership.[36] Privately, the Sandinistas communicated to Washington that they had slowed the flow of material flowing through Nicaraguan territory to Salvadoran guerrillas, and were seeking a reciprocal gesture from the United States.[37]

None was forthcoming. These signals from the Sandinistas only encouraged the Reagan administration in its multifaceted campaign of pressures. Rather than seeing the Nicaraguan moves as an opportunity for a diplomatic solution, the administration took them as an indication that the Sandinistas were becoming weaker and, with continued pressure, could be deposed. Administration officials made clear through the press that they had no intention of making any concessions to Nicaragua, and that the policy of pressures would be stepped up, not reduced. Nicaragua's actions, like the Cuban proposals earlier in the year, were simply declared to be insincere and without meaning.[38]

The administration's diplomatic response was to relay to the Nicaraguan government a proposal developed by the *contras* in their meeting with Reagan's special negotiator, Richard Stone. The *contras* would agree to a ceasefire if Managua would open negotiations with them. "We do not talk to puppets," replied Nicaraguan Foreign Minister Miguel D'Escoto, "We would rather talk to the puppeteers."[39]

Bilateral relations between Nicaragua and the United States worsened in early 1984 when the Central Intelligence Agency began mining Nicaragua's major ports.[40] Nicaragua appealed to the United Nations Security Council, accusing the United States of responsibility for the mining, even though at that time the *contras* were claiming credit for it. Thirteen of the fifteen Security Council members voted in favor of Nicaragua's resolution condemning the mining, Britain abstained, and the United States exercised its veto.[41] Nicaragua then tried to take its case to the World Court, but the United States refused to acknowledge the court's jurisdiction in the matter.

The revelation that the CIA itself was responsible for the mining and that this escalation in the covert war had been undertaken with only the most pro forma notification of the congressional intelligence committees set off a storm of domestic protest. The Republican-dominated Senate voted 84-12 to condemn the mining.[42] Trying to repair some of the political damage done by the mining, the administration denied once again that the campaign of pressures was intended to overthrow the Sandinistas, but rather was aimed at forcing them into "meaningful negotiations" for a Central American peace plan. But to most observers, both in Central America and in the U.S. Congress, the administration's actions spoke louder than its words.

CONTADORA: DRAFTING AN ACCORD

Within the Contadora process, attention moved to drafting a regional treaty to implement the objectives agreed upon in September, but the process encountered repeated delays. In April, just prior to a Contadora meeting, the foreign ministers of Costa Rica, El Salvador, and Honduras met and produced a joint statement calling for Nicaragua reduce its military forces. When Nicaragua rejected this proposal, the United States blasted the Sandinistas for rejecting a "concrete initiative" for peace and accused them of "public relations grandstanding" in their claim to support the Contadora process.[43]

This was too much for Mexico, which had long been convinced that U.S. intransigence was the major obstacle to a regional accord, and that Washington was using its allies in the region to block progress in the Contadora negotiations. On the eve of a visit to the United States by Mexican President Miguel de la Madrid, a "senior Mexican official," blasted Costa Rica, Honduras, and El Salvador for trying to "sabotage" the Contadora process. He left little doubt that Mexico suspected that these countries were not acting on their own.[44] De la Madrid himself lamented the absence of bilateral negotiations between Nicaragua and the United States, noting that the Sandinistas had repeatedly indicated their interest in such a dialogue. He called the mining of Nicaragua's harbors "gravely damaging" to the regional peace process, and criticized the other Central American nations for their "lack for political will" to reach an accord.[45]

De la Madrid's meeting with Reagan in Washington on May 15 began with uncharacteristically sharp and critical words by both presidents about each other's stance in Central America.[46] The outcome of the meeting, however, was agreement that both sides would take some new initiatives in the area. Mexico agreed to upgrade its relations with El Salvador, where Christian Democrat José Napoleón Duarte had just won the presidential election. Washington agreed to open talks with Nicaragua.

On June 1, Secretary of State Shultz travelled without advance warning
to Managua for discussions with Nicaraguan leader Daniel Ortega, and
the two agreed that special representatives be designated by each side
to continue the talks. The United States designated Harry Shlaudeman,
who had just recently replaced Richard Stone as special negotiator for
Central America. Shultz raised four basic issues on which the United
States sought Nicaraguan action: an end to the Sandinistas support for
rebels in El Salvador; a reduction in the size of the Nicaraguan military;
an end to the presence of Cuban and Soviet military advisors in Nicaragua;
and democratization of Nicaragua's internal politics. U.S. officials described
the surprise initiative as an effort to strengthen the Contadora process.[47]

The opening of negotiations with Nicaragua had various salutary effects
for the Reagan administration. It responded to a direct request made by
Mexico, and produced a change in Mexican policy toward El Salvador
as a quid pro quo. By making the administration appear more reasonable,
the negotiations repaired some of the political damage done in Congress
by the mining of Nicaragua's harbors just as debate was resuming on
whether Congress should terminate aid to the contras. No sooner had
the negotiations begun than the administration began to argue that a
cutoff of aid to the contras would weaken the U.S. bargaining position
in the negotiations. Finally, the negotiations allowed Reagan to emphasize
his desire for peaceful political solutions to the conflicts of Central
America just as the U.S. presidential campaign was getting underway,
thus undercutting any Democratic hopes of turning the unpopularity of
Reagan's Central American policy to political advantage. It was this
prospect, in fact, that had convinced Reagan's political advisers to support
the opening of talks with Nicaragua in the first place. All of these gains
could be realized, however, without any real progress in the talks
themselves, which led both the Sandinistas and the Democrats to question
whether the administration was sincere.[48] Nevertheless, the talks went
on through the summer at the Mexican resort of Manzanillo, moving
from procedural to substantive matters, with both sides indicating satisfaction with progress being made.[49]

The administration itself was deeply divided between those who
honestly sought to achieve a negotiated agreement with the Sandinistas
and those who were intent upon deposing them. The State Department,
and in particular its Latin American bureau headed by Langehorne Motley,
hoped to secure concessions from the Sandinistas regarding their foreign
policy (i.e., their support of the guerrillas in El Salvador and their military
relationship with Cuba and the Soviet Union) in exchange for a halt to
U.S. pressures. Administration hardliners concentrated in the CIA, the
Defense Department, and the National Security Council had no interest
in negotiations. They emphasized the U.S. demand for internal political

changes in Nicaragua, knowing that the Sandinistas had repeatedly refused to negotiate this issue as a matter of Nicaraguan sovereignty. So deep was the split within the administration that the State Department kept Shultz's trip to Managua secret from the National Security Council until the last possible moment in order to give the hardliners no opportunity to sabotage it.[50]

The momentum of the bilateral talks between Washington and Managua was interrupted in September when the Contadora nations circulated a proposed peace treaty to the Central American nations, and the Sandinistas unexpectedly agreed to sign it. The treaty was a revision of an initial draft circulated in July, and represented what the Contadora nations thought would be the final act. Its security provisions prohibited foreign military schools or bases, banned international military maneuvers, required the withdrawal of all foreign military advisors, prohibited support for insurgent movements against other nations in the region, and placed limits on the size of military forces and the sophistication of their weaponry.[51]

The political provisions of the proposed treaty committed the five nations to developing representative pluralist democracies, ensuring honest periodic elections, and protecting human rights. Countries torn by civil strife would be required to promote national reconciliation. The economic provisions of the proposed treaty were designed to protect refugees, strengthen regional integration, and promote development.

Washington's reaction to Nicaragua's offer to sign the treaty was immediately negative. Administration officials denounced the Sandinista pledge as a hypocritical publicity stunt that, they feared, would undercut Washington's efforts to isolate the Sandinistas internationally and would cast doubt on the administration's claim that it sought a peaceful solution to its conflicts with Nicaragua. Some people in the administration went so far as to advocate that Nicaragua be punished for agreeing to the peace treaty—even though the administration had been justifying its policy of hostility for two years on the grounds that it was designed to make Nicaragua accept a Contadora agreement.[52]

A large part of the administration's frustration was that Managua caught it off guard. U.S. officials had assumed Nicaragua would not sign the proposed agreement because of Nicaragua's earlier objections, especially to the language on internal political conditions. Washington, therefore, had not carefully followed the drafting and submission of the September treaty, nor had they closely monitored the reactions of Honduras, Costa Rica, and El Salvador, who could always be relied upon to echo Washington's position. Before the Sandinistas agreed to sign the September treaty, these three U.S. allies had all indicated their preliminary support of the text.

The Reagan administration responded to Managua's offer to sign the September treaty by pressing its allies in the region to reverse their initial acceptance of the text and insist upon changes in it. The administration criticized the timing of several security provisions, the provisions regarding internal democracy, and the verification procedures (which were unquestionably weak). The treaty, Washington insisted, would need substantial revision before it would be acceptable.

In addition, Washington charged that Nicaragua was trying to short-circuit the negotiating process by accepting a preliminary draft and then insisting that no changes be made in it. This, the administration argued, was evidence of the Sandinistas' bad faith.[53] In fact, the treaty proposed by the Contadora nations in September was not intended as a draft at all. Based upon a revision of a draft submitted in July, the September version was intended to be the final document, as Washington knew full well and as the Contadora nations clearly said.[54]

Nevertheless, Washington was able to block acceptance of the treaty with concerted diplomatic pressure on El Salvador, Honduras, Costa Rica, and the Contadora nations themselves.[55] In late October, the foreign ministers of all the Central American countries except Nicaragua met in Honduras to draft an alternative version of the September accord, which the United States quickly endorsed. The Tegucigalpa draft omitted the ban on foreign military exercises, reduced the potential limitations on U.S. aid to El Salvador, and made the foreign ministers of the Central American states themselves the judges of alleged violations of the accord.

The Manzanillo bilateral negotiations between Nicaragua and the United States, which had made good progress through the summer, stalled almost as soon as Nicaragua agreed to sign the Contadora agreement. The U.S. position called for major concessions by Nicaragua on the size of its armed forces and its relations with the Soviet bloc, and for a reorganization of Nicaraguan domestic politics to assure democracy. In return, the United States promised only to take Nicaragua's actions "into consideration" in the formulation of its policy toward the region. Moreover, U.S. envoy Harry Shlaudeman was given strict instructions not to explore with the Sandinistas how differences in the two positions could be narrowed. The U.S. attitude, in effect, was, "Take it or leave it." As one State Department official said, "No one will tell Shlaudeman what the end game is, what the road map to a final agreement is. The reason is that the administration doesn't really want a settlement with the Sandinistas. . . . No one knows whether the United States should invade Nicaragua, but people don't want to foreclose that option by signing some kind of agreement." Hardliners within the administration reportedly opposed negotiating with the Sandinistas at all.[56]

No sooner had President Reagan been re-elected than the administration began to plan actions to increase the pressure against Nicaragua.[57] Debate raged within the administration through November and early December between the hard-liners at the Defense Department, CIA, and NSC, and officials at the State Department who favored a diplomatic settlement. In mid-December, the hard-liners prevailed. The administration's new policy began from the premise that the continued existence of the Sandinista government was unacceptable. Concerns about Nicaraguan foreign policy which had previously dominated U.S. posture toward the Sandinistas were relegated to secondary importance, to be resolved as a by-product of changing the Nicaraguan government.[58] Shortly thereafter, the United States broke off the Manzanillo talks, claiming that Nicaragua was trying to reach a bilateral accord with the United States as a way of derailing the Contadora process—despite the fact that Nicaragua had agreed to sign the September treaty.[59] Assistant Secretary of State for Inter-American Affairs Langehorne Motley, who had led the campaign for some sort of accommodation with Nicaragua, resigned shortly after the termination of the Manzanillo talks and was replaced by Elliot Abrams, a neo-conservative hard-liner.

In February and March, the administration's verbal assaults on the Sandinistas reached new heights as the campaign to renew U.S. aid to the *contras* got into full swing. Reagan called the *contras* "our brothers," and the "moral equivalent of our founding fathers."[60] He also acknowledged for the first time that the goal of administration policy was to remove the Sandinistas from power.[61]

The Sandinistas tried to revive the bilateral talks in late February when President Ortega announced he would send home 100 Cuban military advisors as a gesture of good faith and that Nicaragua would unilaterally cease the acquisition of new weapons systems. The action was also aimed quite openly at effecting the growing debate in the U.S. Congress on aid to the *contras*.[62] As Ortega was making these public gestures, Nicaragua privately suggested that Ortega meet with Secretary Shultz at the upcoming inauguration of Uruguayan President Julio Sanguinetti in order to renew the bilateral dialogue.[63] The two met in Uruguay, but did little more than restate their respective positions; no real progress was made and bilateral talks were not resumed.[64]

Attention then returned to the Contadora process, which had been paralyzed since Washington's sabotage of the September draft treaty. Reviving the Contadora process from that trauma proved to be no easy task. In February 1985, Costa Rica, Honduras, and El Salvador refused to attend any further Contadora meetings because Nicaraguan police were holding a Nicaraguan citizen who had sought asylum in the Costa Rican embassy in Managua in August 1983, but was then apprehended outside the embassy by Sandinista police in December. Costa Rican authorities refused to participate in further negotiations unless this individual was allowed to emigrate to Costa Rica.[65] This obstacle was finally overcome when, after several weeks of stalemate, Nicaragua agreed to release the prisoner to Costa Rica in order to proceed with the Contadora negotiations.

In April, the administration launched its effort to convince Congress to resume aid to the *contras* after nearly a year interruption. Reagan proposed a "peace plan" for the region, calling on the Sandinistas to open negotiations with the *contras*. The plan as outlined was essentially a restatement of a plan put forward by the contras themselves in March in San Jose, Costa Rica, and was not well received by the Contadora nations.[66] From this point, onward, however, the administration took the position that it would not resume bilateral talks with Nicaragua unless the Sandinistas agreed to open negotiations with the *contras*. This demand, like the earlier insistence that the Sandinistas agree to negotiate their internal political arrangements, was a pre-emptive demand whose effect was to prevent negotiations.

After the Congress narrowly rejected Reagan's bid to resume assistance to the *contras*, the administration imposed a full economic embargo on Nicaragua. The embargo was widely criticized by U.S. allies in Latin America and Europe, and no other nation in the world joined it. Mexico called the embargo "economic coercion . . . not compatible with the objectives of the Contadora group." Venezuela and Panama criticized it as well, though they were careful to balance their statement with criticism of Nicaraguan President Daniel Ortega's trip to Moscow.[67] Two months later, under intense pressure from the administration, Congress reversed itself and approved $27 million in nonlethal logistical aid for the *contras*. Nicaragua immediately insisted that the Contadora group take up the issue of the escalating war against it, and when the other Central American nations refused, Nicaragua briefly boycotted the negotiations.

Fearful that U.S.-Nicaraguan relations were once again heading toward direct confrontation, the Contadora nations appealed to the United States in late July to reopen the Manzanillo talks. Secretary Shultz refused, explaining that bilateral talks would "undermine Contadora."[68] The Contadora nations grew increasingly frustrated by U.S. opposition and their consequent inability to broker an agreement. Within each of the four, conservative political forces grew stronger in their demand that the process be terminated rather than allowing it to strain bilateral relations with the United States. This was especially true in Mexico, where the debt burden (and later the economic consequences of the earthquake) made the government especially vulnerable to pressure.

In an effort to counter-balance U.S. pressure Brazil, Uruguay, Peru, and Argentina formed a Contadora Support Group (Grupo de Apoyo, also known as the Lima Group) in August.[69] The establishment of Lima Group formally involved the major South American democracies in the peace process in Central America, thereby lending substantial diplomatic weight to the Contadora countries, especially in their dealings with the Washington. Together, the two groups included every major ally of the United States in Latin America.

In September, the Contadora states submitted a new draft of the regional accord to the Central American governments, insisting that they reach a decision on whether or not to sign the document within 45 days.[70] The 1985 draft devoted much greater attention to issues of implementation, verification, and enforcement. It also incorporated changes suggested by Washington's allies in the region which Nicaragua found unacceptable.[71] Specifically, the new draft allowed for the continuation of international military maneuvers within certain limits (whereas the 1984 draft prohibited them) and it redefined foreign military advisers vaguely as foreign personnel capable of playing a military role. The Sandinistas felt, rightly, that the first change would allow the United States to continue its practice of conducting intimidating military exercises in Honduras, and that the second was aimed at forcing the expulsion of Cuban civilian as well as military advisers since most Cuban "internationalists" had some military training.

The biggest problem, however, was Nicaragua's insistence that no Contadora agreement could be signed unless the United States would formally pledge to abide by it—i.e., to stop aiding the *contras* and trying to overthrow the Sandinista regime. "The interventionist and aggressive policy of the U.S. government is playing the central role in the Central American crisis," wrote President Daniel Ortega, "Given this, it is not possible to find a lasting or stable solution to the prevailing conflicts unless the U.S. government agrees to serious and detailed commitments to halt its illegal conduct."[72] Nicaragua's point was logical enough. Once it signed a Contadora agreement, it would have to freeze the size of its military and enventually reduce it to mutually agreed upon levels. The United States, if not formally bound to observe the terms of a Contadora accord, would be free to continue or even escalate its paramilitary pressures against the Sandinistas, and they would be unable to expand their defenses to meet the threat.

The Sandinistas' point was not new; they had long maintained that no Contadora agreement could succeed unless Washington were willing to support it. Indeed, this assumption was shared by all the Central American governments and by the Contadora nations themselves. But until November 1985, when the Sandinistas insisted upon a formal U.S.

pledge as a necessary condition for signing an accord, no one had stated the dilemma so starkly. There could be no accord without Washington's willingness to reach a modus vivendi with the Sandinistas. And that was the one thing that Washington seemed unwilling to contemplate.

The self-imposed deadline of November 20 came and went with the negotiating process still deadlocked. Frustrated by the lack of progress and increasingly preoccupied with internal problems, the Contadora nations accepted a suggestion made by Nicaragua to suspend negotiations for five months until after the election and inauguration of new presidents in Honduras, Guatemala, and Costa Rica.[73]

Mexico, in particular, stated openly that it intended to deemphasize Central America, focusing instead on bilateral relations with Washington—particularly the issue of debt—because the regional conflict had proven so intractable. Neither Washington nor Managua, Mexico insinuated bitterly, had the desire to reach a settlement in Central America. Washington, for its part, continued to pressure the Mexicans to change their regional policy by hinting that a cooperative attitude on the debt issue might depend upon Mexican concessions in Central America.[74]

Colombia's enthusiasm for Contadora had waned as well. President Belisario Betancur had come to office intent upon settling Colombia's internal conflict by negotiations with the guerrillas, especially the powerful M-19. This process, he hoped, would serve as a model for national reconciliation in Central America. When the truce Betancur negotiated with the M-19 collapsed in bloody violence in late 1985, Colombia's interest and energy was diverted from Contadora.

Venezuela had played only a minor supporting role in the Contadora negotiations since the election of Jaime Lusinchi, who was more intent upon addressing Venezuela's internal economic problems. Panama, always a junior partner in the Contadora group, was wholly preoccupied by internal politics; the civilian president, elected by the slimmest of margins in a contest whose honesty was a matter of considerable dispute, was forced to resign in late 1985 by the national guard.

There was much speculation that the Contadora process was finally dead—speculation that seemed confirmed when Secretary Shultz, on his way to an OAS meeting in early December, said that the United States would continue to give assistance to the *contras* even if a Contadora agreement were signed. At the meeting, the eight foreign ministers of the Contadora and Support Groups again called for the United States to resume bilateral talks with Nicaragua, and Washington again refused.[75]

The impetus for reviving Contadora came unexpectedly from Marco Vinicio Cerezo, the Christian Democrat who was elected president of Guatemala in December. Shortly after his election, Cerezo toured Central America expressing his desire to assist in the search for regional peace and affirming that Guatemala's policy would be one of "affirmative neutrality," which was understood to mean that he would not join Washington's crusade against the Sandinistas.[76] Prompted by Cerezo's activism and the positive response he encountered in his travels, the foreign ministers of the Contadora countries and their supporters in the Support Group met in January in Carabelleda, Venezuela where they adopted a communique calling for a resumption of the Contadora negotiations among the Central Americans and a resumption of bilateral talks between Nicaragua and the United States. A few days later, Cerezo's inauguration became the occasion for an impromptu summit among most of the Central American heads of state, and their foreign ministers issued a statement endorsing the Carabelleda declaration.[77]

In early February, the foreign ministers of Contadora and the Support Group assembled once again in Washington to ask the Reagan administration to resume talks with the Sandinistas and to halt aid to the *contras*. Their audience with Secretary Shultz had little impact on U.S. policy; at the same time they were making their appeal, Reagan was telling an interviewer from the *Washington Post* that he was "going to go all out," to convince Congress to approve military aid for the *contras*. Regarding bilateral talks, Shultz simply reaffirmed existing policy: the Sandinistas would have to open negotiations with the contras before Washington would consider a new dialogue.[78]

Yet in the inner councils of the administration, the diplomatic pressure brought to bear by the eight Latin nations was beginning to have some effect. The State Department, which in the past had been more willing than other agencies to see some sort of diplomatic settlement with the Sandinistas, was loath to once again simply reject the appeal of the Contadora eight. Not only was the U.S. posture eroding relations with the rest of the hemisphere, it was also eroding support for the Administration's policy in the U.S. Congress. The State Department proposed that the administration proceed with its plan to see congressional approval for military aid for the *contras*, but that it offer to delay disbursement pending the resumption of the Contadora negotiations. The moratorium would be extended as long as the talks were making adequate progress. Hard-liners in the White House and the Defense Department vetoed the plan, and U.S. policy remained unchanged.[79]

In March, Reagan appointed Ambassador Philip Habib as his new special envoy to Central America. The move was widely viewed as an effort to bolster the administration's flagging credibility on Capitol Hill as Congress was once again considering Reagan's proposal to increase aid to the *contras*.[80] Even within the administration, some saw the appointment cynically. "There's no real interest in negotiations," a senior official observed, "This administration believes that a negotiated settlement with these guys (the Sandinistas) . . . would be a life-time insurance policy for the revolution."[81]

The Contadora nations and the Central Americans resumed negotiations in early April 1986, but found themselves deadlocked around the same issues that had stalled negotiations in November 1985. The Sandinistas continued to insist upon a formal commitment of nonaggression from the United States as a precondition of signing a final agreement. The Contadora nations (including Mexico, which was normally sympathetic to Nicaragua's position) urged Nicaragua to drop this precondition. The United States, they argued, would never give such a guarantee; if the Sandinistas continued to insist upon it, the whole process could collapse. If, on the other hand, Nicaragua agreed to sign the agreement without a pledge from Washington, Congress would most likely cutoff aid to the *contras* anyway.[82] Nicaragua would not give in, and the April meetings ended with Nicaragua unwilling to sign a pledge that would commit it to signing a final accord by June 6.[83]

Just as the April meetings concluded, Ambassador Habib wrote a letter to Representative Jim Slattery (D-Kansas) defining the administration's position regarding Contadora. In the letter, which the Department of State subsequently transmitted to the Contadora nations as an official statement of U.S. policy, Habib noted that the United States would not be a signatory of any Contadora accord and therefore would not be legally bound by it. He went on to pledge, however, that Washington would "as a matter of policy" abide by the terms of an accord that was being fully respected by all the signatories. Most important, he interpreted the draft accord as requiring an end to aid for paramilitary forces (i.e., the *contras*) "from the date of signature" of the agreement.

To be sure, there were various escape clauses carefully crafted into the letter. The United States could make its own determination as to whether Nicaragua was abiding by the accord, and would be free to act accordingly. In particular, the Reagan administration interpreted "national reconciliation" to mean that the Sandinistas would have to negotiate with the *contras*—a very different interpretation than was held in Manauga or in the Contadora countries.[84]

Nevertheless, the Habib letter exploded inside the Reagan administration, leading to open warfare between the pragmatists in the State Department and the hardliners in the Defense Department, CIA, and National Security Council. Congressional conservatives acted as pointmen for the hard-liners. In an April 29 meeting with Habib, conservative House Republicans accused the envoy of "selling out" the *contras*.[85] Representative Jack Kemp (R-NY) and Senator Jesse Helms (R-NC) complained directly to Reagan about Habib, and Kemp even wrote to Reagan calling for Habib's ouster. The White House quickly defended

Habib, but the next day, an unnamed "senior administration official" repudiated the Habib letter, saying that Washington would not end its support of the *contras* until Nicaragua had implemented the full Contadora agreement.[86]

The administration's internal battle broke fully into the public when the Department of Defense released a study entitled, *Prospects for Containment of Nicaragua's Communist Government.* The report was a major attempt by the hard-liners to discredit the Contadora process. It argued that if a Contadora agreement was signed, Nicaragua would violate it and the United States would have no choice but to intervene directly in Nicaragua with 100,000 troops at a cost of $9.1 billion the first year. Outraged, the State Department denounced the report as having "no standing as a United States Government document." Undersecretary of Defense Fred C. Ikle, who had directed the study, called the State Department "plain wrong," insisting that the document had been cleared with senior officials both at State and in the White House.[87] President Reagan did little to reduce the internecine combat, assuring the hardliners that he would never abandon the *contras*, while simultaneously expressing confidence in Habib, whose letter pledged that Washington would abandon the *contras* if Contadora succeeded.

As discussions resumed in May among the Contadora nations and the Central Americans, Washington's allies began to insist on reopening issues which had already been resolved—particularly the procedures and arrangements for verifying the accord, and the meaning of "national reconciliation" and democracy. Both of these were points in the draft that the Reagan administration had complained about, which suggested that the reopening of them was approved if not instigated by Washington.[88] The June 6 deadline for signing an accord had to be postponed, and there was little likelihood that an agreement could be concluded quickly. With the Contadora nations unwilling to see the process fail and the United States unwilling to allow it to succeed, the Contadora negotiations seemed destined to continue indefinitely.

CONCLUSION

From its earliest days in office, the Reagan administration has been divided over whether its primary objective in its relations with Nicaragua should be to find a basis for coexistence with the Sandinista government in Nicaragua or to overthrow it. Those who have favored coexistence have put a high priority on security issues, seeking to contain the Nicaraguan revolution. In effect, they have been prepared to offer the Sandinistas a deal in which they make concessions on security issues of special concern to the United States in exchange for Washington's acceptance of their existence. Those in the administration who reject the containment formula have always insisted that only the elimination of the Sandinista regime is consistent with U.S. interests.

Efforts to find a regional diplomatic solution to the Central American crisis have repeatedly run aground on this schism. Whenever those favoring a policy of containment have sought to move toward a diplomatic solution on the basic security issues, hard-liners have managed to block them. Over time, Washington's policy toward Nicaragua has gradually hardened to the point that U.S. officials are no longer reticent about admitting that they seek the removal of the Nicaraguan government. The unlikelihood of a *contra* military victory and the enormous cost of a direct intervention was all that kept the containment position alive.

Because the administration was unwilling to commit itself to achieving a diplomatic accord with Nicaragua, the Contadora process was primarily a public relations problem. Contadora was widely hailed in Congress and among U.S. allies worldwide as the best hope for peace in Central America. This posed a dilemma; the Reagan administration did not want to be seen as an obstacle to peace, but at the same time did not want to give up the option of waging war. As the covert war came under increasing attack on Capitol Hill, it was essential for the administration to be able to argue that it was supporting Contadora. The administration solved its dilemma by constantly paying lip service to Contadora, but never letting it interfere in the slightest with the policy of hostility toward Nicaragua. So long as Washington could control the direction of Contadora through its allies, Honduras, El Salvador, and Costa Rica, there was little danger that Contadora would produce an agreement that would put Washington's bona fides to the test.

In fact, a successful Contadora agreement along the lines developed in the various draft accords would pose some serious problems for the Reagan administration's policy in Central America. An agreement that excluded any significant foreign military presence from outside Central America would require drastic changes in the U.S. military posture—especially if El Salvador and Honduras, where there were hundreds of U.S. military advisors and a variety of installations used by U.S. military and intelligence forces. The Contadora requirement that all foreign military schools and bases be closed and all foreign military advisors be withdrawn would mean the virtual end of U.S. efforts to retrain the Salvadoran and Honduran armed forces in counterinsurgency warfare. The ban on importing heavy weapons into the region would limit U.S. efforts to modernize the air forces of those two nations.

In El Salvador, in particular, such a cutback in U.S. assistance would constitute a danger to the survival of the regime. Of course, a successful Contadora agreement would also prohibit Nicaraguan aid to the guerrillas, making it more difficult for them to acquire external logistical support. But the outcome of the Salvadoran war would then depend upon which side, the government or the guerrillas, was more dependent upon external aid, and to most observers, the government's position appeared the more tenuous. Certainly Washington showed no interest in wagering otherwise.

Most importantly, though, a Contadora agreement would eliminate Honduras and Costa Rica as bases for the *contras*. Since the *contras* had shown no capacity to survive inside Nicaragua, the closing of their base camps meant the end of the covert war. Nor could the administration expect Congress to continue funding the war if Nicaragua signed a peace accord with its neighbors and sent home all its Cuban and Soviet miltary advisors. And without the *contras*, there was no hope whatever that the Sandinistas could be overthrown. Washington would have to live with them—something that the hard-liners in the administration were simply not willing to do.[89]

The *contras*, however, seemed utterly incapable of unseating the Sandinistas by themselves. Washington's policy of hostility was slowly transforming Nicaragua into another Cuba, and it offered no plausible means—short of a U.S. invasion—for winning. To pragmatists in the State Department, the Contadora agreement seemed to offer a possible exit that would at lease achieve U.S. security objectives in the region. And so the Reagan administration's internecine conflict between the containment camp and the war party continued—the pragmatists willing to accept the revolution in Nicaragua so long as the Sandinistas abstained from a strategic alliance with the Soviet Union, and the hard-liners intent upon rolling back the Nicaragua revolution no matter what.

NOTES

1. By 1986, the administration was more or less publicly providing support to insurgencies against "Communist" regimes in Nicaragua, Angola, Cambodia, and Afghanistan.

2. The literature on Nicaragua and on relations between Nicaragua and the United States is vast and growing rapidly. The best history of U.S.-Nicaraguan relations is still Richard Millet, *Guardians of the Dynasty* (New York: Orbis, 1977). On the internal situation in Nicaragua both before and after the 1979 revolution, see John A. Booth, *The End and the Beginning: The Nicaraguan Revolution* (Boulder, CO: Westview Press, 1982), Thomas W. Walker, *Nicaragua: Land of Sandino* (Boulder, CO: Westview Press, 1986), and Dennis Gilbert, "Nicaragua," in *Confronting Revolution: Security Through Diplomacy*, ed. Morris Blachman, William M. LeoGrande, and Kenneth Sharpe (New York: Pantheon, 1986). A number of recent books focus on developments in Nicaragua since the revolution. Among the best are two volumes edited by Thomas W. Walker, *Nicaragua in Revolution* (New York: Praeger, 1982) and *Nicaragua: The First*

Five Years (New York: Praeger, 1985). Carlos M. Vilas, *The Sandinista Revolution* (New York: Monthly Review, 1986) provides an account sympathetic to the Sandinistas, and Shirley Christian, *Revolution in the Family* (New York: Vintage, 1986) provides one sympathetic to their opponents. Bruce Marcus has edited a very useful volume of key speeches by Sandinista leaders, *Nicaragua: The Sandinista People's Revolution* (New York: Pathfinder, 1985). On relations between Nicaragua and the United States, see the extensive collection of articles and documents in Peter Rosset and John Vandermeer (eds.), *The Nicaragua Reader* (New York: Grove, 1983). For a discussion of the covert war and a first-hand account of the *contras*, see Christopher Dickey, *With the Contras: A Reporter in the Wilds of Nicaragua* (New York: Simon and Schuster, 1985). The broader international implications of the Central American conflict are discussed in Richard E. Feinberg (ed.), *Central America: International Dimensions of the Crisis* (New York: Holmes and Meier, 1982), Joseph Cirincione (ed.), *Central America and the Western Alliance* (New York: Holmes and Meier, 1985), and Andrew J. Pierre (ed.), *Central America as a European-American Issue* (New York: Council on Foreign Affairs, 1985).

3. "It Takes Two to Contadora," (editorial), *New York Times*, May 22, 1986.

4. "U.S. Halts Economic Aid to Nicaragua," *New York Times*, April 2, 1981.

5. Don Oberdorfer, "U.S., in Secret Dialogue, Sought Rapprochement with Nicaragua," *Washington Post*, December 10, 1981.

6. Ibid.

7. For an excellent account of the Enders initiative and subsequent bilateral diplomatic efforts between Nicaragua and the United States, see Roy Gutman, "Nicaragua: America's Diplomatic Charade," *Foreign Policy*, No. 56 (Fall 1984): 3-23. Essentially, Gutman concludes that U.S. efforts to reach an accord with Nicaragua were half-hearted at best.

8. John M. Goshko. "Haig Won't Rule Out Anti-Nicaragua Action," *Washington Post*, November 13, 1981.

9. Marlise Simons, "Mexico Warns Against Attack on Nicaragua," *Washington Post*, November 25, 1981.

10. Barbara Crossette, "Haig Asserts the Nicaraguans May Discuss Resuming Ties," *New York Times*, December 3, 1981.

11. Alan Riding, "Lopez Portillo Urges Talks on Region," *New York Times*, February 22, 1982.

12. Wayne S. Smith, "Dateline Havana: Myopic Diplomacy," *Foreign Policy*, No. 48 (Fall 1982): 157-174.

13. Don Oberdorfer, "Mexican Tells Haig Details of Peace Plan," *Washington Post*, March 7, 1982.

14. Alan Riding, "Nicaragua Ready to Talk with U.S.," *New York Times*, March 19, 1982; Alan Riding, "U.S. and Nicaragua Said to Agree to Hold Direct Talks on Disputes," *New York Times*, March 24, 1982.

15. Bernard Gwertzman, "Nicaragua is Given New U.S. Proposal to Mend Relations," *New York Times*, April 10, 1982; John M. Goshko, "U.S. Considers Aid to Nicaragua to Ease Tensions," *Washington Post*, April 10, 1982; Barbara Crossette, "Nicaragua Accepts U.S. Plan for Talks on Reconciliation," *New York Times*, April 15, 1982.

16. Leslie Gelb, "Central America Talks: Less Than Meets the Eye," *New York Times*, March 25, 1982; John M. Goshko, "U.S. Stalling on Negotiations with Nicaragua," *Washington Post*, April 17, 1982; "U.S. is Said to Rule Out a Plan for Sandinista Talks," *New York Times*, May 1, 1982.

17. Alan Riding, "Mexicans Pessimistic on Talks Between U.S. and Caribbean Leftists," *New York Times*, May 10, 1982.

18. Raymond Bonner, "President Approved Policy of Preventing Cuba-Model States," *New York Times*, April 7, 1983.

19. Joanne Omang and John M. Goshko, "House Members Urge Reagan to Negotiate in Central America," *Washington Post*, October 7, 1982.

20. Marlise Simons, "Latin Plan for Peace Parley Excluding U.S. is Postponed," *New York Times*, April 11, 1983.

21. For a good explication of the Contadora countries' motives, see Tom Farer, "Contadora: The Hidden Agenda," *Foreign Policy*, No. 59 (Summer 1985): 59–72. For a detailed discussion of the foreign policies of the major Contadora states, see Bruce Michael Bagley, *Regional Powers in the Caribbean Basin: Mexico, Venezuela, and Colombia*, Occasional Paper No. 2 (Washington, DC: Johns Hopkins School of Advanced International Studies, 1983).

22. "Four Latin Officials on Peace Tour," *New York Times*, April 13, 1983.

23. Dial Torgerson, "Latin Officials End Central America Peace Tour," *Los Angeles Times*, April 14, 1983; Alfonso Chardy, "Latin Ministers Fail to Find Peace Plan," *Miami Herald*, April 22, 1983.

24. Stuart Taylor, Jr., "U.S. Still Favors Latin Peace Talks," *New York Times*, April 11, 1983.

25. Pamela Constable, "Diplomacy: Mistrust, Posturing Impede Search for Peace," *Boston Globe*, May 15, 1983.

26. Martin McReynolds, "U.S., Castro Urged to Aid Latin Peace," *Miami Herald*, July 18, 1983.

27. "Fidel Castro on Central America," *Cuba Update*, 4, No. 4 (August 1983).

28. Fred Hiatt, "U.S. to Increase its Military Presence in Central America: Exercises' Aim to 'Intimidate' Nicaragua," *Washington Post*, July 21, 1983.

29. "Central America: To Talk or Not to Talk," *Newsweek*, August 15, 1983.

30. Lou Cannon, "U.S. Said to Doubt Cuban Bid to End Latin Arms Aid," *Washington Post*, August 14, 1983.

31. Daniel Southerland, "Administration Sees Progress Toward Negotiations in Central America," *Christian Science Monitor*, August 1, 1983. The administration's refusal to even seriously consider the Cuban offer was simply one in a long series of negative responses to Cuban initiatives on Central America. See Wayne Smith, "Myopic Diplomacy."

32. Text of the Document of Objectives, as reprinted in Inter-American Dialogue, *The Americas in 1984: A Year for Decisions* (Washington, DC: Aspen Institute, 1984), 76–82.

33. Barbara Crossette, "What Hopes for the Contadora Process?" *New York Times*, June 19, 1983.

34. Patrick E. Tyler, "Sandinistas Propose Four Security Accords to U.S." *Washington Post*, October 21, 1983.

35. Hedrick Smith, "U.S. Spurns Peace Plan Offered by Nicaragua," *New York Times*, October 22, 1983.

36. Robert S. Greenberger, "Nicaragua Offers Amnesty to Some Critics as Part of Plan to Hold Elections in 1985," *Wall Street Journal*, December 5, 1983.

37. Leslie Gelb, "Latin Diplomacy: Little Result Yet," *New York Times*, April 29, 1984.

38. Hedrick Smith, "U.S. Policy on Nicaragua: Keep the Pressure On," *New York Times*, December 1, 1983; Don Oberdorfer, "U.S. Officials Doubt Reports of Changes in Nicaraguan Policy," *Washington Post*, November 26, 1983.

39. George Skelton, "U.S. Relays Peace Bid to Nicaragua," *Los Angeles Times*, December 2, 1983.

40. Philip Taubman, "Americans on Ships said to Supervise Nicaragua Mining," *New York Times*, April 8, 1984.

41. "U.S. Vetoes U.N. Resolution on Mines in Nicaragua," *Washington Post*, April 5, 1984.

42. Martin Tolchin, "Senate, 84-12, Acts to Oppose Mining Nicaragua Ports," *New York Times*, April 11, 1984.

43. Don Oberdorfer, "U.S. Says Nicaragua Won't Back Up Claimed Peaceful Intentions," *Washington Post*, May 2, 1984; Robert J. McCartney, "Mexico Says U.S. Allies 'Sabotage' Peace Efforts," *Washington Post*, May 13, 1984.

44. Ibid; "Obstruction of Contadora Efforts Is Charged," *New York Times*, May 13, 1984.

45. Robert J. McCartney, "Mexico Says Peace Moves at an Impasse," *Washington Post*, May 11, 1984.

46. Francis X. Clines, "Blunt Talk Marks Reagan's Welcome for Mexico's Chief," *New York Times*, May 16, 1984.

47. Joanne Omang, "Shultz Meets with Ortega in Managua," *Washington Post*, June 2, 1984.

48. Bill Keller, "Democrats Laud Nicaragua Move But They Question the Motives," *New York Times*, June 3, 1984; Robert J. McCartney, "Managua Wary of Initiative by Washington," *Washington Post*, June 3, 1984.

49. Philip Taubman, "Nicaragua Talks Said to Progress," *New York Times*, August 23, 1984.

50. John M. Goshko and Joanne Omang, "Administration Split: Pursuit of U.S.-Sandinista Pact Is Debated," *Washington Post*, July 8, 1984.

51. "Contadora: A Text for Peace," *International Policy Report*, November 1984 (Washington, DC: Center for International Policy). This report includes the text of key provisions from the September 7, 1984, proposed Contadora treaty and of the U.S. Department of State's objections to it. See also, John Lantigua, "Draft Pact Would Limit Arms in Central America," *Washington Post*, September 25, 1984.

52. Philip Taubman, "U.S. Reported to Fear Sandinista Publicity Coup," *New York Times*, September 24, 1984.

53. John M. Goshko, "Modify Contadora Plan, U.S. Urges Latin Allies," *Washington Post*, October 2, 1984.

54. "U.S. Version of Contadora Draft Disputed," *Washington Post*, October 3, 1984.

55. Joanne Omang, "Washington Plays Contadora Catch-up," *Washington Post*, October 15, 1984; Alma Guillermoprieto and David Hoffman, "Document Describes How U.S. 'Blocked' a Contadora Treaty," *Washington Post*, November 6, 1984.

56. Philip Taubman, "Nicaraguan Talks Are Said to Stall," *New York Times*, November 2, 1984.

57. Philip Taubman, "U.S. Said to be Studying Ways to Increase Pressure on Nicaragua," *New York Times*, November 11, 1984.

58. Joanne Omang, "U.S. Is Hardening Stand on Nicaragua," *Washington Post*, December 17, 1984.

59. Philip Taubman, "U.S. Says It Has Halted Talks with Nicaragua," *New York Times*, January 19, 1985.

60. Gerald M. Boyd, "Reagan Terms Nicaraguan Rebels 'Moral Equivalent of Founding Fathers,'" *New York Times*, March 2, 1985.

61. Hedrick Smith, "President Asserts Goal Is to Remove Sandinista Regime," *New York Times*, February 22, 1985.

62. John Lantigua, "Nicaraguan Says 100 Cuban Advisers to be Sent Home," *Washington Post*, February 28, 1985.

63. Larry Rohter, "Nicaragua Seeks Parley with U.S.," *New York Times*, February 28, 1985.

64. Jackson Diehl and John M. Goshko, "Shultz Sees Ortega in Uruguay," *Washington Post*, March 3, 1985.

65. "Central American Peace Drive Collapses," *Washington Post*, February 14, 1985.

66. Richard J. Meislan, "Reagan Peace Plan for Nicaragua Gets Only Cool Support in Region," *New York Times*, April 12, 1985.

67. "Mexico Joins Critics of U.S. Embargo Against Nicaragua," *Washington Post*, May 5, 1985.

68. Richard J. Meislin, "Shultz Rejects Resumption of Talks with Sandinistas," *New York Times*, July 27, 1985.

69. "Press Release Issued by the Ministers of Foreign Relations of the Contadora Group and Those of the Support Group, Integrated by Argentina, Brazil, Peru, and Uruguay, August 26, 1985," Embassy of Mexico Press Release No. 15/85.

70. "Acta de Contadora para la paz y la cooperacion en Centroamerica" and "Acta de Contadora: Documento explicativo" (Texts of the September 1985 draft treaty and accompanying statement of the Contadora Group, Panama City, Panama, September 12, 1985, mimeograph).

71. Nicaragua's objections to the draft are explained in "Letter from the President of Nicaragua addressed to the presidents of the countries of the Contadora Group and the Support Group, November 11, 1985," United Nations General Assembly document A/40/894 (New York: United Nations, 1985).

72. Ibid.

73. "Latin Peace Meetings Suspendedn Until May," *New York Times*, January 3, 1986. For a discussion of the differing attitudes of the Contadora nations toward the process, see Susan Kaufman Purcell, "Demystifying Contadora," *Foreign Affairs*, [date missing]: 74–95.

74. Robert J. McCartney, "U.S. Seen as Unhappy with Mexico's Policies," *Washington Post*, December 25, 1985; William Stockton, "Reagan Sees Mexican Today," *New York Times*, January 3, 1986.

75. Doyle McManus, "No Stopping Aid to Contras, Shultz Insists," *Los Angeles Times*, December 2, 1985; Alan Riding, "Eight Latin Countries Call for U.S.-Nicaraguan Talks," *New York Times*, December 4, 1985.

76. "New Leader Says That Guatemala's 'Neutrality' Role Will Continue," *Washington Post*, December 16, 1985.

77. "Caraballeda Message for Peace, Security, and Democracy in Central America" (Message of the Foreign Ministers of the Contadora Group and the Support Group, Caraballeda, Venezuela, January 12, 1986, mimeograph) and "The Statement of Guatemala" (Statement of the Foreign Ministers of the Central American States, Guatemala City, Guatemala, January 14, 1986, mimeograph); Robert J. McCartney, "Contadora Peace Efforts Revived," *Washington Post*, January 16, 1986.

78. "Latin Ministers Urge U.S. to Halt Aid to Contras," *The New York Times*, February 11, 1986.

79. Joanne Omang, "Latin Peace Talk Move Vetoed," *Washington Post*, February 16, 1986.

80. Joanne Omang, "Troubleshooter Has a Second Mission: Pacify Increasingly Critical Congress," *Washington Post*, March 8, 1986.

81. Eleanor Clift and Doyle McManus, "Reagan Names Habib Central America Envoy," *Los Angeles Times*, March 8, 1986.

82. Edward Cody, "Latin Envoys Try to Revive Peace Talks," *Washington Post*, April 7, 1986.

83. Daniel Ortega Saavedra (President of Nicaragua),
"Communique," Press Release of the Embassy of Nicaragua, Washington, DC, April 12, 1986.

84. Jim Morrell and William Goodfellow, *Contadora Under the Gun* (Washington, DC: Center for International Policy, 1986).

85. Rowland Evans and Robert Novak, "A Box Called Contadora," *Washington Post*, May 13, 1986.

86. Joanne Omang, "U.S. Reaffirms Desire for Latin Peace Pact," *Washington Post*, May 23, 1986; Joanne Omang, "Habib Called Wrong, Imprecise, in Letter on U.S. Latin Policy," *Washington Post*, May 24, 1986.

87. Leslie Gelb, "Pentagon Predicts Big War if Latins Sign Peace Accord," *New York Times*, May 20, 1986; Bernard Gwertzman, "State Department Assails the Pentagon Over Study of Latin Peace Talks," *New York Times*, May 21, 1986.

88. Edward Cody, "Contadora Talks Go On," *Washington Post*, May 28, 1986.

89. Philip Taubman, "Latin Peace Plan: Why the U.S. Balks," *New York Times*, October 3, 1984.

6

Reagan and Congress: Consensus and Conflict in Central American Policy

Richard A. Nuccio

In the early 1960s, John F. Kennedy offered his now classic characterization of the options for U.S. policy in developing regions undergoing rapid social change:

> We have three choices in descending order of acceptability—a decent democratic regime, another dictatorship, a communist government. We should strive for the first but we can't reject the second until we're sure we can prevent the third.[1]

While JFK may not have been expressing the full range of possible choices of regime for Latin America, he was describing the landscape of political possibilities as it appears from Washington. Striving for decent democratic governments has at times had greater and lesser priority in the United States. But it has almost always been the required goal of high visibility, politically popular, and sustainable policy initiatives toward Latin America.

Writing nearly two decades later, another architect of U.S. foreign policy, Ambassador Jeane Kirkpatrick, faced JFK's dilemma and placed her emphasis on the dichotomy in his original formulation between authoritarian and totalitarian regimes:

> Only intellectual fashion and the tyranny of Right/Left thinking prevent intelligent men of good will from perceiving the *facts* that traditional authoritarian governments are less repressive than revolutionary autocracies, that they are more susceptible of liberalization, and that they are more

compatible with U.S. interests. Although most governments in the world
are, as they always have been, autocracies of one kind or another, no idea
holds greater sway in the mind of educated Americans than the belief
that it is possible to democratize governments, anytime, anywhere, under
any circumstances. . . . Many of the wisest political scientists of this and
previous centuries agree that democratic institutions are especially difficult
to establish and maintain. . . .[2]

She did not dismiss democracy as irrelevant but expressed a more
than robust skepticism for the ability of the United States to protect
its interests and achieve decent democracies among its autocratic allies.
And she worried that in the naive assumptions about democratic possibilities she saw as characterizing the policies of the Carter administration
in Nicaragua, lay the seeds of totalitarian disaster outlined by Kennedy.

The debate over U.S. policy toward Latin America in the 1980s is
focused almost exclusively on a region that does not contain many more
people than the capital city of Mexico. This debate over Central America
is marked by limited public understanding on the one hand and by
partisan recrimination among experts on the other. It is easy to understand
why. Central America emerged again as a preoccupation of the United
States at that precise moment when the consensus guiding U.S. foreign
policy after the Second World War fractured. The loss of the war in
Vietnam caused many to question whether the United States should try
to determine events in the Third World. The fall of the Shah in Iran
and the long ordeal of the hostages indicated to some that the United
States would pay dearly for its unwillingness to stand by its friends.
Afghanistan undermined the hope of others that détente with the Soviet
Union would lead to its restraint in regional conflicts. For these reasons
and others, Central America is the place where a new consensus over
how the United States should deal with revolutionary change in Third
World countries will be forged (or not forged) in the post-Vietnam, post-
Iran, post-Afghanistan era.

Whatever the merits of any approach to the problems of Central
America, no policy will be successful if it is not sustainable over the
long run. This paper is an argument that emphasizes certain aspects of
recent U.S. policy in Central America to make the case that "success"
in Central America has come, even in the midst of our foreign policy
"crisis of consensus," when strong congressional initiatives have produced
compromise by the executive branch. It focuses on the "success" of
policy toward El Salvador and draws lessons for the current failures of
policy in Nicaragua that require a change in the objectives the administration hopes to achieve in that country. Finally, it draws on an analogy
with the Middle East peace negotiations to outline the parameters of a
possible Nicaraguan settlement.

CONSENSUS OF EL SALVADOR

In the perceived emergency of the guerrilla offensive in El Salvador in late 1980 and early 1981 and perhaps flush with November victory, the Reagan administration forgot for a time the fundamental lesson of North American politics identified by JFK: "decent democracies" must be the goal of a sustainable U.S. policy toward Latin America. It allowed its ideological distaste for a reformist politician like Napoleón Duarte and its preoccupation with the Soviet specter to reduce its options to the Kirkpatrick dichotomy. But the unprecedented slaughter conducted by the military-civilian junta during 1981, including that of North American churchwomen, galvanized the human rights lobby in the United States sufficiently to exert pressure through the Congress on the conduct of policy toward El Salvador. El Salvador's was an overt, not covert, war. Congressional approval for funding of the war effort was crucial to administration policy. And so, over time, the administration made many of the goals of Congress its own for El Salvador: support for the reformist Duarte and reform policies including such ideologically unpalatable measures as land reform and the nationalization of the banking sector and foreign trade; attention to massive human rights abuses by the Salvadoran armed forces called for by aid-contingency legislation; and the promotion of democracy as the ultimate objective of U.S. policy. In the process it advanced from the Kirkpatrick dichotomy to return to the JFK dilemma.

The consequence of this merging of the administration's agenda for El Salvador with that of Congress was "success." Duarte survived the military-civilian junta with his reformist credentials somewhat intact. He could still not be elected president in 1982, but neither could the administration allow Roberto D'Aubuisson to hold the office. Duarte's election in 1984 was desirable and achievable. By the legislative elections of 1985, after a "dialogue" with the guerrillas had been initiated, Duarte and the Christian Democrats were so powerful that they created a new concern that they aspired to the single-party state model once tried by the military and the PCN (Partido de Conciliación).

With Duarte came congressional funding for the war effort, virtually without restrictions. The military situation stabilized for the government and even appeared to have turned in its favor. Human rights abuses decreased and the aerial bombardment that was essential to the counter-insurgency strategy produced civilian deaths in guerrilla controlled areas far from cameras and news stories. The military seemed increasingly comfortable and convincing in its new role as defender of the constitutional order.

At this precise moment of its greatest advance in El Salvador, the administration set in motion the policies that may ultimately snatch defeat from these jaws of victory. Instead of using its position of strength to sue for peace, the administration raised its objectives in El Salvador. Military defeat of the guerrillas became the goal of U.S. policy, not their elimination as a political threat. That might have been achieved by encouraging Duarte to make a proposal so generous and accommodating to the guerrillas and their civilian allies that it would have undercut all but the most fanatical adherents. But diplomatic accommodation was undesirable; it would send a message to other guerrilla movements that they could wage war until stalemate and then negotiate at the table what they could not achieve on the battlefield.

For a time in 1985 it looked as if military victory might be at hand. The army's tactics were more effective and prevented the guerrillas from mounting a dry season offensive or even operating regularly in large-scale units. Official estimates of their strength decreased to roughly half of what they had been a year earlier. U.S. military trainers spoke of reducing the guerrillas to bandits and extending government control to 90% of the country in three to five years. The dialogue begun with the guerrillas by President Duarte in October 1985 and suspended after the hard-line positions of each side became clear during the second meeting at Ayagualo, seemed unimportant. Like El Salvador's own conservatives, the United States believed it could win a whole loaf on the battlefield; why negotiate for half a loaf?

By the beginning of 1986 the optimism that had prevailed just six months earlier seemed misplaced. Changes in guerrilla tactics brought their operations back to the front pages. Attacks on U.S. marines and Salvadoran training bases and the kidnapping of local Christian Democratic majors and the daughter of President Duarte demonstrated the guerrillas' ability to hold out for the long run and to conduct successfully the "low intensity conflict" that is the new buzzword of military thinkers. The guerrillas extended operations to virtually all parts of El Salvador and, through greater coordination of their factions, became more adept at simultaneous sabotage that can cut off electricity or disrupt transport to major parts of the country.

The Salvadoran economy, never healthy, is now reeling. Five hundred million dollars in U.S. aid annually is no longer even able to keep the economy limping along. Massive austerity measures have had to be taken at a time when Duarte's political strength is noticeably weaker. Destruction of the Brazilian coffee crop may help El Salvador squeak through in the short run by raising prices for the country's primary export product, but is unlikely to resolve President Duarte's fundamental political difficulties.

The decline in Duarte's political fortunes can be traced to several causes. Distrusted by the military and the civilian right, Duarte has waged a campaign of accommodation with the interests of the right. He had been quite successful with the military until his negotiations with the FMLN to obtain the release of his daughter undermined his standing with them. The civilian right had never trusted the Christian Democrat who nationalized the banks and the coffee export sector. Less seduced by Duarte's ability to produce U.S. aid, they are ready to desert the president the first time he seriously threatens their interests. As Duarte moved toward accommodation with the right his traditional source of political support in the Christian Democratic labor unions became more tenuous. Expressing the nub of Duarte's political dilemma, one labor leader commented after the recent austerity measures that, "Now we will not only die because of the war. They're also condemning us to die of hunger." In the political space opened up by Duarte's election, the FMLN intended to move back into the cities to organize political support in the universities, labor unions, and other "popular organizations." Amidst the economic downturn it could expect to find more fertile ground for protest than at any time since the late 1970s.

Pessimists, especially on the left, have not proven to be correct about El Salvador in the recent past. Pointing accurately to potential problems, they have underestimated Duarte's own personal capabilities as well as the pragmatism displayed at key junctures by the Reagan administration. Countervailing trends to the negative developments cited above are also in evidence in 1986. Splits have emerged more publicly than ever before between the FDR and the FMLN over tactics, and some middle-level FDR supporters have returned to El Salvador to test the waters for overt political activity.

However, another pessimistic judgement will be offered here: that the high point of administration policy was reached in El Salvador in 1985 both militarily and politically. Because of the negative developments of 1985 and early 1986, both a military and a political solution will be more difficult to achieve in the future. An opportunity to cut a deal with the more moderate elements of the left in El Salvador that would have preserved essential U.S. interests while reducing direct U.S. involvement was passed over in 1985 for the ideologically more desirable goal of total victory. It may be some time before such an opportunity to bargain from strength returns again.

CONFLICT OVER NICARAGUA

Nicaragua policy has never displayed the agility on the part of the administration that was demonstrated in El Salvador. A fundamental reason for this is that the administration has never been confronted with an alternative policy by Congress. Because the war against Nicaragua was "covert," congressional funding has, until recently, not been as crucial, as public, or as massive as it was for El Salvador. In the case of Nicaragua the administration has consistently been on the offense and Congress on the defense. Supporters of official policy could more accurately and effectively than in El Salvador threaten to charge those in opposition to administration policy with having "lost" Nicaragua. The human rights abuses by the U.S.-backed government in El Salvador embarrassed the administration and emboldened the opposition. In Nicaragua, the administration can rely on a "secret" speech by Arce here or a Moscow trip by Ortega there to do their work for them with Congress. Human rights violations by the *contras* were never as massive or as embarrassing as those by the "death squads" in El Salvador. And the Sandinistas themselves have moved to decrease progressively political space within Nicaragua.

Still, administration policy in Nicaragua has not ultimately been as "successful" as it was in El Salvador. A congressional consensus for pressure on Nicaragua has been established after intensive lobbying by the administration (and gaffes by the Sandinistas), but it is quite fragile. It is true that there are no longer any friends of the Sandinistas in Congress. (Perhaps there is literally one, Ron Dellums.) Thanks to President Ortega's trip to Moscow and earlier spade work by the administration, the Congress has approved "humanitarian" assistance to the *contras*. Yet it is possible to imagine a *contra* atrocity, a blown CIA operation, or other embarrassment that will threaten the support which exists for "humanitarian"—i.e., overt but politically clean—assistance to the *contras* and prevent military aid from being voted in the future.

If the essence of the compromise wrought by congressional opposition in the case of El Salvador was the pursuit by the administration of "decent democracy" in El Salvador, the equivalent for Nicaragua would be the acceptance by the administration of a political solution to the Nicaraguan conflict that would not remove the Sandinistas from power as a prior condition. This is because of the other pole of sustainable policy initiatives toward Latin America: the United States can not be overtly engaged in the overthrow of a legally constituted government that does not appear to be an immediate threat to the security of the United States.

Some may argue that the administration is, in fact, not pursuing the overthrow of the Sandinistas. Ignoring for the moment the inhibitions on frankness about overthrowing the legal government of a country with which the United States maintains full diplomatic relations and the "Say Uncle" remark by President Reagan in his news conference of February 21, 1985, it is still possible to demonstrate that current policy toward the Sandinistas is either duplicitous or contradictory in its intentions.

The syllogism of official current policy goes something like this:

The Sandinistas are Marxist-Leninists. Marxist-Leninists will only make concessions to democracy if forced to by pressure. With current levels of U.S. pressure the Sandinistas have become ever more totalitarian. Therefore, Congress needs to approve funding for much higher levels of pressure.

Most students of international affairs will recognize in this characterization of current policy the familiar restatement of a great policy principle: an ineffective policy can be made more effective by increasing the amount of pressure with which it is applied.

A more accurate statement of actual policy toward Nicaragua would probably be as follows:

The Sandinistas are Marxists-Leninists. Marxists-Leninists will never willingly surrender power; it must be taken from them. Current measures are not sufficient to remove the Sandinistas from power, but public support does not yet exist for the direct U.S. role that would be required to remove them. Therefore, interim measures must be adopted to preoccupy the Sandinistas until public support for their removal becomes manifest.

The dilemma of U.S. policy toward Nicaragua in 1986 is that if this second rendition of administration thinking is accurate, it cannot be publicly supported by a majority in Congress. Many U.S. citizens and a significant number of their representatives in Congress have difficulty with an attempt by the United States to overthrow a legal government that is not a direct threat to the security of the United States. The result of this dilemma is a series of very elaborate dances around the real issues:

1. Everyone supports Contadora. But the goal of Contadora is to reach a negotiated settlement between the conflicting parties in Central America that would accommodate the Sandinistas. This goal is unacceptable to the administration, but the administration cannot openly reject Contadora so it works within Contadora to oppose any treaty that would leave the Sandinistas in power.
2. The administration opposes the Sandinistas because they are undemocratic. But it pays only the most superficial attention to the issue of democratization within the Nicaraguan opposition.
3. The administration promotes a prominent role for civilian leadership of the *contras* with democratic credentials. Yet, taking a page from the great democrat, Fidel Castro, it discourages pluralism among *contra* groups in the interest of greater military effectiveness. By

emphasizing a military approach it sets up the potential for a repeat of the 1979 experience—should the *contras* ever come to power—when the FSLN literally outgunned its civilian allies. By increasing the opposition's reliance on U.S. aid it encourages the historical pattern in Nicaragua of dissidents looking more to the United States to solve their political disputes than to their own political resources.

FACING THE REAL ISSUES

There are various ways to resolve this dilemma of U.S. policy toward Nicaragua. The Congress could decide to accept the administration's view of the Sandinistas, override public concern about a direct U.S. military involvement in Central America, and vote much higher levels of United States aid to the *contras* and whatever other assistance is necessary—including U.S. air cover and/or troops—to overthrow the Sandinistas. This would "remove" the communist threat in Central America in at least as effective a manner as it was "removed" in Guatemala in 1954. Such an action would also have certain costs.

Some analysts, such as the Rand Corporation's David Ronfeldt, have argued that a reassertion of U.S. hegemony in the Caribbean Basin would be welcomed by many in Latin America. Others, however, assume that much of the rest of Latin America would be horrified by such an action on the part of the United States. The Sandinistas have vowed that, if invaded, they would retaliate, Qadaffi-like, by sending terrorists "hit-teams" throughout Latin America and to the United States itself. In addition, there are the actual costs of the invasion itself which were estimated, before the recent acquisition of a great deal more military equipment by the Sandinistas, to require 61,000 men and result in 2,000 to 5,000 American dead and between 9,000 to 19,000 American wounded.[3]

Another solution would be that suggested by the evolution of U.S. policy toward El Salvador: the presentation by Congress of a strong alternative to administration policy. This alternative would place enforceable limits on U.S. tolerance of Sandinista practices, but not actively seek their overthrow unless those limits are violated. Such a congressional alternative would not be taken seriously by the administration unless it were backed by a consistent refusal to grant administration aid requests for the *contras* until the administration signaled its willingness to reject overthrow of the Sandinistas unless they take specific aggressive steps. Such steps might include massive levels of support for the export of revolution; installation of Soviet bases; acquisition, with proximate intent to use, of large amounts of purely offensive weapons; etc.

This alternative, if successful in deterring the administration from pursuit of the overthrow of the Sandinistas, would also have its costs. It would alarm the right in the rest of Central America, though it would be warmly received by the governments of virtually the rest of Latin America (Chile and Paraguay excepted).[4]

It would hearten the Sandinistas and perhaps encourage a spirit of triumphalism that they had tweaked the nose of the *yanqui* twice in a decade and lived to tell about it. However, more moderate elements of the Sandinistas would gain ground if they were inclined to battle with more doctrinaire members of the ruling group. The perverse cycle of the ideological right in Washington feeding on the ideological left in Managua and vice versa might thus be broken.

Some parts of the Nicaraguan opposition would feel disillusioned; others, betrayed and abandoned. The *contra* fighters in particular would become a massive problem for the United States, Honduras, and the surrounding Central American countries if provision were not made for the return of some to Nicaragua and the migration of others to the United States or other third countries. An emphasis on political rather than military opposition would, however, be encouraged and a tradition of elite reliance on Uncle Sam to "fix" Nicaraguan internal disputes broken.

NEGOTIATING SOLUTIONS TO INTRACTABLE DILEMMAS

Because Central America is a quagmire, a conundrum, and an apple of discord, a solution to the Central American policy dilemma will have to be similar to that adopted in other intractable policy arenas such as the Middle East. A la Kissinger, a diplomatic accord over Nicaragua will be one that is consciously misperceived by all parties to the dispute. Just as in the Middle East peace agreement between Israel and Egypt, each side will have to assume that the final agreement is ambiguous enough to be interpreted as favoring them over their opponents. In the case of the United States and Nicaragua the formulation of a negotiated solution would be as follows:

The Sandinistas would make concessions to the opposition and the United States that they believed could possibly remove them from power, but probably would not.

The United States and the Nicaraguan opposition would make concessions to the Sandinistas that they believed could possibly leave the Sandinistas in power, but probably would not.

122 Richard A. Nuccio

As in the case of the Middle East, such a simultaneously misinterpreted treaty would lead to a great deal of maneuvering on the part of the parties involved to increase their leverage against their adversaries and to potential stalemate. It would have the advantage of emphasizing political over military competition.

This type of agreement in the Middle East was possible because significant actors in the conflict recognized that their maximum objectives were either no longer achievable or too costly to national survival to continue to pursue. All parties to the Nicaraguan conflict now appear to believe that their maximum objectives are within grasp without significant compromise. Until these perceptions (or realities) change, a negotiated outcome is unlikely. However, Congress is an institution uniquely qualified to evaluate the costs of the pursuit of maximum objectives in Nicaragua and to impose a negotiation alternative that could preserve essential U.S. interests at reduced costs.

NOTES

1. Lester D. Langley, *Central America: The Real Stakes* (New York: Crown Publishers, 1985), p. 24.

2. Jeane Kirkpatrick, "Dictatorships and Double Standards," *Commentary*, Vol. 68 (November 1979), pp. 34–45.

3. Theodore Moran, "The Cost of Alternative U.S. Policies Toward El Salvador 1984–1989," in Robert S. Leiken, ed., *Central America, Anatomy of Conflict* (New York: Pergamon Press, 1984), p. 156.

4. Official statements by administration spokespersons that most Latin American governments really want the United States to overthrow the Sandinistas, but that they cannot say so publicly, is no basis on which to build U.S. policy in the region. Many of the same Latin officials cited by the United States as secret adherents to administration policy say exactly the opposite to Western European officials who disagree with U.S. policy. This leads one to the conclusion that Central Americans continue their historic and entirely understandable tendency to act as all small powers must and tell big powers whatever they want to hear.

7
Contadora and the U.S. Congress

Cynthia Arnson

In the congressional debate on Central America, the Contadora initiative has been widely embraced by Democrats, Republicans, conservatives and liberals, proponents and opponents of President Reagan's Central America policies. And it is easy to see why: Contadora provides for the peaceful settlement of the regional conflict through a negotiating framework constructed by the United States' major democratic allies in Latin America. Because the concept of the peaceful resolution of disputes is so appealing, members of Congress of widely divergent political persuasions could claim support for Contadora's objectives without compromising their basic positions on Central America.

Yet beneath the surface of broad support for Contadora lie profound differences over what the negotiations meant and how best to foster them; these reflected differences over how best to approach the conflict in Central America and guarantee the protection of U.S. interests. With respect to Contadora, Congress was divided in two major ways:

1. between those who favored a predominantly U.S. solution in Central America along the lines articulated by the Reagan administration, and those who preferred a multilateral approach devised and implemented by leading Latin American nations with U.S. support; and, related to the first.
2. between those who viewed U.S. military pressure (the *contras*) against Nicaragua as inhibiting the Contadora process and the achievement of U.S. goals in Nicaragua, and those who believed U.S. military pressure was essential in forcing the Sandinista government to moderate its internal and foreign policies, including acceptance of the Contadora treaty.[1]

While it is true that all in Congress claimed support for Contadora, a small group of liberals and moderates (Representatives Barnes, Alexander, Solarz, Hamilton, Levine, and Gephardt, and Senators Kennedy and Cranston) were the true carriers of its banner.[2] This is not only because Contadora provided liberals and moderates a way out of their own impasse in proposing a comprehensive alternative to Reagan's Central America policies, but also because this handful of individuals concretely did the most to promote Contadora, meeting with Contadora officials in Latin America and Washington, conveying the perspective of these diplomats to the Congress, introducing resolutions on behalf of the negotiation process, and promoting legislation and amendments—at times success-fully—limiting U.S. military involvement in Central America in order to facilitate the Contadora negotiations.

To make the distinction between groups of congressmen and the entire body, however, is to state a basic tension in Congress' role vis-a-vis Contadora. While small groups of liberals and moderates (both Democrat and Republican) were able to make symbolic expressions of political support for Contadora and at times to mobilize their colleagues in support of the negotiations, Congress as a whole continued to fund most of the Reagan policies in Central America which critics and Latin American leaders themselves decried as militaristic and contrary to the search for diplomatic solutions in the region. Moreover, given the executive branch's dominance in the formulation of U.S. foreign policy, and the fact that the United States was not even a direct party to the talks, the role of the U.S. Congress in facilitating the negotiations could, at best, be secondary. However, in politics, process and debate themselves often play an important role in shaping and limiting outcomes, and in this sense, Congress played at times a positive role in support of Contadora, acknowledged even by the leaders of the Contadora nations themselves.[3]

EVOLUTION OF CONGRESSIONAL INVOLVEMENT

A brief overview of congressional activism regarding Contadora shows that it was determined not only by developments in the negotiating process and the pace of the U.S. legislative calendar, but by the overall search for an alternative U.S. Central America policy.

1983, the year that Latin American leaders launched the Contadora initiative, was one of tremendous struggle between the Congress and the administration over Central America, not only over aid levels to the region, but over the desirability of continuing the covert operation against Nicaragua. By the time that President Reagan delivered a speech to a joint session of Congress on April 27, 1983, majorities of the House Foreign Affairs Committee and the Senate Foreign Relations Committee favored drastic cuts in the administration's request for military aid to El Salvador. Only hours before Reagan's address, Representatives Boland and Zablocki, Chairmen of the House Intelligence Committee and House Foreign Affairs Committee, respectively, introduced legislation to terminate U.S. support for the covert war against Nicaragua.[4] The dominant fear among liberals and moderates in both parties was that the Reagan emphasis on stark ideological portrayals of the conflict and reliance on military instruments of policy was polarizing the region even further, and drawing the United States into a deeper and deeper quagmire. The road of military escalation ". . . will mean greater violence . . . greater bloodshed . . . [and] greater hostility. And inevitably, the day will come when it will mean a regional conflict in Central America," said Senator Christopher Dodd, who delivered the Democratic response to President Reagan's speech. Then, referring to dialogue initiatives in El Salvador and Nicaragua, Dodd made the first congressional reference to Contadora: "Every major ally of ours in the region—Mexico, Panama, Venezuela, and Colombia—is anxious for such a step and has offered to make the arrangements."[5]

The search by administration critics for dialogue and negotiations in Central America was not new. In 1981 the Congress included in its "certification" requirement for El Salvador a provision that the President report the extent to which the Salvadoran government:

> . . . has demonstrated its good faith efforts to begin discussions with all major political factions in El Salvador which have declared their willingness to find and implement an equitable political solution to the conflict. . . .[6]

In 1982, just prior to President Reagan's meeting with new Mexican president Miguel de la Madrid, a bipartisan group of 106 members of the House called on President Reagan to "respond positively" to a Venezuelan-Mexican dialogue proposal to reduce tensions in Central America.[7] In early 1983 the Chairman of a key House subcommittee required the President to name a special envoy to promote negotiations in Central America as a condition for further military aid to El Salvador.[8] Support for Contadora was thus a natural step in the search by opponents of Reagan's policies to direct U.S. efforts down the path of peaceful negotiation, rather than what was viewed as a military approach to the region.

In a June 6, 1983 report to House Speaker Thomas P. O'Neill, Jr., House Deputy Majority Whip Bill Alexander summarized the dominant mood of Reagan's critics in the House in the conclusions of a May trip to visit with Contadora Foreign Ministers and heads-of-state. Citing the "apparent political-military stalemate in Central America that has been brought about by the policy of the last two and a half years," Alexander stated that:

> . . . a perception exists among principals of the Contadora nations that a real danger of general hostilities exists, that these countries see the United States position hardening, and that despite differing emphases on what the American role should be, they are all interested—almost desperately so— in efforts toward mediation and conciliation. . . .

> The impression exists among the spokesmen for these nations that both the United States and the Soviet Union are stepping up their preparations for a military showdown in Central America, and that this confrontation is inevitable unless immediate steps are taken to avert it. . . . The key question that must be addressed: *Is war inevitable, as recent developments in administration policy would indicate and as Latin American spokesmen fear? Or can war be avoided? And if so, how?* (emphasis added)

Then, echoing a sentiment expressed repeatedly over the next several years, that the United States was giving only tepid and verbal support to the Contadora effort, Alexander charged:

> It is obvious that Mr. Reagan is articulating a policy of negotiations on the one hand, while administering a policy of military build-up on the other.[9]

This perception was rooted in concrete Administration actions: in the first six months of 1983 the Administration requested a quadrupling of military aid to El Salvador, announced the replacement of Assistant Secretary of State Thomas Enders (a move seen as favoring administration hard-liners), and sent an additional 100 military advisers to Honduras. U.S.-backed *contra* leaders spoke publicly of their desire to overthrow the Sandinista regime. Plans for large-scale maneuvers in Honduras involving thousands of U.S. troops did not become public until July.

Throughout the remainder of 1983 Democratic critics of Reagan's policies in Central America continued to be the most outspoken champions of Contadora. Introducing H. Con. Res. 151 "in support of the Contadora initiative," Representative Leon Panetta stressed "the limits of acting unilaterally in Central America" and that ". . . it is time we expressed our unqualified support for the Contadora plan."[10] Representatives Barnes and Alexander and Senators Bingaman and Inouye went beyond rhetorical expressions of support and introduced a resolution (H. Res. 282 and Sen. Res. 181) linking the success of Contadora to specific U.S. policies: ". . . the United States government should cease the funding of guerrilla forces fighting against the present Government of Nicaragua."[11] Neither resolution was ever considered on the House or Senate floor.

Then, on July 28, 1983, the House voted to end U.S. support for the covert operation against Nicaragua. The bill, H.R. 2760 stated that:

> The United States shall support measures at the Organization of American States, as well as efforts of the Contadora Group, which seek to end support for terrorist, subversive, or other activities aimed at the violent overthrow of the government of countries in Central America."[12]

Following the "Boland-Zablocki" vote, House supporters of Reagan's policies in Central America attempted to prevent support for the Contadora negotiations from being used as a way to criticize the administration. On August 4, 1983, Representatives Hyde, Lagomarsino, and Bereuter introduced a resolution (H. Con. Res. 159) ". . . in recognition of the President's stated support for the four-nation Contadora peace initiative."[13] Although that resolution was never brought to a vote, Republicans could join Democrats later in the year in approving H. Con. Res. 197 "strongly support[ing] the initiatives taken by the Contadora Group." Representative Mel Levine, a junior member of the House Foreign Affairs Committee, introduced the resolution following the October 1983 agreement by the Contadora foreign ministers on a Document of Objectives. On November 17, 1983, the House adopted the resolution by voice vote, with four Democrats (Barnes, Levine, Panetta, and Zablocki) and five Republicans (Lagomarsino, Gilman, Conte, Leach, and Broomfield) making statements in its favor. The House thus went on record in favor of a negotiated settlement in Central America, with each side in the policy debate able to claim that its approach to the region was fostering the talks.[14]

1984 proved to be as inconclusive as 1983 in terms of congressional words and actions regarding Contadora: members of Congress across the spectrum continued to voice strong support for the peace initiative, while marshalling different reasons for doing so, and in support of quite different U.S. policies. Symbolic of those differences were remarks by Representatives Robert Lagomarsino and Stephen Solarz during consideration of H. Con. Res. 261, "expressing support for the initiatives of the Contadora Group and the resulting agreements among the Central American nations."

> Solarz: . . . the Contadora process may well be the last best hope that we have for peace in Central America. . . . I fear that if the Contadora process should fail, the stage would have been set for a significant escalation of the conflicts now underway both in El Salvador and in Nicaragua. There is a very real possibility that such escalation could spill over to neighboring

countries of the region, leading to a conflagration throughout all of Central America.

Many of us believe that . . . the best way, and perhaps the only way, to solve the problems in Central America is through a process of negotiation, rather than through elusory efforts to achieve military victories that are not in the cards.[15]

Lagomarsino: Last year, my Republican colleagues on the Western Hemisphere Subcommittee and I introduced a resolution commending the President and expressing the support of the Congress for the President's efforts in support of the Contadora process. At that time, it appeared that too many critics overlooked or ignored the president's efforts at encouraging a negotiated settlement of the Central American crisis. I have believed all along that the president's intention and policies have been directed at achieving a peaceful, political settlement in the region and his support for the Contadora initiative is one element of that process.[16]

The resolution passed the House on May 1, 1984, 416-0, and was approved by the Senate by voice vote on June 29, 1984. Of the many bills and resolutions introduced on Contadora beginning in 1983, H. Con. Res. 261 was the only one to be considered on the floors of both the House and Senate.

During 1984, however, there emerged cracks in the facade that anyone could endorse Contadora regardless of his or her position on U.S. policy in Central America. Latin American leaders themselves began to express their view that specific U.S. policies were contrary to the search for peace. Following a meeting with former Latin diplomats in Washington for the non-governmental Inter-American Dialogue, for example, Representative Barnes reported to his colleagues in March that:

These distinguished Latin American friends of the United States were unanimous in their view that our country must stop escalating Central America's conflicts militarily and give real support to the Contadora process— not as a way of abandoning our security objectives, but as the only way to achieve those objectives. . . .[17]

In May, following a furor in Washington over the U.S. mining of Nicaraguan harbors, Mexican President Miguel de la Madrid expressed a thinly-veiled criticism of the Reagan administration when he made a speech to a joint session of Congress: ". . . we therefore reject, without exception, all military plans that would seriously endanger the security and development of the region."[18] Only days before de la Madrid's address to the U.S. Congress, former president of Venezuela Carlos Andrés Pérez complained during a visit to Washington that State Department officials "speak of support" for Contadora, "but when we dig a little deeper, we find that they do not really believe in Contadora." Carlos Andrés Pérez quoted U.S. officials as saying that "Nicaragua is a communist regime and Nicaragua is not going to comply with the agreements of Contadora."[19]

The effect of these statements was to lend credence to the arguments of Reagan's critics that his administration had, in the words of Senator Kennedy, "only paid it [Contadora] lip service, while pursuing actions that Contadora group members have criticized for harming their efforts."[20] That sentiment was heightened by press reports in October 1984 that the Reagan administration had reacted negatively to Nicaragua's decision to sign a proposed Contadora draft treaty, an action, said ranking Democrat on the Senate Foreign Relations Committee Claiborne Pell which "must have the Sandinista leadership and our friends in the area thoroughly confused and perplexed."[21]

Yet criticism of U.S. policies by active Contadora officials remained private, a fact that prolonged a stalemate in the Congress over which advocates of policy were helping or hindering the talks. Lack of clarity also stemmed in part from the use of language: critiques of "military intervention" and support for "self-determination" by Latin American leaders were often meant as references to the U.S. covert war against Nicaragua as much as they were references to presumed Nicaraguan support for Salvadoran rebels. In the United States, however, "intervention" is usually understood by policymakers to refer to the direct introduction of troops. When members of the Reagan administration, including the president himself, stated publicly that they had no intention of "intervening" in Central America, the Latin American distinction fell on deaf ears.

During the principal debates in 1984 over Central America—a rebuke to the president over the mining of Nicaraguan harbors, a supplemental funding request for the *contras* and for El Salvador, and an annual foreign aid bill—Contadora at best hovered in the background. The negotiations were virtually absent from discussions of whether or not to aid (and under what conditions) the newly-elected government of José Napoleón Duarte in El Salvador, while debates over Nicaragua policy continued to focus principally on such questions as the nature of the Sandinista regime, the nature of the *contras*, the ends of U.S. policy and the means for achieving them. Because war and peace questions were most intimately linked with the covert operation in Nicaragua, however, Contadora remained a factor in that debate. In the view of Republican Senator Arlen Specter, for example:

I voted against the funding . . . for covert aid to Nicaragua because I believe that such covert aid which is essentially directed to harass or to overthrow the Nicaraguan Government is counterproductive to a long-range solution in the region. As previously noted, it is my view that negotiations should be undertaken through the Contradora (sic) process with the participation of the United States.[22]

Moreover, when House Democrats succeeded in October in including a cut-off of the covert operation in the Fiscal Year 1985 Continuing Resolution (while allowing the president to request renewed funding after February 1985), they required the president to consider the impact of a new request on the Contadora negotiations.[23] Implicit in the wording of the law was an observation made earlier in the year by Senator Kennedy:

> Rather than moving the region toward peace, the secret war had undermined the Contadora process and damaged the prospects for a negotiated solution to the problems of the entire region.[24]

THE CONTRA DEBATE: REVISED AND REVISITED

As specified in the 1985 Continuing Resolution, the president announced in April a drive to secure $14 million in military aid for the *contras*, linking the request to a "peace plan" involving negotiations between the Sandinistas and their armed and unarmed opponents. In reacting to the president's request, House and Senate legislators pushed an alternative policy based on Contadora beyond words and non-binding resolutions into the arena of potentially-binding law. A Senate Democratic proposal stipulated that the president could give $14 million in non-military aid to the *contras* if:

> . . . a) bilateral conversations between Nicaragua and the United States are resumed. In such conversations the relations between the two countries would be discussed so as to normalize bilateral relations and in this way contribute to the Contadora process; and b) the *contras* and the Nicaraguan government each agree to institute a mutual, monitored cease-fire. . . .[25]

Two House "Democratic alternatives" replaced or linked new money for the covert operation to the Contadora negotiations. The first, the "Barnes-Hamilton" amendment in April 1985 (the full list of bipartisan sponsors included Representatives Jim Jones, Hamilton Fish, Ed Zschau, and Jim Leach) replaced a presidential request for $14 million in military aid with $4 million to implement a finalized Contadora treaty and $10 million for refugees outside Nicaragua. The second, the "Gephardt" amendment in June 1985, sought to postpone congressional consideration of renewed *contra* funding for six months, in order to allow the Contadora countries to proceed at a particularly critical moment in the negotiations.

The story of the success or failure of these amendments is part of the larger drama surrounding the House "switch" in June 1985 in favor of non-military aid to the *contras*. But it is a story in which the lines between the majority supporting a Contadora negotiating alternative and a growing majority supporting some form of aid to the *contras* began to blur. The myth that one could have Contadora and the *contras* too began to replace a former cleavage between those who believed that the *contras* were a major, if not fatal impediment to Contadora, and those who believed Nicaragua would only submit to a Contadora treaty under the pressure of *contra* attacks.

A summary of the Barnes-Hamilton proposal reveals its central orientation towards multilateralism: in place of $14 million in military aid requested by President Reagan, the bipartisan alternative found that:

> . . . the Contadora 21 principles provide an appropriate framework for achieving peace and security in the region . . . [and] U.S. policy should encourage a cease-fire and peace negotiations among the combatants as part of a regional settlement through the Contadora process or the OAS. . . .[26]

The prospects for passage of Barnes-Hamilton were given an inadvertent boost by President Reagan, when he claimed that President Betancur of Colombia had responded positively to his "peace plan" accompanying the request for $14 million in military aid. In an interview with the *New York Times* which was widely quoted during the House and Senate floor debates, Betancur issued a rare public denunciation of the Reagan proposal, calling it "preparation for war." Then, stopping just short of an outright condemnation of the *contra* policy, Betancur stated that he:

> firmly believe[d] that any foreign support to guerrilla groups, whatever the origin, is clearly in opposition to the prevailing doctrine in Latin America regarding foreign intervention in the internal affairs of our continent.

Asked whether the administration was using his statements to gain renewed military aid for the *contras*, Betancur responded succinctly: "there would be a contradiction by whomever attempts to do so."[27] All this from a man who only two weeks before had voiced his opposition to military approaches in Central America by quoting House Democrats Lee Hamilton and Bill Alexander.

The president's proposal for $14 million succeeded in the Senate after the military aid component was changed to non-lethal "humanitarian" aid; in the House the Barnes-Hamilton proposal won 219-206, but a subsequent "Michel" amendment (named for House Minority Leader Robert Michel) to provide non-lethal assistance to the *contras* lost by only a narrow two-vote margin.[28] Republicans such as Senator Jake Garn and Representative Henry Hyde linked the *contras* and Contadora in the following way:

> Garn: The centerpiece of diplomacy has been the Contadora process and I strongly support these ongoing efforts. Several drafts of a final regional settlement have been prepared and progress is being made. In hopes of facilitating the Contadora process, bilateral negotiations occurred between the United States and Nicaragua. Diplomatic channels such as these should remain necessary components of a regional peace settlement.
>
> The vote today, whether it be for economic or security assistance, is an indication of our commitment to freedom fighters the world over. . . .[29]
>
> Hyde: We no longer understand the relationship between force and diplomacy. You say you want negotiations? But you need an instrument of negotiation. With whom will the Sandinistas negotiate if we turn the democratic resistance into refugees?
>
> This legislation does direct and deadly damage to the democratic resistance in Nicaragua. It is retreat. It is surrender. How are you going to have tough-minded diplomacy, having vacated the field altogether boggles the mind. . . .[30]

Senator Richard Lugar, Chairman of the Senate Foreign Relations Committee summed up the position: "We must have a reasonable policy, but one with substance behind it."[31]

In perhaps the pre-eminent statement that the Contadora leaders themselves saw a contradiction between their negotiations and U.S. support for the *contras*, Chairman of the Western Hemisphere Subcommittee Michael Barnes stated forcefully that:

> If they were here tonight, if the democratically elected presidents of the democracies of Latin America were standing here in the well tonight, they would plead with all of us to vote against this military approach, and they would plead with us to give their effort an opportunity to work.
>
> They say—and they have said it to many of us in this room—they say that when the United States holds a gun against the head of the Sandinistas and says "Cry uncle or we'll shoot," there is no better way to assure that the Sandinistas will not do what we all want them to do. . . .[32]

That the Barnes-Hamilton alternative prevailed on April 24, 1985 by such a narrow margin ensured that the issue would be dealt with again; Daniel Ortega's trip to Moscow on the heels of the congressional vote guaranteed that the debate would be re-opened sooner rather than later. Adding to the frustration of moderates and liberals in both parties was the House failure to secure final passage of the resolution containing the Barnes-Hamilton proposal: liberal Democrats voted against final passage to prevent the bill from going to conference with the Senate, which favored non-lethal aid; Republicans voted against the resolution in disgust over a series of high-stakes defeats. All of this meant that Contadora was being sidelined by issues related to a domestic U.S. agenda: from anger over legislative procedures, to a visceral desire among congressional moderates and conservatives to "get even" with Ortega, to the perception of House moderates that "switching" from the predominant Democratic position would either elevate their personal visibility or protect them against domestic recriminations of being "soft on communism." Over the next several months, congressional votes on a series of bills—Fiscal Year 1986 authorizations for the State Department, intelligence, and foreign assistance, and the Fiscal Year 1985 Supplemental Appropriation—reflected a new consensus on "humanitarian" aid, votes which were taken in the flood of heated emotions and rhetoric, and over the expressed desires of U.S. democratic allies, if not the Contadora leaders themselves.[33]

"I can't remember one meeting when anyone affiliated with Contadora has ever expressed gratitude to the U.S. for the *contra* program," said a policy analyst who had followed the negotiations closely. "Even the ones that dislike the Sandinistas the most say 'no' to the *contras*."[34]

As Contadora negotiators made progress in the spring and early summer toward agreement on key provisions of the treaty, House Democrats in particular became convinced that a reversal of the House position on *contra* aid would represent an overwhelming obstacle to the talks. Sensing the shift in the House mood, Democratic leaders sought a formula which would at least be able to delay what all acknowledged would be approval of non-lethal aid. House Democratic Caucus leader Representative Richard Gephardt wrote to his colleagues describing an amendment he intended to offer to the upcoming supplemental appropriations bill:

Let's give the Contadora peace process in Central America a chance to work before we consider resuming aid to the *contras*.

The Contadora process is at a crossroads. Negotiators are currently working on a final compromise draft, and discussions at the ministerial level are scheduled for the near future. There is a genuine possibility of success in the coming months, and strong U.S. support is vital.

This opportunity for peace could be greatly harmed by an immediate resumption
of aid to the contras. . . . (emphasis in original)[35]

But in this instance, the inability and/or unwillingness of Contadora
leaders to go public with their criticisms allowed House proponents of
non-lethal aid to usurp the banner of Contadora.[36] In the words of two
legislators who voted in favor of non-lethal aid to the *contras*:

McCurdy: The issue is not whether we support Contadora. We provide
$2 million for the Contadora nations and support the regional settlement...the
only real issue today is whether we provide real incentives for both sides
and particularly the Sandinistas to negotiate with their people.[37]

McKinney: I strongly endorse Michel-McCurdy. I think it is a chance for
us to state several things: we do support the Contadora process; we do
support humanitarian aid; we do support negotiations; and that we do
want peace talks.[38]

In reply, Representative Barnes pleaded that: "Three of the five documents
have now been agreed to by all five of the Central American countries
as well as the four Contadora countries. . . ."[39] while Representative
Matthew McHugh quoted an earlier Betancur letter to Reagan stating
that ". . . military aid to the groups in opposition to the government
of Nicaragua troubles me. . . ."[40] In the end, the House defeated the
Gephardt amendment to delay *contra* funding for six months, 172–259.
President Reagan, meanwhile pledged to "pursue political, not military
solutions in Central America."

RAISING THE STAKES

The House decision in the summer of 1985 to renew *contra* funding
may have contributed to a resurgence of diplomatic activity in Latin
America around Contadora.[42] The diplomatic push, which began in late
1985, was undertaken with new urgency; and for the first time Contadora
leaders were willing to oppose U.S. funding for the *contras* as inimical
to a regional peace settlement. These public remarks, in turn, served
the Reagan administration's opponents, who continued to press for the
negotiations as an alternative to wider war.

On January 11 and 12, 1986, the Contadora and "Support Group"
Foreign Ministers met in Caraballeda, Venezuela. The document they
produced—the "Caraballeda Message"—contained the most explicit language about aiding the *contras* used by the Contadora nations to date.
The eight Foreign Ministers called for the "termination of external
support to the irregular forces operating in the region," an unmistakable

reference to U.S. support for the anti-Sandinista rebels. The document also called for the "termination of support to insurrectionist movements in all countries of the region," a thinly veiled appeal to Nicaragua to cease its support for guerrilla movements in Central America.[43]

Then, on January 14, 1986, meeting at the inauguration of President Vinicio Cerezo in Guatemala City, the five Central American Foreign Ministers expressed their "adhesion to the initiatives and actions proposed in the Caraballeda Message."[44] Rumors that the Reagan administration intended to ask for $100 million in military aid to the *contras* thus surfaced as South and Central American countries reinvigorated their multilateral search for a diplomatic settlement, and went on public record in opposition to aspects of U.S. policy.

The renewed Latin American activity had a predictable effect in Congress. A flurry of letters from congressional Democrats urged the Reagan administration to withhold any decision on aid to the *contras* "so that the Contadora process may be given a chance to work."[45] On January 22, 1986, Rep. Barnes wrote the president that "to renew lethal military aid to the *contras* at this time would be a direct slap in the face to Latin American leaders."[46] A week later, 39 liberal members of the House again asked the president not to request "any form of aid" until "the Contadora process [had] been given a chance."[47] In mid-February, nine Democratic Senators, including four members of the Senate Foreign Relations Committee, stated that it would be "a particularly bad time" to request new aid for the *contras*, given Contadora diplomatic activity."[48]

Perhaps the key letter during this time was initiated by Rep. Jim Slattery (D-KS) and signed by 31 members of the House, of whom 25 had voted for aid to the *contras* in June 1985. Noting that "Contadora has reached a crossroads," the letter asked President Reagan for "a major diplomatic initiative by the U.S., in support of Contadora." They proposed that ". . . the Sandinistas . . . be tested by a diplomatic initiative . . . to determine, in clear and decisive terms, whether a diplomatic solution based on the Contadora principles is viable."[49] By sending the letter, key "swing vote" moderates were in essence notifying the president that their support for *contra* funding would be contingent, at least in part, on demonstrated administration willingness to pursue a negotiated settlement. Twenty-one of the thirty-one co-signers of Rep. Slattery's letter ultimately voted against the president's request for $100 million in military aid.[50]

Lingering hopes about the administration's support for a Contadora settlement were dealt a severe blow on February 10, 1986. Eight Latin American Foreign Ministers from the Contadora and Support Group countries met with Secretary of State George Shultz in Washington, to urge him not to seek renewed funding for the *contras*, to reopen talks with Nicaragua, and to back the Contadora negotiations. According to press accounts of the meeting, "eyes glazed over around the table" when Shultz repeated the demand that Nicaragua open talks with the *contras* at the same time that the U.S. reopen bilateral talks with the Nicaraguans.[51] The Contadora Foreign Ministers returned home empty-handed. Within fifteen days of their visit, President Reagan transmitted a formal request to the Congress for $100 million, including $70 million in military aid, for the anti-Sandinista rebels. President Betancur of Colombia denounced the proposal as "wrong" and "counter-productive."[52]

The unprecedented activity by the Contadora leaders in response to U.S. policy moves had a critical, if indirect, impact on the ensuing congressional debate. Specific references to Contadora were less important than the overall impression that, in the words of Sen. James Sasser (D-TN), the president was "seizing military options before he has exhausted the hope of a peaceful solution."[53] This perception, together with the fear that approval of the president's aid package meant a downpayment on deeper U.S. military involvement in the Nicaraguan conflict, was an important—if not the dominant—factor leading to House rejection of the president's request on March 20, 1986.[54]

"We have an obligation to demonstrate our commitment to a political, rather than a military solution," said Rep. David McCurdy (D-OK), a key "swing vote" who supported the President in June 1985 on *contra* funding and opposed him in March 1986. "Proponents of funding the *contras* overestimate what war can do and underestimate what diplomacy can achieve," said Chairman of the House Intelligence Committee Lee Hamilton (D-IN). "I see us becoming engaged, step by step, in a military situation that brings us directly into the fighting," said Speaker of the House Thomas P. O'Neill, Jr., in a rare appearance before a packed House chamber. O'Neill concluded by quoting a plea from Ambassador Edelberto Moreno of Venezuela that all member states of the OAS "remain committed to [solving] their controversies exclusively by peaceful means, and to abstain from the use of force directly or indirectly."[55] The House defeated the president's request, 222–210.

On March 27, 1986, the Republican-controlled Senate approved President Reagan's aid request 53–47, the narrowest margin on any Senate *contra* vote during the Reagan administration. A Democratic proposal offered by Sen. Sasser attempted to delay military aid for six months, to allow for direct bilateral negotiations between the United States and Nicaragua, through Contadora or independently. The proposal failed by a wide 33–67 margin, and was vigorously opposed by the Reagan administration.[56]

A BALANCE SHEET

President Reagan failed in his all-out attempt in February and March 1986 to secure military aid for the *contras*. But in subsequent months, the Congress seemed certain to approve additional funding, including perhaps military training and assistance. The reason for this is two-fold:

1. a majority (albeit narrow) in the Congress came to believe that internal change in the character of the Sandinista regime—not just "containment" of it—was a legitimate, even necessary goal of U.S. policy; and
2. internal democratization in Nicaragua (the opposite of the consolidation of a Marxist regime) would only occur if external pressure (i.e., physical force) were applied.

Where some congressional proponents of "pressure" differed from the administration was perhaps only in the ultimate goal of U.S. policy—that is, reform of the Sandinista regime, rather than its ultimate replacement.

Seeking democratization within Nicaragua was not incompatible with the Contadora formula; indeed, contained in Contadora's Document of Objectives was a provision committing treaty signatories to the "improvement of democratic, representative and pluralistic systems." Coupling that goal with *contra* "pressure," however, was incompatible with the Contadora approach, as it sanctioned a policy of unilateral U.S. military pressure against Nicaragua, outside and in opposition of the efforts of major regional powers to negotiate a multilateral peace. Proponents of a unilateral policy thus revealed a basic distrust of the ability of the Contadora nations to resolve and guarantee regional security issues, as well as a lack of confidence in diplomacy to exact concessions from the Sandinistas over the internal composition of their regime.

Since the launching of the Contadora initiative in 1983, the negotiations have been used in Congress as a basic counterweight to Reagan administration policy. As privately expressed fears among Latin American leaders became public condemnations of aspects of U.S. policy, Contadora blunted the administration's ability to secure backing for its approach in Central America, particularly the *contra* war.

Ultimately, however, there remained a central irony: that while Reagan administration insistence on the *contra* policy posed an impediment to Contadora, it also contributed to Nicaraguan intransigence regarding key provisions of the draft treaty. A vicious circle was thus created: the Reagan administration policy fueled Nicaraguan resistance to aspects of the Contadora agreement (particularly regarding arms reductions), while Nicaragua's refusal to sign a draft agreement intensified congressional doubts about the Sandinistas'commitment to a negotiated solution.

Whether that impasse can be broken remains unclear in mid-1986. What seems clearer, however, is that prospects for finalizing a Contadora treaty diminished as Congress moved closer to the Reagan administration's support of the *contras*. As Senator Claiborne Pell (D-RI), ranking Democrat on the Senate Foreign Relations Committee had noted prophetically in September 1984:

". . . if the United States does not really want a Contadora treaty, there is no chance in the world that the Contadora peace process would produce anything but a meaningless pile of papers."[57]

NOTES

1. See the excellent Congressional Research Service Issue Brief, *The Contadora Initiative: Implications for the Congress*, by Nina Serafino, September 22, 1985, for a different formulation of the varying positions in Congress.

2. Several Republicans, Representatives Leach and Fish, as well as Democrat Jim Jones were co-sponsors of the April 24, 1985 "Barnes-Hamilton" amendment; yet they were not major activists in support of the Contadora negotiations before or after that time.

3. Mexican President Miguel de la Madrid wrote Representatives Solarz and Barnes thanking them for the May 1, 1984 vote on H. Con. Res. 261. He stated that it was a "political incentive that we greatly appreciate. The U.S. Congress is without a doubt a factor that can contribute in an important manner to strengthening the search for political and peaceful solutions."

4. *Congressional Quarterly*, April 30, 1983, p. 819.

5. *Congressional Record*, April 28, 1983, pp. E1952-3.

6. Section 728(d) of the International Security and Development Cooperation Act of 1981.

7. *Washington Post*, October 7, 1982.

8. Then-Chairman of the House Foreign Operations Subcommittee Clarence Long proposed the special negotiator, and led efforts to cut Reagan's military aid request to El Salvador by half.

9. Representative William Alexander, "Report to the Speaker," *Congressional Record*, June 6, 1983, pp. H3579-81.

10. "Panetta Dear Colleague" (a way of communicating views by letter to the entire House or Senate membership), July 28, 1983. Panetta also introduced two bills regarding Contadora.

11. "Barnes and Alexander Dear Colleague," July 29, 1983.

12. The failure of the Senate to follow the House in terminating aid to the *contras* led to a compromise figure of $24 million for the covert operation.

13. Hyde, Lagomarsino, and Bereuter "Dear Colleague," August 4, 1983. On July 27, 1983 the *Washington Post* published the text of a July 26 Reagan letter to the Contadora Group claiming that his Administration "consistently expressed strong support for the Contadora process."

14. It is indeed a tribute to the universal preference for diplomacy in international relations that only one member of Congress in the entire period since the launching of Contadora publicly spoke ill of its efforts. That distinction falls to Republican Representative Eldon Rudd, who stated on August 2, 1983: ". . . for the past eight months the so-called Contadora group . . . has been running around Central America telling the world how peace can be achieved in that region in our hemisphere. So far the only thing that the four countries that make up the Contadora . . . have been able to achieve is the establishment of a forum for our enemies to take pot-shots at our Government . . . we do not need the Contadora group and its highly suspicious motives." *Congressional Record*, pp. H6218-9.

15. House Committee on Foreign Affairs, Mark-Up, *Legislation Concerning Latin America: Colombia, the Contadora Process, and El Salvador*, 98 Cong., 2nd Sess., April 5, 1984, p. 5.

16. *Congressional Record*, May 1, 1984, p. H3199.

17. *Ibid.*, March 30, 1984, p. E1345.

18. *Ibid.*, May 18, 1984, p. S5795

19. *Congressional Quarterly*, May 12, 1984, pp. 1094-5.

20. *Congressional Record*, May 15, 1984, p. S5758.

21. *Ibid.*, September 25, 1984, p. S11780-1.

22. *Ibid.*, April 4, 1984, p. S3853.

23. The Fiscal Year 1985 Continuing Resolution required the president to report to the Congress as to, among other things, ". . . how the proposed assistance would further [U.S.] goals, including the achievement of peace and security in Central America through a comprehensive, verifiable, and enforceable agreement based upon the Contadora Document of Objectives." *Congressional Record*, October 10, 1984, p. H11884.

24. *Congressional Record*, April 4, 1984, p. S3761.

25. *Ibid.*, April 23, 1985, p. S4552.

26. Representatives Barnes, Hamilton, Jones, Fish, Zschau, and Leach, memorandum, "Summary of the Bipartisan Alternative," April 1985.

27. *New York Times*, April 16, 1985.

28. In a letter to House Speaker Tip O'Neill on April 24, 1985, President Reagan stated that ". . . the proposal to be offered by Mr. Barnes and Mr. Hamilton would divert funds from existing economic assistance and refugee accounts for humanitarian assistance to refugees outside Nicaragua and for the expenses of implementing an eventual Contadora agreement. Members of Congress should be under no illusion about this proposal. Its adoption would damage our national security and foreign policy interests. By providing a financial inducement for members of the resistance to ˙leave Nicaragua and become refugees in other countries, it relieves pressure on the Sandinistas while, at the same time, it increases the burdens imposed on the neighboring democracies. As a result,

fragile democracies would be weakened, their economic recovery would be stalled, their security would be diminished–and the civil war in Nicaragua would go on." *Congressional Record*, April 24, 1985, p. H2490.

29. *Congressional Record*, April 23, 1985, p. S4607.

30. *Ibid.*, p. H2332.

31. *Ibid.*, June 6, 1985, p. S7593.

32. *Ibid.*, April 23, 1985, p. H2424.

33. In a joint press conference with Mexican Foreign Minister Bernardo Sepulveda Amor, Spanish Foreign Minister Fernando Morán stated that "U.S. financing of the *contras* is an error. European and other Latin American countries have also asked the U.S. government to be more flexible." *Foreign Broadcast Information Service*, June 11, 1985. Later in the year, Sepulveda referred to "progress" in the Contadora talks ". . . despite the fact that on innumerable occasions the negotiations have been hindered by an atmosphere of political intolerance among the parties directly involved, or by external interference that does not solve, but rather intensifies, the regional and international political conflicts of the Central American countries." Remarks at the "Dialogue on Central America," Roosevelt Center, Chicago, Illinois, October 28, 1985.

34. Interview, January 20, 1986.

35. "Gephardt Dear Colleague," June 7, 1985.

36. Explanations for this reticence might include (1) the reluctance to interfere directly in the U.S. political process, provoking potentially hostile and counter-productive responses from the Reagan administration and Congress, and (2) the fear of antagonizing the Reagan administration to such a degree that other bilateral interests—trade, debt, drug control, etc.—would be jeopardized.

37. *Congressional Record*, June 12, 1985, p. H4131.

38. *Ibid.*, p. H4137.

39. *Ibid.*, p. H4156.

40. *Ibid.*, p. H4159.

41. Letter from President Reagan to Rep's. Michel and McCurdy, June 11, 1985.

42. A Contadora "Support Group" formed in late 1985 by the governments of Argentina, Brazil, Peru, and Uruguay gave a critical boost from Latin American democratic governments. The late 1985 elections in Guatemala and Costa Rica brought center and center-left governments to power who sought peace talks with the Sandinistas.

43. *Mensaje de Caraballeda*, January 12, 1986.

44. *Declaracion de Guatemala*, January 14, 1986.

45. Letter from Rep. Richard Gephardt (D-MO) to President Reagan, January 16, 1986.

46. Letter from Rep. Barnes to President Reagan, January 22, 1986.

47. Letter from Rep's. Levine, Panetta, et al., to President Reagan, January 30, 1986.

48. Letter from Sen's. Harkin, Pell, et al., to President Reagan, February 10, 1986.

49. Letter from Rep. Slattery, et al., to President Reagan, February 3, 1986.

50. Thirty-three members of the House "switched" in June 1985 from an anti-aid position to a pro-"humanitarian aid" position. Of these 33, 17 signed Rep. Slattery's letter. Of these 17, 15 voted against President Reagan's $100 million aid request on March 20, 1986.

51. According to the *Washington Post* of February 16, 1986, Shultz had lost an important intra-administration battle with the White House and Pentagon over the timing and conditions of any aid request for the *contras*. According to a State Department official quoted by the *Post*, the White House rejected Shultz's proposal "in part out of fear that the Sandinistas would accept it this time."

52. *Washington Post*, March 10, 1986; *Congressional Record*, March 18, 1986, p. H1276.

53. Sen. Sasser delivered the official Democratic response to President Reagan's television address on Nicaragua, March 16, 1986.

54. Moderate Democrats and Republicans also resented the administration's attempts to paint opponents of the aid request as pro-Communist. On March 5, 1986, White House Communications Director Patrick Buchanan wrote an editorial in the *Washington Post* in which he accused the Democratic Party of becoming "with Moscow, co-guarantor of the Brezhnev doctrine in Central America. . . . With the vote on contra aid, the Democratic party will reveal whether it stands with Ronald Reagan and the resistance–or Daniel Ortega and the communists."

55. *Congressional Record*, March 20, 1986, pp. H1466, H1477, H1491.

56. Several liberals joined conservatives in voting against the Sasser amendment, because it contained $30 million in non-lethal aid for the Contras.

57. *Congressional Record*, September 25, 1984, p. S11781.

8
The United States, Nicaragua, and Consensus Decision Making
Roy Gutman

In July 1982, shortly after the Israeli army encircled Beirut, the chief U.S. representative at the scene, Philip Habib, proposed bringing in a detachment of U.S. Marines to oversee the departure of Palestinian fighters from the city. He wanted the marines to stay 60 days. Secretary of State George Shultz agreed. Over at the Pentagon, Caspar Weinberger, reflecting the cautious attitude of the Joint Chiefs of Staff, said he did not want to send troops under any circumstances. President Reagan told his two top aides to get together and come up with something both could live with. And that is how the marines came to be sent to Beirut for 30 days. Because, however, the underlying logic of either position had been abandoned, halfway through those 30 days Weinberger was able to go to Beirut and announce that the marines had done their job and would be coming home. It was an impulsive action, never cleared with Shultz, Habib, the multilateral forces nor the Lebanese government. The marines came home. Beshir Gemayel was assassinated, the Israelis entered West Beirut, and the marines returned, this time for an indefinite time and purpose.[1]

The process is called consensus decision making. It is a method of splitting the differences. It has the dubious merit of preserving the appearance of harmony in the cabinet and the grave defect that it has no bottom line. It can lead to erratic actions, loss of control over rhetoric and eventually loss of control over events.

It is a risky way of doing business. It is also in U.S. national security issues the prevailing way of doing business. President Reagan, acting as "chairman of the board," applies the same approach to arms control, where he manages to pursue both arms reduction and its antithesis, "Star Wars," either of which would undermine the other. The latest example is Angola, where the president wants to remain the mediator in the dispute while actively supplying one side with sophisticated arms. Everyone in the government is equally happy or unhappy in these actions, which are not decisions so much as examples of indecision.

This is the context in which I would like to discuss U.S. policy vis-a-vis Sandinista Nicaragua. To some degree any government makes decisions based on a consensus of the various power centers; but this administration has carried the practice to new heights.

To understand better the application of the rule, it is worth looking at an exception: U.S. policy in El Salvador. In July 1981, Thomas Enders, the Assistant Secretary for Inter-American Affairs, in his first speech after being confirmed set out a balanced policy position. He pledged support for land reform, called for an end to violence on the right as well as left, threw his weight behind elections, and called for continued military assistance.

A month later, a high level decision was made to ask Major General Fred Woerner to head a U.S.-Salvadoran team to make recommendations on revamping the Salvadoran army.[2] These two documents form the basis for policy today. The matter has not been settled but it has been handled with a modicum of success.

By comparison, U.S. policy toward Nicaragua has been a good deal less successful. Some of the more thoughtful people in Congress, after studying the issue, have been unable to divine just what U.S. strategy in Nicaragua is. There are no such milestones as the Enders speech and the Woerner report. Instead, there are four points—democracy, disarmament, expulsion of foreign advisers, and a halt in support of external insurgent groups. But, according to State Department officials, the order of the four for a long time has kept changing, because no agreement could be reached on priorities.

Early in the Reagan administration policy makers examined El Salvador in a serious, rigorous manner and put enormous energy and planning into crafting long-term policy. It was regarded as "salvageable."

But Nicaragua, the serious money had it, was already "lost" and the revolution was more or less consummated. What happened in the view of many State Department officials is that Nicaragua policy was thrown as a "bone" to the right. Of course you cannot do that and not pay the price somewhere down the line. 1986 is supposed to be the year of decision in U.S. policy toward Nicaragua but in a very real way things are up for grabs: no one in Washington can say what the next move will be in American policy or in the Congress or what the effects will be; so much depends on what the Sandinistas do, undo or do not do.

How long will Honduras tolerate the ambiguities that increasingly disturb its internal political and military equilibrium?

Not a great deal longer, Honduran officials say, and the resignation of the armed forces chief in January 1986 is an important omen.

The goal until recently was described as the avoidance of two negatives: Vietnam and Cuba. It could not be expressed in positive terms for two reasons: the deep internal division within the administration and the fear there would be no public support for any stronger position. Today the goal is more positive sounding—democracy in Nicaragua. That is a codeword for overthrow.

The means at hand is an over-sized, ill-trained, and under-equipped army of insurgents whom the U.S. Congress has fitfully supported over the past four and a quarter years. I do not know anyone who thinks it will work; plainly the United States either must alter its means or its ends. A U.S. intervention will replace the Sandinistas and could install a "democracy." But the president himself, citing the costs of such an action both at home and in the region, has ruled it out.[3] It is an unlikely course unless there is an obvious provocation. There are many officials who expect, or hope, something will happen. But it very well may not. As Daniel Ortega told Thomas Enders in August 1982, "we are romantics but not suicidal."[4] What the United States does then is a question no one can answer.

About the only way to merchandise this muddle is to speak of policy outcomes in terms of best case/worst case scenarios. The U.S. best case for the *contras* is that they will create enough havoc in the countryside to convince the population that they have support in the cities. The U.S. worst case for the Sandinistas is that the Nicaraguan economy will collapse and the government leave. One high U.S. official describes such expectations as a case of "self-delusion." The Sandinistas, convinced that U.S. policy is based on a personal obsession of the incumbent president, feel they must only wait out his term in order to survive. And the administration, aware that its means may not achieve its ends for the foreseeable future, is busy at work trying to lock in a policy that will bind future presidents. Perhaps the most realistic expectation of current policies is that they will lead to a prolonged civil war in Nicaragua.

Now what has brought the United States to this point? I would argue it is the president himself, by stating broad goals that cannot be implemented, by splitting the differences among his aides and by pursuing several policies at the same time rather than making the tough choices that will stand up in the medium and long term.

In 1981, the agenda of the right was to oust the Sandinistas and reverse the course of history. The uniformed military wanted to avoid direct involvement in Central America, contain the Nicaraguan revolution and avoid another Cuba. The agenda of the State Department policy-level people was to save El Salvador. The agenda of the White House was domestic: tax reductions, budget cuts, and higher defense spending. The agenda of the CIA or at least its director was in flux: a desire to become far more active and effective and to shake off the taint of the past. This agenda shifted as the agency acquired its own instrument and became its champion. The agenda of Secretary of State Alexander Haig was strategic as well as personal. He wanted to go to the source—to scare Cuba and probably cut off its pipeline to the Soviet Union and Nicaragua—but also to be firm and tough, and personally to take charge.

It would be difficult to hammer out a policy from this variety of agendas in the best of times. But imagine the result if the president does not force his people to sit down, take stock, think out what is doable and at what price, decide the goals, and set out a plan. The fact is, he did not. To paraphrase Henry Kissinger, they never thought this one through.[5] Instead, they agreed on what they could and put off the real decision.

There are those who would say U.S. policy has achieved at least limited aims such as forcing the Sandinistas to focus on their own problems and slowing consolidation of the revolution or achieve a stalemate of forces. Besides begging the question how to define a consolidated revolution, this ignores the fact that the most basic U.S. policy decisions have been merely put off, the choices are now extremely limited and time is running out. The policy process could be characterized as one of contradictions begetting contradictions.

In 1981, Haig wanted to act forcefully in Central America but was thwarted by the White House domestic agenda. Enders tried a peace effort with Nicaragua, then backed the armed insurgency, but both efforts were a distraction from Haig's desire to "go to the source." Enders viewed the *contras* as a means of pressure to achieve diplomatic goals. The approach which might be called "coercive diplomacy," was politically tenable at home but it was unrealistic to expect third country nations to risk their lives for limited U.S. goals. As the insurgency developed, the policy took on a life of its own in Washington, regardless of what it achieved on the ground.

In mid-1982, despite Enders' concerted resistance, U.S. goals were expanded to include a call for democratization of the government of Nicaragua. But it was at a time of growing congressional concerns, and the means as measured by U.S. financial support for the *contras* were never adjusted to this ambitious new goal. From that time forward, the gap between means and ends steadily widened.

1983 was a year of upheaval in the region and hyper- activity in Washington. For six months there was interregnum at the State Department as Langhorne Anthony Motley, Enders' successor, struggled to gather up the reins of power. Decisions were made in the White House.

The whole series of U.S. activities culminating in the invasion of Grenada in October unleashed a mighty fear in Nicaragua, where leaders ousted the Salvadoran guerrilla leaders and cut their supply lines. But because these actions had never been coordinated, the administration could not conceivably have cashed in on them even if it wanted to. It was an unnerving experience for George Shultz, in office just one year, to learn about the biggest set of military maneuvers in history in this region from the newspapers.

This was coercion without diplomacy. On the covert side, the CIA was faring no better. It went through a series of tactical shifts in short order as it struggled to get control of the no longer secret war. Another problem for the CIA in 1983 was political: Congress had let itself be misled in 1981 when the CIA said it would support the *contras* to interdict arms coming from El Salvador to Nicaragua. In 1983, the Republican-dominated Senate Intelligence Committee rejected Casey's attempt to broaden the goals.

1984, a presidential election year, was a disaster for the covert war, not because of anything the *contras* did or did not do; indeed it was a year they came into their own and began causing grave military problems for the Sandinistas. It was the mining of Corinto that destroyed their case of support in Congress, an action they did not even carry out, even though the CIA credited them with it. The action went well beyond what Congress had knowingly approved; moreover it was a failure. Ships kept coming despite the warnings to mariners that the *contras*, as part of the plan, had transmitted to Lloyds of London.

It was at this point that prodded by public urging from Mexico and other countries, Secretary of State George Shultz went to Managua and arranged the first serious effort at negotiations in three years. U.S. policy by this time was becoming incongruous. The president had begun using far harsher rhetoric toward the Sandinistas, but he had lost control of the stick. And in the meanwhile, the Sandinistas had developed a counterinsurgency strategy and began altering their military force structure to implement it.

The military momentum began to shift. By the time of the U.S. and Nicaraguan elections in November, political power also began to shift once again inside the administration from the State Department, which was trying to contemplate a world without *contras* or *contra* aid, to the White House, which could not imagine anything of the kind.

By the spring of 1985, when Reagan was able to get aid restored in the form of overt humanitarian assistance administered by the State Department instead of the CIA, the Sandinista army was gaining momentum, and by the end of the year, its Operation Sovereignty had achieved most of its aims. As this is written in early 1986, there is no sign of a southern front. In the north, the *contras* were mostly sitting in their camps in southern Honduras without boots, blankets, hammocks, and so on. The Hondurans simply couldn't swallow the publicity that attended overt aid to a group whom they officially deny is in their country. There is a fair-sized force in eastern Nicaragua, Boaco, and Chontales, but what they are doing there, far from their supply sources, far from the centers of population, is not completely clear. It may seem strange for a great power, but as the situation on the ground all has worsened, U.S. policy goals today are more ambitious than ever. It is now nothing short of full democracy in Nicaragua.[6]

But the ground beneath this demand is shaky at best. Honduras wants the *contras* out, although its new government seems willing to allow resupply if it leads to that end. To move entirely into Nicaragua would require an enormous expenditure for offensive and defensive arms, transport, and air support. It will require American military training not just in weaponry but in leadership and in small unit tactics. It is not clear even with all this support that the *contras* can achieve enough of a sanctuary to survive not to mention taking effective control of territory, which is essential if they are to be taken seriously. Militarily, it is a very bleak situation which cannot be resolved by throwing money at it; in addition, the political leadership of the FDN, the principal rebel group, is deeply divided.

Trying to represent these ends and means to the rest of the world as a foreign policy has put a real burden on American diplomacy. Invariably, leaders and opinion makers abroad ask whether the United States exhausted diplomacy before proceeding down the path it has taken. U.S. diplomacy toward Nicaragua has gone through five phases in the past five years, which are briefly enumerated below.

Offered first is an example of effective diplomacy, then an example of hurried and ineffective diplomacy. Third an example of phony diplomacy is given; followed by an example of furtive diplomacy. And fifth is the current situation of no diplomacy.

As an example of effective diplomacy, I would cite the efforts of Larry Pezzullo, the U.S. ambassador to Managua, in the spring of 1981. The administration had what it considered irrefutable evidence that Nicaraguan territory was being used in the supply of Salvadoran rebels who launched their final offensive just days before Ronald Reagan took office. This offensive, which was as ill-timed as it was ill-named, provoked Haig into over-reaction. It soured his relations with the White House in Reagan's first days in office.

Less well known is the secret diplomacy of those first few months, a glimpse into which has been provided in the recent State Department publication "Revolution Beyond Our Borders," which was the U.S. response to Nicaragua's case at the World Court last September.

On January 9, 1981, on the eve of the Salvadoran "final offensive" and in the last days of the Carter administration, Pezzullo went to Tomas Borge, one of the most powerful of the *comandantes*. U.S. intelligence had picked up signs of a major arms resupply of the Salvadoran guerrillas and Pezzullo reminded Borge of promises the previous autumn not to become involved in the Salvadoran conflict. Borge acknowledged that some arms had passed through Nicaragua en route to Salvador. This set the stage. A few weeks after Reagan took office, Pezzullo went to see Daniel Ortega, coordinator of the junta, and bluntly accused Nicaragua of failing to carry out its promises. On February 17, Ortega responded that the Sandinistas understood U.S. concerns and that Nicaragua would not risk its revolution for an uncertain victory in El Salvador. "Not a single round" would transit Nicaragua thereafter, he promised Pezzullo. Ortega also acknowledged that the Sandinistas had been very permissive in allowing the Salvadoran rebels to mount operations in Nicaragua. These promises were reiterated later in February and in early March.[7]

It worked. According to high State Department officials and sources monitoring intelligence data at the U.S. Southern Command, the reduction in the arms flow after Pezzullo's demarches was dramatic. What is puzzling is that the administration failed to use this as a jumping off point for coming to terms with Managua but instead announced on April 1 that it was cutting off U.S. aid to Nicaragua. This was of course a mixed signal to the Sandinistas, suggesting that their compliance with U.S. demands would not be reciprocated. The reasons for the action are still not clear, but other events going on that month, such as the March 17 visit to Washington of the Argentina military leader, General Viola, may offer a clue. The Argentines were just getting started in backing an irregular group who later would come to be known as the *contras*, and that visit at least symbolically established the link between the Reagan administration, the Argentines, and the insurgents. On the diplomatic side, however, this went down as a missed opportunity for the United States.

My second example is one of hurried diplomacy. Enders went to Managua in mid-August for two days of talks with the Sandinista leaders. Many of the sessions were testy, particularly with Father Miguel D'Escoto, the foreign minister. D'Escoto recalled one such exchange.[8] Enders said he did not want to blame the Nicaraguan government directly for the arms flow to the Salvadoran guerrillas, but that obviously some people within the Sandinista army must be looking the other way. D'Escoto replied that "this was not happening because if it was happening in a significant degree, we would necessarily know about it, and we knew nothing about it." To which Enders rejoined: "how could you claim to have the right to govern a nation if you don't know what is happening in your territory?"

D'Escoto asked Enders how Nicaragua was supposedly sending the arms. Enders replied that the greatest bulk was "going through your common land border with Honduras." D'Escoto saw his opening. "Look, by your own admission, all of this is going through Honduras. Have you ever questioned the right of the Hondurans to govern? Because you have to believe they either know that this is happening and they are accomplices or that they don't know, and have you questioned their right to govern?" But in asking the question, D'Escoto effectively conceded Enders' original allegation.

The final session with Daniel Ortega seemed to end on a cordial note with both sides committing themselves to exchange proposals in five areas of relations to resolve differences. Enders did that up to a point. He began by sending proposals he thought contained incentives to the Sandinistas, such as commitments of nonintervention and U.S. enforcement of the neutrality law regarding Nicaraguan exiles in the United States. He never got to draft the proposal on economic aid, but the one that proved to be the sticking point concerned security. It proposed that the Sandinistas send their heavy arms, at that time primarily some Soviet tanks, back to the countries of origin. So radical was this proposal that when Craig Johnstone, Enders' director for Central American affairs, showed this to Arturo Cruz, then the Nicaraguan ambassador, Cruz asked Johnstone to withdraw it. Cruz never even informed his government he had seen it.[9]

On the Nicaraguan side, officials now express regret that they did not do more to entertain Enders' proposals because in the context of everything that followed, this was the most serious opportunity they had had. Of course had the security proposal been sent, the talks might have come to a halt immediately. In any case, not to have probed the American position was a missed opportunity for the Sandinistas. The reason may lie in the nature of the leadership system that has been created there, in which as many as nine individuals—really four or five—must reach consensus on policy and any one of the stronger ones therefore has a veto. U.S. actions, which from this side seem inconsequential, were blown up there. In early September 1981 with one of the Enders papers came a notice that another aid program was being suspended. A small U.S. military exercise called Halcon Vista was scheduled, raising concerns in Managua that U.S. quiet diplomacy was to be accompanied by the big stick. There was no one on the U.S. side at the top level in Managua to coax the talks through. Pezzullo had left Managua and there was no replacement until March 1982. Finally, and most tellingly, is the reason the foreign ministry now gives for the delay in a Sandinista response: "we weren't so pragmatic in those days."[10]

The fact is the Sandinistas would have had to come forward quickly with developed proposals, a team of negotiators, and a sophisticated strategy within days of Enders' return to Washington for it to have worked. Enders came under immediate pressure in Washington for failing to push the Sandinistas hard enough in their internal democratic development. In retrospect, his visit, far from opening a diplomatic process that would extend over many months as any real effort must, was a last gasp effort before the boom came down.

Not long after this, Enders himself would become the champion of giving U.S. aid to the rebels. His purpose was quite limited: pressures that would lead back to negotiations. But in fact what happened is that the purpose broadened in 1982 and 1983. William Baez, a Nicaraguan economist, summarizes the progress of U.S. policy as three R's: reconciliation, then reform, and finally removal.

Enders had championed the idea of working to build democratic institutions in El Salvador, and this developed partly because of events in Honduras into a region-wide approach. But as stated earlier, policymakers at the State Department viewed Nicaragua as a lost cause. And when democracy became part of the U.S. negotiating agenda with Managua as it did in 1982, it was over Enders' objections. The new U.S. position was presented shortly after Anthony Quainton, the new U.S. ambassador, arrived in Managua in March, 1982. He made an oral presentation and didn't follow it up in writing for about six weeks and only on request. But there is little evidence of any serious American diplomacy at this point. Indeed, a national security council document on Central America policy approved in April 1982 and leaked to the New York Times the following year states the administration attitude. U.S. strategy was to increase pressure on Nicaragua and Cuba to increase the costs of interventionism and to isolate Nicaragua. There is no reference to seeking a negotiated solution with Nicaragua, and indeed the only reference to negotiations concerns heading them off. It calls for a step up in "efforts to co-opt the negotiations issue to avoid Congressionally mandated negotiations, which would work against our interests." I suspect this was intended to refer to Salvador although it might well be to both. Suffice to say, Quainton's presentation in Managua did indeed coopt the negotiating process.

The fourth example of diplomacy is the one that all sides may view in retrospect as the most frustrating. It took place in Manzanillo, Mexico, involved Harry Shlaudeman, a veteran U.S. diplomat, and Victor Hugo

Tinoco, the Nicaraguan vice minister of foreign affairs, and ran from June until December 1984. The talks opened and closed in an atmosphere of distrust. The Sandinistas assumed that this was a political ploy by the administration to hold off critics in an election year; and the rest of the administration thought the State Department was about to sell out their "policy." This was a classic case where the internal negotiation was every bit as tough as the external one, perhaps more so. In retrospect, Manzanillo seems to have been a missed opportunity for both sides, if only to prove whether either side was serious. The United States made a very complex proposal involving a timetable of reciprocal actions by both countries and included in this the arrangements for Nicaragua's elections and a reconciliation of the government with the *contras*. It left U.S. responses to these Nicaraguan actions vague, in part because they could not be agreed on in Washington. The Nicaraguans replied with a proposal that excluded any reference to internal issues; but they indicated a willingness in the course of those months to come to terms on security issues.

Unlike August 1981, this was a negotiation that lasted long enough to be serious; but it failed nonetheless. My theory is that Manzanillo began with the endorsement of the four who made up the mediating group known as Contadora, but they quickly and inadvertently came into conflict with Contadora's own mediation. U.S. efforts at Manzanillo dealt with most of the same issues as Contadora; both processes operated in secrecy; the two were never coordinated. So the Nicaraguans in mid-September 1984 accepted the Contadora treaty draft and rejected the U.S. Manzanillo proposal. It provided a short-lived public relations boost for the Sandinistas and an adrenalin shot for the Contadora countries, but ultimately led to the demise of the negotiating process. There is enough blame to go around: the Americans; the Contadora countries and the Nicaraguans. The reason it failed, I believe, is because the American side had to be so furtive at Manzanillo in good measure because of the internal pressures in Washington. The Americans did not know that Contadora was going for a final document; and Contadora did not know how serious the Americans were or how the two processes would fit together.[11]

This brings us to the present situation, which is one of no diplomacy at all. It is true that both countries have embassies in the respective capitals, and the Nicaraguans do call at the State Department and vice versa. But U.S. diplomats say that the relationship is maintained largely to provide the figleaf that discussions are continuing for the benefit of Congress. The fact is that no serious diplomacy is being conducted. No high U.S. official has gone to Managua to talk to Sandinista leaders since Shultz in June 1984. Even Congressional delegations stopped visiting

Nicaragua or Honduras from the summer of 1985 until the eve of the vote on Reagan's request for $100 million in *contra* aid in March 1986. Manzanillo ended in January 1985, but as part of the trade-off to obtain resumption of aid to the *contras*, Reagan agreed to consider resumption of talks with Nicaraguans.

In case there are any lingering expectations about U.S.-Nicaraguan diplomacy, the back and forth in September 1984 should disabuse the notion. As described by Father D'Escoto, this was a situation of protocollary one upmanship. As a preface, it should be noted that Shultz told a Contadora foreign minister before the Nicaraguans that the talks would be held, and an American reporter conveyed the word to D'Escoto. About a week before Ortega's arrival in New York, the U.S. side proposed that Abrams, accompanied by Shlaudeman and ambassador to Managua Harry Bergold, call on Ortega in New York. The Sandinistas responded that Ortega was willing to call on Reagan or to receive Shultz. But if Abrams wanted to see Ortega, he would have to travel to Managua. On the other hand D'Escoto, who is after all, the foreign minister, was willing to receive Abrams in New York. If the Americans wanted a meeting in Washington, D'Escoto would send his deputy, Nora Astorga. Miss Astorga was denied agreement when proposed as the Nicaraguan ambassador to Washington because of allegations she lured a CIA asset into her house where he was murdered. The Americans said no to all of the above, but proposed for Shlaudeman to call on D'Escoto. Now it was the Nicaraguan turn to demur. They instead suggested that Miss Astorga meet Shlaudeman in New York. The Americans declined. A few weeks later, Shlaudeman met the Nicaraguan ambassador to Washington, Carlos Tunnerman. Both sides reiterated their already stated positions.[12]

In view of the choppy and fleeting nature of U.S. diplomacy, it may reasonably be asked where Contadora fit into the American schema. Essentially it did not. The process came to life because of the diplomatic vacuum of 1982, the tense situation on the Honduran–Nicaraguan border and the desire of the participating countries to prevent a regional war that might lead to a U.S. military intervention. It was a time when Mexico was still attempting to project its influence, a new Colombian president was launching a domestic plan to pacify a longstanding insurgency, and Venezuela had residual oil wealth and aspirations of regional influence. All these motivating factors have since subsided, and Panama, which is closest to the conflict and most familiar with the players, is itself in political turmoil.

The strategic problem throughout Contadora's brief history is that it is a multilateral forum which has attempted to resolve things without U.S. participation. Meanwhile the Reagan administration approach has been largely unilateral. Reagan is in a position to block Contadora, but the converse does not necessarily hold true. Contadora's first accomplishment, the 21 Points, was achieved at the time of interregnum in the State Department. State was cool to the developments; the White House was the first to react. In fact Jeane Kirkpatrick, who did not believe the United States should come to terms with Sandinista Nicaragua but should overthrow that government, ironically emerged as the champion of Contadora within the administration. But others on the conservative side such as Constantine Menges were openly scathing about its efforts.

The Contadora foursome committed tactical mistakes as they went along that made it hard for the Reagan administration to take them seriously and easy for the administration to look the other way. They never found a way to engage public opinion in this country, either in Congress or the U.S. press, and today Contadora remains one of those stories that put newspaper editors to sleep. They went through three iterations of the draft treaty without forcing the protagonists to bargain it out until the very end when the momentum was lost. The four maintained an awkward distance from the United States and vice versa. Surely Washington should have been invited publicly to send an observer to all meetings, and if this was vetoed by one of the participants, then Contadora should have faced the decision of whether it made sense to continue. Cuba had an observer. The Contadora countries were remarkably coy about informing Washington of what happened; for example, in producing the revised *Acta* in September, 1984, the four did not present a copy to Washington immediately, but gave it first to the United Nations for distribution to this country among others. A similar procedure was followed in 1985.

In any negotiation that has as its goal a treaty on largely security issues, there has to be active and continuing involvement of the military establishments of the countries. Yet in each of the Contadora countries with the exception of Panama, this process was carried on by the foreign ministries almost exclusively. It would be difficult for a mediator to be a foursome anyway. The four countries simply have too many of their own interests to uphold to be neutral in the same measure. One would imagine the problem of how to proceed is four times as difficult as having one mediator; it will double again if the group enlarges as it seems to be in the process of doing.

That being said, those involved worked extremely hard and are understandably frustrated at the lack of results. There is a tendency to look for a scapegoat. But in truth, this would be a thorny issue no matter who handled it; each side has missed opportunities, and before the process is resurrected, if it is, it would be worth considering just how it could proceed in a manner that will be taken seriously.

Meanwhile, the fact remains that Contadora is still the only diplomatic game in town and its drafts may one day provide the basis for an agreement. Ironically the parties were at a situation in early 1986 in which a treaty draft was sitting on the table that contained features unacceptable to Nicaragua but possibly would achieve ultimately the aims of that country, namely to force the U.S. Congress to cut aid to the rebels. But instead, the Nicaraguans are insisting on a prior commitment from the United States before signing any treaty. Their response, while understandable, clearly lacks in imagination or foresight. Indeed the Sandinistas seem to have lost touch with the attitudes of Congress and public opinion in this country. Washington for its part continues to demand prior negotiations between the Sandinistas and the armed opposition before it will talk with Managua. This is a condition the Sandinistas say they never will accept.

One lesson of the past three years will be lost because no one has the capacity to deal with it. It is structural and relates to the decision-making processes of the major actors. Consensus decision making does not work on issues of national security. But three key actors—the United States, Nicaragua with its nine-man directorate and the Contadora four-some—rely on this kind of process as their method of decision making.

Consensus decision making in Washington has resulted in a situation where the U.S. policy choice is war or withdrawal. Consensus decision making in Managua has resulted in a lack of imaginative diplomacy in the face of clear dangers. And consensus decision making by the Contadora countries has forced a reliance on diplomacy by public statements and gestures and an excessive number of tactical misfires. If the United States seems to be in a situation of no exit, the Sandinistas appear modestly better off for having kept the door open a crack in that they have not foreclosed the Contadora option. As for the Contadora countries, I fear that the result of consensus decision making may prove not to be a situation of no exit, just exit.

NOTES

1. This is drawn from my article: "Battle over Lebanon: The War in Washington," *Foreign Service Journal*, June 1984.

2. Interview with Woerner, Panama, June 1985.

3. See for example, his March 23, 1986 interview with the *New York Times*, in which he said he was the "last one in the world that would ever want to put American troops into Latin America. . . . We'd lose all our friends if we did anything of that kind."

4. From a transcript of the talks—obtained by the author.

5. He said this during the deliberations of the Kissinger commission on Central America, according to a U.S. embassy source in Tegucigalpa.

6. "The purpose of our support for the democratic opposition is to pressure the Sandinistas into permitting an open society, a democratic society, into fulfilling their promises to the people of Nicaragua." Interview with Elliot Abrams, Asst. Secy. of State, December 1985. By "democratic opposition," Abrams was referring to the *contras*.

7. Department of State, "Revolution Beyond Our Borders," Special Report No. 132, September 1985, pp. 21–22, including footnotes.

8. Interview with D'Escoto, New York, October 1985.

9. For a more detailed account, see my article "Nicaragua: America's Diplomatic Charade," *Foreign Policy*, fall 1984.

10. Interview with a foreign ministry official, Managua, January 1986.

11. These conclusions are based on interviews with high officials in the four Contadora countries, Nicaragua, Costa Rica, Honduras and the United States as part of research for a forthcoming book.

12. Interview with D'Escoto, op. cit.

Part 3
The Contadora Process

9

Demystifying Contadora
Susan Kaufman Purcell

Contadora is a code word used to mean the pursuit of peace in Central America through negotiations. Its main alternatives are widely believed to be a U.S. invasion, a regional war or both. Like motherhood and apple pie, Contadora is liked and supported by everyone.

Why, then, has a negotiated settlement within the Contadora framework proved so elusive? Critics of U.S. policy in Central America argue that a diplomatic solution requires support from Washington and that, despite rhetoric to the contrary, Washington opposes Contadora because a Contadora treaty would prohibit unilateral action by the United States in protection of its interests. The facts are more complex than this reasoning conveys. The U.S. government remains divided, with some saying that an imperfect treaty is better than no treaty and others arguing that no treaty is better. For their part, the countries of the Contadora group—Mexico, Venezuela, Colombia and Panama—are divided in their interests and strategies. Some of them share the fears and ambivalence of the United States, though they have taken great pains to conceal this fact; the domestic political costs of agreeing with the United States in Central American matters are not negligible.

The impression that the United States and the Contadora Four have few shared interests leads to two opposite conclusions: either the Contadora process is a waste of time, since the United States will ultimately impose its own solution on Central America, or Contadora still offers a good solution, if only the United States would support it. The reality is somewhere in between. Over the past two and a half years, the Contadora Four have been obliged to move beyond empty rhetoric to deal with the complexities of designing a treaty that takes account of the interests

---

of the Central American countries and the United States. In the process, despite all the significant obstacles that remain, they have increased the possibility of a negotiated settlement in Central America.

Contadora refers to both a regional grouping and the negotiating process in which it is engaged. The Contadora group was originally created in January 1983, at the initiative of Colombian president Belisario Betancur, as a diplomatic alternative to the conflict escalating in the region. Nicaragua was aiding the Salvadoran guerrillas. In response, the United States organized the *contras*, who were increasing their forays into Nicaragua from Honduras. The U.S. military presence and activities in the region were beginning to expand. The Contadora countries feared that the Sandinistas would retaliate against the *contras* and draw Honduras, and then the United States, into open armed conflict that might eventually spill over into the rest of Central America.

Contadora aimed to fill a diplomatic vacuum. The Sandinistas have preferred not to work with the Organization of American States (OAS) since they believe the United States still controls its members, despite considerable evidence to the contrary. They favor the United Nations, where the dominant Third World coalition is sure to favor Nicaragua over the United States. For this reason, the United Nations has been an unacceptable mediator for the United States, which strongly advocates hemispheric solutions to hemispheric problems.

By joining forces under the Contadora umbrella, the regional powers believed that they might be able to constrain the United States from its habitual unilateral actions and thereby enhance their own role. They also hoped to offer a different interpretation of events in Central America. They believed that the United States, as a global and non-Latin power, tended to impose an East-West perspective on conflicts that essentially involved such North-South issues as poverty, inequality and exploitation. Their de-emphasis of the Soviet threat was understandable, since the United States, not the Soviet Union, had traditionally been seen as the danger to the countries of the region.

Finally, the Contadora countries had a record of successful joint efforts. In 1976, Omar Torrijos of Panama had enlisted the support of Mexico, Venezuela, Colombia, as well as Costa Rica, to generate Latin American support for the Panama Canal treaties. Three years later, these same countries persuaded the not-yet-victorious Sandinistas to commit themselves to political pluralism, a mixed economy and international non-alignment in return for their support. In 1981, Torrijos again brought the group together, shortly before his death, to pressure the Sandinistas to abide by their commitment.

In January 1983, the presidents of Mexico, Venezuela, Colombia and Panama met on the Panamanian island of Contadora to discuss the deteriorating situation in Central America. Their meeting marked the formal beginning of the Contadora group.

The Contadora Four were not interested in protecting U.S. security interests in Central America. On the contrary, they were reluctant to acknowledge publicly that the United States even had legitimate security interests in the region. They had no such qualms about speaking publicly of the legitimate security interests of Nicaragua. In fact, the regional powers had joined forces precisely to counter a real or imaginary U.S. military threat against Nicaragua.

Since then, observers have repeatedly pronounced the Contadora process dead or dying. They take at face value the frustration of the participants who keep encountering new, seemingly intractable problems each time they solve old ones. They fail to understand that Contadora's mere existence is useful. It allows the four participating governments to affirm that they have kept the United States at bay and have avoided a regional war. This makes it difficult for any of them to desert the negotiating process. At the same time, the costs of failure are relatively low. If diplomacy leads nowhere, the Contadora countries can say that they did their best, but the hegemonic pretensions of the United States made their best not good enough.

The Contadora Four had first become active in Central America in the late 1970s. Venezuela, Colombia and Panama had helped arm Nicaraguan president Anastasio Somoza's opponents and all four had worked hard to isolate Somoza internationally. Yet the Four's familiarity with Central America remained limited. Contadora has helped teach them about Central America and about each other. It has also shown them that it is far easier to call for a diplomatic solution than to create one.

Contadora has forged a consensus around a number of objectives that could constitute the basis for a negotiated settlement. These are embodied in the 21 Points of the Document of Objectives of September 1983, calling for democracy and national reconciliation, an end to support for paramilitary forces across borders, control of the regional arms race, reduction of foreign military advisers and troops, and prohibition of foreign military bases. These goals were incorporated into the draft treaty or *Acta* of September 7, 1984, which Nicaragua quickly accepted and the United States just as quickly rejected. These starkly different reactions created the impression that Nicaragua favored a negotiated settlement and the United States did not.

In fact, the United States rejected the *Acta* because it was a vague statement of goals without concrete limits on Nicaraguan action. Its provisions for verification and enforcement were totally inadequate, and it deferred negotiations on foreign military and security advisers and arms and troop reductions until after signature of the treaty. On the other hand, it required the United States upon signature to cease military exercises and support for the *contras*. Further military aid to El Salvador and Honduras was frozen, while Nicaragua was allowed to maintain its military advantage over these two countries. The provisions for democratization and internal reconciliation were hortatory and unenforceable as drafted. They would have allowed the Sandinistas to claim that the Nicaraguan elections scheduled for November 1984 were in compliance with the *Acta* despite charges by the democratic opposition, led by Arturo Cruz, that the electoral process was rigged.

Nicaragua accepted the *Acta* as a final document, not a draft for discussion, because it asked little of Nicaragua immediately and left no possibility for Nicaragua to be pressured in postsignature negotiations. Accepting the *Acta* also improved Nicaragua's image internationally, just as the U.S. Congress was to vote on aid for the *contras* and Nicaraguan President Daniel Ortega was to address the U.N. General Assembly.

When Nicaragua surprised U.S. friends in Central America by accepting the *Acta*; Honduras, El Salvador and Costa Rica began drafting what became the Act of Tegucigalpa of October 1984—a substitute draft that sought to correct what they and the United States had seen as the main problems of the September 1984 *Acta*. The timetable for disarmament and demilitarization procedures was changed to produce more simultaneous action on these issues, and the role of the Central American governments in the verification and enforcement processes was enhanced. The Nicaraguans immediately rejected the October draft and repeated that they would not accept any substantive changes in the September *Acta*. Their position remains unchanged at this writing.

With the process at an impasse, the Contadora countries looked to the bilateral talks in Manzanillo, Mexico, between the United States and Nicaragua to achieve a breakthrough. In the penultimate round in late 1984, Nicaragua hinted that it was willing to be flexible on key security issues in a strictly bilateral agreement. The United States pointed out that Nicaragua logically could not enter into two contradictory agreements, and eventually concluded that Nicaragua was proposing at Manzanillo the substitution of a limited bilateral agreement on security issues for a comprehensive Contadora agreement. The United States therefore suspended the bilateral talks in January 1985 to emphasize multilateral discussions within Contadora.

This tactic worked for a time. In April 1985 an agreement in principle was reached on revised verification procedures involving concessions by both Nicaragua and the Central American drafters of the Tegucigalpa Act. But the negotiations bogged down again in the summer of 1985, when Nicaragua once more tried to substitute a series of bilateral security agreements for Contadora's comprehensive agenda. Nicaragua favors such an approach to avoid the issue of democratization and internal reconciliation, a shorthand term for talks between the Sandinistas and their armed and unarmed opponents (including the *contras*) leading to the eventual incorporation of the opposition into a democratized political process.

Democratization and internal reconciliation may well be the most difficult issue of all, because it would, in the words of President Reagan, "overthrow the Nicaraguan government, in the sense of changing its structure." The Sandinistas, however, say it is a non-issue; they will not deal with the contras and Nicaragua is already democratic.

The democratization–internal reconciliation issue is also at the heart of the division within the U.S. government. While there is consensus that a more democratic Nicaragua would be more likely to abide by a negotiated settlement, the debate is over the more fundamental question of whether it is possible to democratize Nicaragua at all. Some argue that Nicaragua can be made to accept democratization and internal reconciliation under pressure and want the United States to hold firm for such an outcome. Others doubt that the Sandinistas will ever incorporate the rebels and democratize. They believe that the United States should therefore accept a treaty that deals with the conventional security issues but not with democratization and internal reconciliation.

The so-called Reagan Peace Plan of April 4, 1985, came out squarely in favor of continuing to press for democratization and internal reconciliation. President Reagan was not about to abandon the Nicaraguan "freedom fighters"; he called for a cease-fire and talks between the Nicaraguan government and the rebels. At the same time, he asked Congress to release an appropriation of $14 million in humanitarian aid for the rebels, which the United States would only make available if the talks did not succeed by June 1, 1985. The plan failed to obtain sufficient backing: Congress which denied aid at that time and the Contadora Four wanted nothing to do with a plan that included aid for the *contras*. The Reagan administration continues to emphasize the need to include democratization and internal reconciliation in any treaty. Progress thus depends on whether the Contadora process can devise such a treaty.

The Contadora Four enjoy an image of unity. They oppose a military solution and unilateral action by the United States. They seek a negotiated settlement to end the fighting. They also believe that the Sandinista government of Nicaragua is here to stay and that its future, particularly its international alignment, can be influenced by outside actors. Beyond this consensus, however, there are important differences among the Four, which reflect their particular historical experiences as well as the political constraints they face domestically.

Mexico. Mexico's position has been most at odds with that of the United States. Although critical of Washington for supporting right-wing dictators in Central America and for failing to help eradicate poverty and injustice, in policy terms Mexico has not behaved very differently from the United States. Mexico has not actively supported right-wing dictators, but it did nothing to undermine their rule until the late 1970s, when it withdrew recognition from the disintegrating Somoza regime. Nor did Mexico pursue an active or generous aid program toward the area. In fact, Mexico "discovered" Central America at about the same time the United States did, belying the myth that Mexico knows and understands Central America better than the United States does.

Mexico's policy toward the Sandinistas has been protective and empathetic. As a country that has experienced its own modern revolution, Mexico could not condemn other revolutions. Mexico had also suffered multiple U.S. interventions and lost half its territory to its northern neighbor. It therefore sympathized with the Sandinistas' fear of a U.S. invasion or intervention in their affairs. Precisely because of its historical relationship with the United States, Mexico had earlier adopted a foreign policy based on the principles of nonintervention and self-determination. It applied them to the Nicaraguan revolution when it occurred in July 1979.

Mexico's definition of nonintervention, however, was tailored to its policy preferences. Mexico did not consider itself to be intervening in Central American affairs when it withdrew recognition from Somoza or joined in the Franco–Mexican declaration of August 1981 that recognized the Salvadoran rebels as a "representative political force."

Mexico's support of the Sandinistas and the Salvadoran rebels reflected its belief that revolutionary governments in Central America, including communist ones, would not threaten Mexico's interests. It felt confident that it could establish friendly relations with such governments, as it had done earlier with Cuba. Mexico might even gain influence if left-wing governments triumphed in Central America. The United States would have little, if any, influence over such governments; Mexico, in contrast, could work with them and possibly replace the United States as the most important power in the region.

Finally, Mexico rejected the theory that it was the "last domino" that would fall if Marxist revolutionaries were successful in Central America. Mexico correctly viewed itself as different from its southern neighbors, considerably larger and more developed, with a more differentiated social structure. And, with the exception of Costa Rica, its political system was more effective and responsive than those in Central America.

Mexico's actions were, nevertheless, marked by a gap between rhetoric and reality. The Mexicans pursued a very different policy toward the right-wing military regime of Guatemala than toward other right-wing governments in the region. Mexico has neither broken with nor publicly criticized the government in Guatemala City; nor has it called Guatemala's Marxist guerrillas "a representative political force." Also, despite Mexico's rejection of the domino theory, it has reinforced its military presence along its southern border and implemented the so-called *Plan* Chiapas to help improve the standard of living of Mexican peasants in the lands bordering on Guatemala.[1]

Over the past year, the perception has grown that Mexico's policy toward both the Sandinistas and Central America in general has changed. The presence of Mexico's foreign minister at the inauguration of President José Napoleón Duarte in El Salvador is often cited. The fact that Mexico no longer supplies petroleum to the Sandinistas on terms more favorable to Nicaragua than to other clients is another example. Mexico also has become less tolerant of the political representatives of the Salvadoran guerrillas operating in Mexico. President Miguel de la Madrid has also begun to balance references to U.S. intervention in Central America with references to Cuban intervention.[2] And he seems less eager than his predecessor, José López Portillo, to engage in high-level meetings with Fidel Castro.

Mexico claims that its policy has not changed, but that circumstances in Central America and Mexico have changed. Yet the policy has also evolved. Under López Portillo, Mexico's initial unquestioning support for the Sandinistas, as well as its de-emphasis of the need for political pluralism in Nicaragua, had made Mexico ever more isolated within the Contadora group. Also, as growing numbers of refugees crossed the border into Mexico, Central America increasingly became transformed from a foreign policy issue to a domestic one. Ministries other than the foreign ministry became involved, weakening the previous consensus behind the government's approach and pushing it to adopt a more balanced policy toward Central America.

This shift does not mean that Mexico has abandoned the Sandinistas. Mexico does not want to drive the Sandinistas out of the negotiating process and into total isolation. Mexico was therefore critical of the October 1984 treaty drafted by the Central American allies of the United States because it feared that Nicaragua would abandon the Contadora process if it did not get favorable treatment. Mexico also supported the Sandinistas' stress on the importance of having bilateral talks with the United States. The Manzanillo talks were in part the result of a personal initiative by President de la Madrid during his visit to Washington in May 1984. Mexico therefore continues to work for a balanced settlement in Central America.

Venezuela. The Contadora country whose position has been most at odds with that of Mexico and closest to the United States is Venezuela. Unlike Mexico, Venezuela does not consider itself a revolutionary country; instead, its sense of identity is strongly based on its evolution into one of the most important democracies of the hemisphere. Support for the principle of democratization has been considerably more important in Venezuela, therefore, than it has been in Mexico. Venezuela has also been much more distrustful of Marxist revolutionaries than Mexico, since for years the survival of Venezuela's democracy was threatened by Marxist guerrillas. Venezuela believed that democratic government could not develop in El Salvador if the guerrillas remained unchecked.[3] Venezuela also has been wary of Cuba because of Havana's earlier support of Venezuelan guerrillas.

Unlike Mexico, Venezuela admitted from the beginning that the Central American conflict had implications for Venezuelan security and required a strategic, as well as an economic, political and social response. For this reason, Venezuela sent military advisers to El Salvador. (The decision was facilitated because Christian Democratic presidents were in power in both Venezuela and El Salvador.) This policy became politically unsustainable after the United States sided with Britain during the 1982 Falklands War. Nevertheless, even after the transfer of the presidency to a Social Democrat, Venezuela's policy toward Central America did not change dramatically. Venezuela distanced itself initially from the interim government of Alvaro Magaña in El Salvador, when right-wing elements seemed ascendant. But once Christian Democrat Duarte was elected president, even Venezuela's Social Democratic regime supported him.

Venezuela also favored the incorporation of the Salvadoran guerrillas into the electoral process and, like the United States, opposed negotiated power-sharing. Venezuela had, after all, successfully incorporated its own guerrillas into its electoral process, and some had even been elected to important public offices.

As the Sandinistas became more authoritarian and closely tied to Cuba and the Soviet Union, Venezuela became more openly critical of them. More recently, it has terminated shipments of subsidized petroleum to Nicaragua and has increased its assistance to democratic elements in the labor movement, the church, universities, and the private sector in Nicaragua. Former President Carlos Andrés Pérez, a prominent leader of the Latin American Social Democratic movement who has been highly critical of U.S. policy in the region, refused to attend Ortega's inauguration as president of Nicaragua in expression of his displeasure with the path that the Sandinistas were taking. Still, Venezuela has not yet given up on the possibility of some degree of political pluralism in Nicaragua.

The dramatic differences between Venezuela and Mexico demonstrate the fallacy in the judgment that the Contadora Four are united in opposition to the U.S. approach to Central America. Venezuela, in fact, shares some of the basic premises that underlie U.S. policy toward Central America.

Yet neither Venezuela nor Mexico wishes to see the United States return to the highly interventionist role it played in Latin America in the past. Both would like a solution that would avoid U.S. military intervention or other forms of unilateral U.S. action. The main differences between the Venezuelan and Mexican positions is that Venezuela seems more willing and able to cooperate on military and security dimensions with the United States than is Mexico, and Caracas places more importance than does Mexico City on the need to democratize the Nicaraguan government. At the very least, Venezuelans are divided over whether a Marxist regime poses a security threat and if so, whether Venezuela should play a military role in changing or containing it.

Colombia. The country whose attitudes and behavior changed most substantially with a change of governments is Colombia. Under former Liberal president Julio Cesar Turbay, Colombia was supportive of U.S. policy toward Central America. In part, this reflected a traditional tendency on the part of his party to work closely with the United States. Turbay himself distrusted the Sandinistas' expansionist inclinations, particularly toward a number of Colombian islands claimed by Nicaragua. President Reagan backed Colombia in its conflict with Nicaragua, which reinforced cooperation between the two governments.

Colombia is the only Contadora country with an immediate guerrilla problem. Turbay had promulgated a national security statute less than one month after his inauguration in 1978. The attempted military solution to Colombia's guerrilla problem failed and so Turbay's successor, Belisario Betancur, tried a completely new tack when he took office in 1982.[4]

Betancur's goal was to negotiate amnesty for the guerrillas in return for their peaceful incorporation into the political system. The new president believed that such a deal would not be possible while Colombia continued to align itself with the United States, whose Central American policy seemed to emphasize defeat of guerrillas by military means. On his inauguration day, he distanced himself from the United States by announcing that Colombia would apply for admission to the Non-Aligned Movement, chaired at that time by Fidel Castro. He also called for the restructuring of the OAS so as to exclude the United States and include Cuba. These steps paved the way for a new strategy for dealing with the guerrillas at home.

In pursuit of his new domestic policy, Betancur successfully engaged the services of Nobel Prize laureate Gabriel García Márquez, who was close to Castro as well as to the Sandinistas. The idea was to get Castro and the Sandinistas to encourage Colombia's guerrillas to negotiate the terms of an amnesty with the Colombian government. If successful, the strategy would end Colombia's guerrilla problem and neutralize Cuba and Nicaragua, in the sense of ensuring their noncooperation with guerrilla groups in Colombia.

Betancur was trying to "Mexicanize" Colombia's foreign policy. By pursuing a "progressive" foreign policy that included friendly relations with Cuba and Nicaragua, Betancur hoped to discourage their support for the Colombian guerrillas and encourage them to cooperate with his government.

Betancur paralleled his domestic strategy toward the guerrillas with a more active role for Colombia within the Contadora group. Attracted to the role of international peacemaker, Betancur traveled incessantly throughout the region, engaging in marathon talks with governments and rebels, as well as with the other three Contadora countries and the United States. The last such effort ended in Washington, D.C., in April 1985, the same day President Reagan announced his peace plan. President Betancur endorsed the plan, but qualified (or some would say retracted) his endorsement several days later by stating that he could not side with the United States in supporting the *contras*. Since the plan clearly included a role for the *contras* from the beginning, Betancur had either endorsed it before reading it carefully or was persuaded to distance himself from the United States once the other Contadora countries objected to it.

Betancur's domestic policies continue to be debated within Colombia. Critics contend that they are failing. Although Betancur succeeded in signing truces with Colombia's two main guerrilla groups, one of them subsequently changed its mind. There is also evidence that some of the guerrilla groups used the amnesty to regroup and rearm. Betancur has so far rejected the use of force or pressure to achieve his objectives at home and abroad. The guerrillas, however, have not. Their use of force and negotiations has therefore put the Colombian government at a disadvantage.

Presidential elections are scheduled in Colombia for 1986. If guerrilla violence continues to increase, Colombia will probably return to a more hard-line policy toward the guerrillas after the election, whoever is elected. Colombia's role and posture within Contadora would also probably change, toward a lower profile and a more centrist approach.

Panama. The fourth Contadora country, Panama, resembles the Central American countries themselves; it is small, poor and weak. Yet Panama has never regarded itself as part of Central America, and neither can it be considered a regional power like Mexico, Venezuela and Colombia.

Its membership in the Contadora group is mainly a reflection of the leadership qualities of Omar Torrijos, who regarded Panama as too small a stage for his ambitions and talents, and so played an active role in regional politics. Since his death, Panama has been governed by four different presidents, a symptom of the domestic political instability that has focused Panama's attention inward.

Panama's diminished role in Contadora also reflects ambivalence regarding developments in Central America and in its relationship with the United States. On the one hand, Panama does not wish to see the Sandinistas extend their influence in the region. The traits that Panama shares with its Central American neighbors, in addition to its geographical proximity, make it more immediately vulnerable than are its Contadora partners to the destabilizing impact of regional conflict. Furthermore, the Panamanian national guard shares many of the anti-communist sentiments that underlie U.S. policy toward Central America.

On the other hand, Panama does not want to appear too closely aligned with the United States for fear of fanning domestic anti-U.S. sentiments. The United States has been a kind of colonial power in Panama, where its ownership of the canal gave it extraordinary influence, if not control, over the course of events. Despite a reduction in the U.S. role in Panama since the signing of the canal treaties, the United States remains very involved. The U.S. Southern Command is headquartered in Panama and has grown considerably during the course of the Central American conflict.

Panama has resolved these tensions by focusing within Contadora on getting an agreement that would increase Panama's international prestige. Consistent with this goal, its position on specific issues has been flexible and pragmatic.

In view of these differences among the four Contadora countries, how could they claim to be united in support of the September 1984 *Acta* that the United States and the Central American countries found unacceptable? Mexico took the lead in pressing for a draft treaty prior to the U.S. presidential election. It hoped that if a draft treaty were in place prior to Ronald Reagan's expected reelection, the chances for unilateral action by the United States would be diminished. Colombia agreed. Venezuela believed it important to have a treaty prior to the Nicaraguan elections, which were also scheduled for November 1984; after the elections it would be difficult to press Nicaragua to democratize. Nicaragua also wanted to move before its elections so the result would seem to be blessed by Contadora. There was no time to work out a perfect treaty before November. The decision was made, therefore, to leave the most difficult problems, such as arms negotiations, a timetable of withdrawal for security advisers, verification and processes for implementation, for later negotiations. Meanwhile, a treaty ending U.S. military exercises and support for the *contras* would protect Nicaragua and reduce the chances of direct intervention.

This strategy involved a decision to win Nicaragua's support at the expense of that of the United States, a reasonable decision in view of the fact that there was considerable doubt among the Contadora Four that the United States would ever find any draft treaty acceptable. Obtaining Nicaragua's acceptance of the draft, however, could probably be counted on to increase international pressure on the United States to go along as well. This is exactly what happened.

The Contadora Four did not accept the idea that an unenforceable treaty would threaten their security. This highlights a major problem that confronts the United States in the search for a negotiated settlement in Central America. Underlying any negotiations is the assumption on the part of the Contadora Four that if their security is *really* threatened, the United States will do something about it. Thus, they can take risks in the negotiating process that the United States is unwilling to take.

But there are, of course, players beyond the Contadora Four. Any negotiated settlement in Central America would have to win the approval of the Central American countries. Yet these countries do not see eye to eye with the Contadora countries, and the latter, especially Mexico, virtually ignore them in the mediating process. Costa Rica, Honduras and El Salvador are pitted against Nicaragua; Guatemala is also, but it seeks to project itself as more neutral than the other three.

Because the positions of Costa Rica, Honduras and El Salvador are congruent to the United States' position, the conventional wisdom is that the United States has pressured these small, weak countries to do its bidding. This view is, at the least, an oversimplification.

The postures of the governments of Costa Rica, Honduras and El Salvador reflect the common reality they face. They all feel vulnerable to the activities of Marxist guerrillas operating in Central America and accept the much-maligned "domino theory." They do not trust the Sandinistas and, together with the United States, fear that Nicaragua will continue to support radical insurgents throughout the region. Their support of the *contras* is due to their belief that the Sandinistas will change only under outside pressure. A negotiated solution to the conflict that requires the United States to stop providing military assistance to them is unacceptable because they need U.S. military, economic and political support to survive. Thus, they agree with the United States on the root of the problem and its solution.

Nevertheless, these countries are ambivalent toward Washington. The United States cannot be too closely supported without undermining the still fragile domestic legitimacy of their governments. They also view

U.S. policy toward the region as erratic and undependable. For these reasons, they need to hedge their bets in order not to irreparably damage their relations with the Sandinistas or the Contadora Four.

Toward the Contadora Four, their attitude is quite negative. Mexico, Venezuela, Colombia and Panama have little understanding of Central America, they feel, and are more interested in protecting their own interests and assuring the survival of the Sandinista government than in protecting them. Like the Contadora Four, these Central American countries want to avoid a regional war, but they doubt that the way to do it is by siding with the Sandinistas against the United States.

As the Contadora Four have become more involved with the specifics of a negotiated settlement, the Central American countries have become more resentful of what they regard as unwarranted intervention in their internal affairs. Costa Rica, El Salvador and Honduras believe that current trends are in their favor; Contadora, therefore, is seen as increasingly obstructionist. This resentment is directed most against Mexico, which is their "Colossus of the North."

Despite the general consensus that Costa Rica, Honduras and El Salvador share, there are some differences. As with the four Contadora countries, these variations grow out of the different historical experiences and current realities of each country.

Costa Rica. Costa Rica is unique in Central America as the only institutionalized democracy without a military establishment. Costa Rica also has a tradition of distrust of Nicaragua, stemming from Somoza's repeated attempts to intervene in his neighbor's internal affairs. Anti-Somoza sentiments ultimately led Costa Rica to join with Venezuela, Colombia, Panama and Mexico to help oust the dictator. Costa Rica, however, soon found the Sandinistas to be authoritarian and interventionist as well.

Officially neutral toward the Central American conflict, Costa Rica is not ideologically neutral; it is profoundly anti-communist. This helps explain the unofficial support that Costa Rica has given to Edén Pastora, the former Sandinista and current leader of the Nicaraguan rebel group that operates in the border region between Costa Rica and Nicaragua. Costa Rica also supports the need to democratize the Nicaraguan government and incorporate the rebels into the political system. It does not want a Contadora agreement that allows the further consolidation of a communist regime in Nicaragua. Costa Rica distrusts the ability of any treaty to contain the expansionist tendencies of the Sandinistas and believes, as does the United States, that democratization and internal reconciliation are the best guarantors against the export of revolution by the Sandinistas. Finally, without an agreement that integrates the *contras* into Nicaraguan politics, Costa Rica fears it will receive thousands of refugees in addition to the approximately 40,000 that it already hosts.

El Salvador. The government of El Salvador is engaged in a civil war and needs uninterrupted military assistance from the United States in order to hold its own against the guerrillas, let alone defeat them. The government also needs to prevent the Sandinistas, the Cubans and their other allies from supplying the rebels with training, munitions and other supplies. Therefore, the Salvadoran government is most concerned with the security-related issues of the Contadora process. It supports an end to arms trafficking and is against provisions that would limit military assistance from the United States to El Salvador.

El Salvador also supports the need for internal reconciliation and democratization in Nicaragua. It opposes a double standard implicit in much of the Contadora discussions: the belief that pressure is legitimate if used to get the Salvadoran government to democratize, but is interventionist and illegitimate if applied to the Nicaraguan government. Although the process has not yet gone far, the Duarte government has held talks with the Salvadoran guerrillas and sees no reason why the Sandinistas should not be required to do the same with their guerrillas.

Honduras. As the only immediate neighbor of Nicaragua with a military establishment, Honduras is the one most concerned with the strength and size of the Nicaraguan armed forces. Thus, Honduras took the lead in Central America in opposing the September 1984 *Acta*, which provided for a freeze of military force levels. Honduras does not want a freeze, since that would freeze Nicaragua's military superiority over Honduras. It wants reduction.

A reduction would also assuage Honduran fears over the growing strength of the Salvadoran military. Although Honduras and El Salvador are currently cooperating with each other, they have traditionally been competitors, if not enemies. The perception of a common threat from the Sandinistas has enabled them to bury their differences for the moment. The Hondurans believe, however, that the chances of Honduran–Salvadoran cooperation enduring would be increased if El Salvador's armed forces were not allowed to become vastly superior to those of Honduras. As the country from which most of the *contras* operate, Honduras is also strongly supportive of a treaty that does not abandon the Nicaraguan rebels. Like Costa Rica, it supports talks between the *contras* and the Sandinistas leading to the eventual incorporation of the former into the Nicaraguan political process.

Finally, like El Salvador, Honduras fears a treaty that would deprive it of U.S. military support, and has thus sought a bilateral military agreement with the United States. At the same time, Honduras does not wish to be taken for granted, and so periodically attempts to negotiate more favorable terms of cooperation with the United States.

Why had the Central American allies of the United States originally seemed willing to accept the September *Acta* that Washington opposed? In part, they were posturing. They had serious problems with the *Acta*, but they chose to adopt a positive stance in order to impress favorably a group of European foreign ministers scheduled to meet in San José, Costa Rica, on September 28, 1984, to discuss economic assistance for the region. They believed that their objections to the *Acta* could be concealed for the time being, since they were convinced that Nicaragua would reject it. They were wrong. Nicaragua's unexpected acceptance of the *Acta*, on the condition that it not be changed in any way, led them to withdraw their support and to draft the Act of Tegucigalpa, which more accurately reflected their interests.

Guatemala. Since October 1984, when Honduras called together the other Central American governments to draft a substitute treaty, Guatemala has sought to distance itself from the others. Appearances are deceiving. The Guatemalan government is as anti-Sandinista as the other three Central American governments. It also does not want to freeze arms levels within Central America at current levels, thereby giving Nicaragua an advantage. It too wants an end to arms shipments to guerrilla movements, and it does not want the United States to withdraw from the region. Furthermore, although Guatemala sent only a vice-minister to the October meeting of foreign ministers and failed to endorse the draft treaty publicly, the vice-minister participated actively in its drafting.

Guatemala's ambivalence is explained by its unique situation. It is the only Central American country that shares a border with Mexico, the country that has been most sympathetic to the Sandinistas. Relations between Guatemala and Mexico have never been easy. The Guatemalan government's anti-guerrilla campaign created a serious refugee problem in southern Mexico. Because some refugee camps were used as safe havens for the Guatemalan guerrillas, Guatemala wanted the camps removed from the border. To achieve Mexico's cooperation, Guatemala needed to improve its relations with its neighbor.

The Guatemalan government also had been upset with the United States for some time, largely because of U.S. criticism of its human rights performance and the related cutoff of economic and military assistance. Although Guatemala basically agrees with the United States on Nicaragua and its potential threat to the region, it wants the United States to pay a price for its cooperation with the other Central American countries.

Finally, the behavior of Guatemala's military rulers has made the country a pariah within Latin America. The civilian governments of

Latin America all publicly supported the efforts of the Contadora Four and regarded the opposition of Honduras, Costa Rica and El Salvador to the September *Acta* as an obstructionist move masterminded by the United States. By withholding public support from the October draft treaty, Guatemala could partially reintegrate itself into Latin America.

Nicaragua. Nicaragua has consistently preferred bilateral over multilateral negotiations to resolve the conflict in Central America. It has believed it could better protect its interests by dealing with its neighbors individually and avoid the issues of democratization, national reconciliation and regional arms control. A series of bilateral agreements would also make it more difficult for the United States to coordinate its policies with its Central American allies. Facing a Central American refusal to accept bilateral negotiations, and therefore a choice between multilateral negotiations or nothing, Nicaragua reluctantly joined the Contadora process. Negotiations would help forestall a U.S. invasion, which the Sandinistas regarded as otherwise inevitable. And multilateral negotiations could possibly produce a treaty that would legitimize the Sandinista regime and formally circumscribe the U.S. military role in Central America.

The Nicaraguan government, however, does not have faith that a multilateral treaty would constrain Washington. It therefore demanded bilateral talks with the United States, toward the goal of a separate U.S.-Nicaragua treaty that would, among other things, prohibit the United States from invading Nicaragua. When these talks began in Manzanillo in June 1984, Nicaragua's purpose was to preclude U.S. support for the *contras.* Nicaragua was willing to make a number of concessions to achieve that goal; it saw the *contras* as the main obstacle to the rapid consolidation of Sandinista rule. In the course of the talks, Nicaragua therefore agreed in principle to send home its Cuban advisers, refrain from supporting guerrilla movements in neighboring countries and prohibit the installation of foreign bases on its territory.

The issues of internal reconciliation and the democratization of the regime were raised by the United States in the first meeting. The Sandinista position, however, was that internal reconciliation between the government and unarmed opposition groups was already occurring, and that the government would never talk with the *contras,* who were traitors. They added later that there was no need to discuss democratization since Nicaragua already had a democratically elected president and a pluralistic political system. Finally, the Sandinista government argued that the current internal reconciliation and democratization demands went beyond those that former Assistant Secretary of State Thomas Enders had originally stated to the Sandinistas in August 1981. At that time, the United States had not insisted on talks between the Sandinistas and the rebels. Enders had demanded that the Sandinistas stop sending arms to El Salvador, cease their own military buildup, loosen their ties with Cuba and the Soviets, and generally increase political and economic pluralism. In exchange, the United States would resume economic aid and not help the rebels.

The United States ultimately suspended the Manzanillo talks in January 1985, after the ninth session. It argued that Nicaragua was using the talks to extricate itself from Contadora and was exploiting fears among Washington's Central American friends of a separate deal between the United States and Nicaragua. Finally, the United States argued that it was demanding more from the Sandinistas than Assistant Secretary Enders had because Nicaragua had become more authoritarian and allied with the Soviet Union since 1981.

The Nicaraguans claimed that the United States suspended the Manzanillo talks because progress toward an acceptable treaty was being made, and the United States had no intention of negotiating a settlement of its conflict with Nicaragua. Since the suspension of the talks, Nicaragua ostentatiously sent 100 Cuban soldiers home and agreed to halt both the military draft and the acquisition of new weapons systems. It hoped that these gestures would keep the U.S. Congress from supporting the *contras* and pressure the United States to resume bilateral talks. President Ortega's trip to Moscow undermined the strategy; Congress voted in favor of humanitarian aid for the *contras*, and Nicaragua then reversed its positions on the draft and the acquisition of new weapons systems.

Within Contadora, Nicaragua holds firm in its support for the September 1984 *Acta*, as originally drafted, and continues to press for a resumption of bilateral talks with the United States. In the meantime, it has intensified its military campaign against the Nicaraguan rebels. Nicaragua continues to refuse to talk with the *contras* or consider additional steps to democratize its political system. Instead, the Sandinistas have tightened their control over the country. They also continue to argue that they have the right to ally with the Soviet Union, Cuba or any other country and to take whatever steps are necessary to protect themselves against their enemies. Nicaragua has reversed its position before. Whether it will do so again will depend on internal and external pressures on the regime.

Contadora is stalemated once again. The immediate stumbling block concerns timing; Nicaragua first wants an end to U.S. support for the *contras*, and then it would be willing to negotiate both the terms and timetables of other issues such as a reduction in the number of military advisers, arms control and maneuvers.

The other Central American countries want "simultaneity." Agreement must first be reached on all outstanding issues and all should then enter into effect simultaneously. The Nicaraguans do not like the Tegucigalpa draft treaty because they do not want to negotiate under military pressure. The other Central American countries do not like the September *Acta* because they are convinced that the Sandinistas will not negotiate in good faith if the *contras* are first disbanded and the U.S. military presence in the region is reduced.

Even if the disagreement over timing could be resolved, much work remains to be done to convert agreement on principles into the detailed provisions of a negotiated settlement. To their credit, Contadora's numerous working groups are already giving serious attention to the question of how to stop arms trafficking and outside support for so-called liberation movements of the right and left. The negotiators are also grappling with the problem of how to verify arms levels, military reductions and the like.

Even if these details are worked out, the problem of what happens if and when treaty provisions are violated still remains. None of the Contadora countries wants the United States to act unilaterally. On the other hand, the regional powers have traditionally been reluctant, if not opposed, to taking collective action, including military action. They cannot have it both ways.

If the Contadora Four want a negotiated settlement in Central America that will be more than cosmetic, they must be willing to take responsibility for assuring compliance with the treaty. They cannot continue to hide behind the principle of nonintervention. They must be prepared to intervene collectively, including militarily, against violators of the treaty.

Once a treaty draft is available that resolves the timing issue and deals adequately with the problems of verification and enforcement, the problems of internal reconciliation and democratization will remain. At that point, what happens at the negotiating table will depend on what is happening on the ground and in Washington.

If the Sandinista government is able to resist pressure from the *contras*, either because it has won the timing issue or because of its own military capabilities, it will also be strong enough to maintain political control of Nicaragua and to refuse to sign a treaty providing for democratization and internal reconciliation. In such a situation, the U.S. government would be hard put to justify an invasion and the casualties and high political costs that it would entail. More likely, the United States would eventually decide to drop its demand for democratization and internal reconciliation and settle instead for the kinds of security arrangements that are currently being worked out by Contadora. It would not be an ideal solution. Contadora would have produced a negotiated settlement of the Central American conflict, but the United States would have accepted the consolidation of another communist regime in the Western hemisphere.

NOTES

1. For a fuller discussion of the Mexican military's role in southern Mexico, see Cesar Sereseres, "The Mexican Military Looks South," in David Ronfeldt, ed., *The Modern Mexican Military: A Reassessment*, Center for U.S.-Mexican Studies, University of California, San Diego, 1984, pp. 201–213.

2. Miguel de la Madrid H., "Mexico: The New Challenges," *Foreign Affairs*, fall 1984.

3. Margaret Daly Hayes, "Regional Perceptions of the Central American Situation," working paper for the November 8, 1983 meeting of the Council on Foreign Relations Study Group on Central America.

4. For a more detailed discussion of Colombia and Contadora see Fernando Cepeda Ulloa, "Contadora, Colombia y Centroamérica," a paper presented at a conference on regional approaches to the Central American crisis, co-sponsored by El Colegio de México and the International Institute for Strategic Studies, in Toluca, Mexico, May 1985.

Part 4
Conclusion

10
The Failure of Diplomacy
Bruce M. Bagley

INTRODUCTION

In mid-1986, the Contadora Group's search for a negotiated settlement of the conflicts in Central America had once again reached a seemingly insurmountable impasse and an intensification of the war in Nicaragua and surrounding countries appeared inescapable. Despite the last-ditch negotiating efforts undertaken by the Contadora Four—Mexico, Venezuela, Colombia, and Panama—to meet their self-imposed treaty deadline of June 6, 1986, they were unable to produce a final draft acceptable to all five Central American republics. In the wake of this failure, on June 25, the U.S. House of Representatives reversed its long-standing opposition to overt military assistance to the Nicaraguan counterrevolutionaries (*contras*) and voted to provide $100 million (70 in military and 30 in "humanitarian" aid) to the rebel forces at war with the Sandinista regime. In August, President Reagan publicly acknowledged for the first time that it might ultimately be necessary for the *contras* to "take over" (i.e., overthrow the Sandinista government militarily).

While the Contadora process is not dead—the member countries announced on June 7, 1986, that the deadline for achieving a treaty would be extended indefinitely and that they would continue to seek a negotiated peace—the group is clearly comatose and its vital signs are ebbing. Since June, regional peace negotiations have been at a virtual standstill while the *contras* and the Sandinistas have been gearing up for a major escalation of the war in late 1986 and beyond.

This essay seeks to explain why Contadora has thus far failed to achieve a negotiated peace in Central America and why it is unlikely to succeed in the foreseeable future. The analysis begins with an effort to clarify the origins and objectives of the Contadora Group and then examines the dynamics of the negotiation process from its inception in January 1983 through mid-1986. In this review the negotiating positions of each of the principal actors involved in the Contadora process are mapped out in detail in order to establish the basic contours of the Contadora's present impasse. Although the United States is not a direct participant in the peace talks, special attention is focused on the evolution of U.S. policy towards Contadora and the crisis in Central America because of the dominant role played by Washington in the region. The essay concludes with a discussion of the limits of the Contadora negotiations and of the alternatives the region faces if, as now appears likely, a Contadora peace treaty does not materialize.

OBJECTIVES AND ORIGINS OF CONTADORA

OBJECTIVES

The Contadora Group was formed on January 8-9, 1983, when the foreign ministers of Mexico, Venezuela, Colombia and Panama met on Contadora Island in Panama. The declared purpose of this meeting was to seek "Latin American solutions to Latin American problems." Specifically, these four nations sought to provide a diplomatic alternative to the rapidly intensifying armed conflicts in the region.[1]

In late 1980 and early 1981, the Nicaraguan and Cuban governments had provided extensive aid to the Farabundo Martí National Liberation Front (FMLN) in El Salvador. In 1981, the Reagan administration responded by organizing the *contras* to oppose the Sandinista regime and by supplying them with "covert" military aid. Throughout 1982 the fighting along the Nicaraguan-Honduran border continued to escalate, leading the Contadora countries to fear the spread of warfare in Central America and the possibility of a direct U.S. military intervention in the region.[2]

The desire to avert unilateral U.S. military action in either Nicaragua or El Salvador was clearly one of the principal motivations that brought the Contadora Group together. Less frequently understood, especially in the United States, is that the Contadora countries were also unanimous in their desire to moderate and contain the revolutionaries in Nicaragua and El Salvador and to limit the growing involvement of Cuba and the Soviet Union in the region. Although some U.S. observers have complained that the Contadora Four were "not interested in protecting U.S. security interests in Central America,"[3] in fact the group was, from the outset, keenly aware that the United States did have legitimate security concerns in the area and worked assiduously to assure that the peace negotiations would produce a settlement that safeguarded those interests. In the final analysis, the Contadora leaders, anti-communists to a man, were just as concerned as Washington with preventing the spread of Soviet-Cuban influence on the region.

The Contadora governments did, however, disagree fundamentally with the Reagan administration over both the strategies and tactics best suited to achieve their common goals. These disagreements were rooted in the Latins' differing interpretations of the underlying causes of the turmoil in Central America and in their rejection of the traditional American presumption of U.S. hegemony in Central America. From the perspective of the Contadora countries, the basic reasons for the region's crisis were internal—poverty, injustice, repression—rather than external—Soviet-Cuban subversion—as the Reagan administration claimed.[4] Moreover, they blamed the United States for supporting, or at least tolerating, repressive right-wing dictatorships in the region and thereby contributing to the long-term instability which the Soviets and the Cubans sought to exploit. Rather than a solution to the Central American crisis, a return to the hegemonic pattern of U.S. intervention was viewed as a dangerously destabilizing response that could trigger explosive undercurrents of nationalism and anti-Americanism throughout the region.[5]

Given this understanding of the roots of the Central American crisis, the Contadora Group unanimously opposed unilateral U.S. military actions and proposed instead a comprehensive negotiated settlement designed to end the fighting, contain the Sandinista regime, and demilitarize the region; thus removing it altogether from the arena of East-West conflict. This strategy implicitly challenged the traditional hegemony of the United States in its Central American "backyard." First, it required not only the removal of Cuban and Soviet military advisors from Nicaragua, but also the elimination of the U.S. military presence throughout the region (in El Salvador and Honduras, as well as U.S. aid to the *contras*). Second, it proposed guarantees for the survival of the radical Sandinista regime in exchange for Sandinista agreement to refrain from entering into military alliances with Cuba and the Soviet Union and to cease its support for revolutionary movements in El Salvador and elsewhere in Central America. Third, by its very existence the Contadora Group implied a modification of the long-standing hegemonic U.S. role in hemispheric affairs and a shift toward a more collective pattern of leadership in which Latin America's regional powers would have a much greater role than in the past.[6]

To argue that the Contadora nations simply were not interested in protecting U.S. security interests in Central America is not only inaccurate, but very much beside the point. It is inaccurate because from its inception Contadora sought to eliminate all Soviet-Cuban military presence in the region and to prohibit Nicaragua from destabilizing its neighbors. It is beside the point because it confuses the problem of protection of U.S. security with the broader question of the preservation of U.S. hegemony in Central America.

ORIGINS

The Contadora initiative was not born overnight, but rather was the product of a lengthy series of previous, more limited efforts undertaken unilaterally, bilaterally and multilaterally by various regional actors interested in reducing growing tensions in the region. Colombian President Belisario Betancur Cuartas (1982–1986) played an important catalytic role in the formation of Contadora, when in October and November 1982 he sent his Foreign Minister Rodrigo Lloreda Caicedo first to the United Nations and then to Mexico City to inform the Mexicans and Venezuelans that his government would be willing to join forces with them to seek negotiated settlements to the conflicts in Central America.[7] But Betancur's initiative was possible only against the backdrop of previous diplomatic efforts undertaken by various governments in the region.

In 1976, Venezuela and Colombia had joined Mexico in supporting Panama's quest for a new treaty with the United States that would return the Panama Canal to Panamanian sovereignty. In early 1979, the Andean Pact countries, led by Venezuela and Colombia, along with Mexico withdrew recognition from the Somoza government; thereby contributing to the regime's growing diplomatic isolation. They then joined forces in the Organization of American States (OAS) to block a Carter administration initiative for the creation of an OAS-sponsored joint peacekeeping force, designed to prevent the Sandinistas from coming to power in Nicaragua. In June, just weeks prior to the July 1979 Sandinista victory over the Somoza regime the group worked together to convince the Sandinistas to promise the OAS in writing that they would sponsor democratic elections in Nicaragua "as soon as possible."[8] In August 1980, Mexico and Venezuela drew up the "San José Accords" in which they jointly pledged themselves to supply petroleum on concessionary terms to nine Central American and Caribbean countries, including both Nicaragua and El Salvador, in an effort to ameliorate the negative economic effects of the 1979 oil price hikes on the already turbulent Caribbean basin.

In July 1981, Mexico and Venezuela, along with Canada and the United States, met together in Nassau, Bahamas, to consider the possibilities of better coordinating their aid programs in the Caribbean Basin. Subsequently, in February 1982, in a meeting in New York, Colombia joined the "Nassau Four," converting the group into the "New York Five." From the outset, Mexico was skeptical about this initiative because of U.S. insistence that "Communist" countries (such as Nicaragua and Grenada) be excluded and no effective coordination ever resulted.[9]

In August 1981, Mexico allied with France to present a joint declaration to the United Nations on the Salvadoran civil war in which both governments recognized the FDR-FMLN as a "representative political force" and urged that foreign involvement be avoided by all parties. In February 1982, Mexican President José López Portillo announced that his country would be willing to offer its good offices to facilitate direct negotiations between the United States and both Nicaragua and Cuba, as well as between the FMLN rebels and the government in El Salvador. On September 7, 1982, in the wake of the Falklands/Malvinas War between Argentina and Great Britain, Mexico joined with Venezuela to call for direct negotiations between Nicaragua and Honduras, that were to include the United States as well, in order to resolve the intensifying conflicts along the Honduran-Nicaraguan border.[10]

Two future Contadora participants—Colombia and Panama—participated, along with Costa Rica, Honduras, El Salvador, Belize, the Dominican Republic, and the United States, in the October 1982 meeting in San José, Costa Rica, that produced the Declaration of San José and the proposal for the creation of a pro-peace and democracy forum to negotiate a settlement to the Central American conflicts. Fearing that this meeting would be dominated by the United States, and thus biased against Nicaragua, neither the Mexicans nor the Venezuelans participated. Such concerns were also shared by the Betancur government in Colombia and the de la Espriella administration in Panama in the aftermath of the San José meeting. Indeed, the subsequent creation of the Contadora Group just two months later was in many senses a preemptive effort to ensure that the mediation process in Central America would not be controlled by the United States and its closest Central American allies.[11]

Mexican president López Portillo was clearly the most vocal champion of peace negotiations in Central America in the early 1980s. In the face of growing Reagan administration hostility towards Nicaragua and the rapid U.S.-sponsored military buildups in Honduras and El Salvador, Mexico sought to bolster its individual diplomatic efforts with a series of bilateral initiatives (such as those undertaken with France and Venezuela), in a conscious effort to increase the constraints on unilateral U.S. action and thereby enhance the chances for a successful negotiated agreement. Mexico's willingness to join forces with Venezuela, Colombia, and Panama in Contadora was the logical outgrowth of that country's earlier efforts to enlist additional allies in the search for a diplomatic solution to the deepening conflicts in Central America.[12]

Although each Contadora nation was motivated by its own individual domestic and geopolitical concerns, they all shared a unanimous distaste for previous unilateral U.S. interventions in the region—Guatemala in 1954, Cuba in 1961, and the Dominican Republic in 1965—designed to "resolve" hemispheric problems and feared a repeat in the Nicaraguan case. They were also collectively troubled by the potential spillover effects of intensifying conflicts in the area. Finally, they shared a common desire to prevent expanding Soviet and Cuban involvement in Central America and thereby avoid the conversion of the region into an epicenter of East-West tensions.

THE DYNAMICS OF CONTADORA: 1983–1986

Contadora has often been likened to a cat with nine lives because of its remarkable ability to recover from seemingly fatal setbacks. During the last three and one half years, the negotiation process has passed through four basic phases. The first, beginning with the initial January 1983 meeting and extending through early September, produced the approval of a consensus Document of Objectives by the Contadora Four and all five Central American governments. The second, lasting from mid-September 1983 through mid-September 1984, culminated with Nicaragua's announcement that it was willing to sign Contadora's Revised Act. The third, stretching from October 1984 through December 1985, was characterized by continuing stalemate and ended with Nicaragua's request for a six-month suspension of the negotiation process. The fourth, from January to June 1986, began with Contadora's Caraballeda declaration, intended to revitalize the negotiations, and ended on June 6 with the failure to meet Contadora's self-imposed deadline for final passage of a treaty. Since June 1986, despite the Contadora Group's vows to persist in its search for a peaceful settlement, the Contadora process has been overshadowed by the U.S. House of Representatives' approval of funding for the *contras* and the Reagan administration's preparations for an escalation of its proxy war on Nicaragua's leftist Sandinista government.

THE DOCUMENT OF OBJECTIVES

Encouraged by the overwhelmingly positive international reaction to their January call for peace negotiations in Central America, the foreign ministers of the Contadora Group made joint visits to all five Central American republics in mid-April 1983 to consult with the governments of the region on how to begin the peace process and the key issues to be negotiated. On April 21, the Contadora foreign ministers met in Panama City with their Central American counterparts to clarify further the principal areas of dispute and to establish the basic procedures of consultation and negotiation to be followed. A subsequent meeting in late May, attended by all nine foreign ministers, led to the creation of a "technical" group, charged with studying the various proposals that had been put forward.[13]

By mid-July 1983, at a meeting held in Cancún, Mexico, in an atmosphere of deep concern over the Reagan administration's intentions, the presidents of the four Contadora nations were able to announce that agreement had been achieved on the general guidelines of a peace program that would be submitted to the governments of Central America for their approval.[14] Unanimous approval was given at a third Contadora ministerial meeting held in Panama in late July and a final consolidated "Document of Objectives" was subsequently signed at a fourth ministerial meeting held in early September.[15]

Commonly known as Contadora's Twenty-one Points, this Document of Objectives called for a halt to the Central American arms race, prohibited foreign military interference, bases, and advisors, and committed the nations of the region to adopt pluralist democratic systems and to institute free elections. It concluded with a proposal for continued negotiations to iron out the agreements and mechanisms required to implement these objectives and to assure adequate systems of verification and control.[16]

THE CONTADORA ACT FOR PEACE AND COOPERATION IN CENTRAL AMERICA

While doubtlessly an important symbolic achievement for Contadora, especially in the context of escalating military conflicts in both Nicaragua and El Salvador, securing approval of these general objectives was a relatively easy task, for formal endorsement imposed no specific obligations on any of the signatories. A refusal to sign would have inevitably exposed the country involved to intense international criticism.

A similar logic prevailed in Washington. Despite the Reagan administration's well-publicized policy of covert military support to the *contras*, its extensive military assistance to El Salvador and Honduras, and its obvious skepticism about Nicaragua's willingness to adhere to any treaty commitments it might undertake; the U.S. government embraced the Twenty-one Points and pledged its continuing support for the Contadora Group's peace efforts in order not to appear publicly as the key stumbling block to peace negotiations.[17] A chorus of domestic critics accused the Reagan administration of merely paying lip-service to Contadora while pursuing policies designed to overthrow the Sandinista regime militarily. Administration officials repeatedly denied that the U.S. government was seeking a military victory in Nicaragua and argued that a two-track policy involving *contra* "pressures" on Nicaragua was entirely compatible with negotiations, for it provided credible "incentives" for the Sandinistas to end their support of insurgents in El Salvador and to move towards democracy at home. Indeed, according to Reagan spokesmen, such pressures were the *sine qua non* of successful negotiations, for without them the Sandinistas would have no need to make any concessions.[18]

During the remainder of 1983, the Contadora Group met repeatedly in order to hammer out an agreement on the procedural questions involved in the implementation of the Document of Objectives. The sense of urgency surrounding these negotiations was greatly heightened by the Reagan administration's October 25, 1983, invasion of Grenada in conjunction with the countries of the Organization of Eastern Caribbean States (DECS). In the immediate aftermath of this stunning action, many observers speculated that its success might embolden the United States to undertake a similar direct intervention in Nicaragua. U.S. efforts to reactivate the moribund Central American Defense Council (CONDECA) in late 1984 added fuel to such suspicions, for it appeared that efforts to revive CONDECA were designed to provide an invitation similar to the one proffered by the DECS in the Grenadan case.[19]

By January 9, 1984, at the close of the twelfth meeting of the Contadora nations (the fifth involving the Central American foreign ministers), the group celebrated its first anniversary with the announcement of a new accord on procedural norms. This agreement created three working commissions (dealing with regional security issues, political matters, and economic and social cooperation), assigned the function of coordination to the previously established "technical" group, and set up a timetable that required the commissions to complete their recommendations by April 30, 1984.[20]

Contadora's success in obtaining this agreement on procedures was, however, almost immediately overshadowed by the public release of the "Kissinger Commission" findings that were submitted to President Reagan on January 10, 1984.[21] In this report, very little attention, and even less credence, was given to Contadora. The Contadora Group's efforts were ambiguously described as "constructive"; but the commission went on to warn that Contadora nations' interests "do not always comport with our own" and that the Contadora process should not be considered as a "substitute" for U.S. policies. Indeed, the report concludes that if Nicaragua proves unwilling to make changes in its internal affairs, along the lines demanded by the Reagan administration, it must be aware "that force remains an ultimate recourse of U.S. policy."[22]

At the April 30–May 1 Contadora meeting (convened to discuss its commissions' reports), Costa Rica, El Salvador, and Honduras challenged Nicaragua to match them in agreeing to disclose military units and major weapons systems, military agreements and arms deliveries from third countries, and foreign military personnel. They proposed that the Inter-American Defense Board be assigned responsibility for verifying the disclosures. The three countries also called on Nicaragua to agree to reduce troop levels, foreign military advisors, and weaponry to agreed levels, prohibit the importation of advanced weapons systems and eliminate trafficking in arms and the "exportation of subversion" to antigovernment guerrillas.[23]

After the meeting, Honduran Foreign Minister Edgar Paz Barnica publicly charged that Nicaragua had refused to accept arms limits. The Reagan administration seconded these criticisms, accusing Nicaragua of reconfirming "their usual pattern" of rejecting Latin initiatives for arms reductions, while "playing the aggrieved party and proclaiming peaceful intentions before international audiences."[24]

During May, domestic and international pressure on the Reagan administration to demonstrate that it was willing to give more than lip-service to the Contadora efforts increased substantially. In April, the U.S. Senate had approved the administration's request for $21 million in aid to the *contras*, before it became known that the Central Intelligence Agency had been directly involved in the mining of Nicaragua's harbors. The House subsequently refused to approve the request and many senators joined with the Democrat-controlled House in criticizing the mining operations. Additional pressure was added by Mexican President Miguel de la Madrid during his May visit to Washington. In his meeting with President Reagan and in his address to a Joint Session of Congress, he emphasized the importance of talks with Managua to revive Contadora's flagging negotiations.[25]

In response, U.S. Secretary of State George Shultz made a surprise visit to Nicaragua in early June for discussions with Sandinista junta leader Daniel Ortega. Although congressional opponents contended that Shultz's trip was made only to disarm domestic critics in anticipation of the upcoming Senate debate over *contra* aid, the State Department insisted that the visit was a bilateral effort intended only to push the regional negotiation effort along. In these talks, Shultz reiterated that the United States had four basic objectives regarding Nicaragua. "The United States wants Nicaragua to reduce its military force, sever its military and security ties with Cuba and the Soviet Union, end its support for Salvadoran leftist guerrillas and permit democratic pluralism to flourish at home."[26] As a result of this initial contact, the United States and Nicaragua subsequently undertook a series of bilateral talks in Manzanillo, Mexico.

Following additional consultation with Central American leaders, on June 9 the Contadora Group submitted its first draft treaty—the Contadora Act for Peace and Cooperation in Central America—for comments and amendments from the five Central American governments. After an additional three months of consultations, designed to produce a consensus document, a Revised Act was transmitted on September 7, 1984, to the

Central Americans for final "improvements" and, "in the not too distant future," for signatures.[27]

The U.S. reaction to the Revised Act was initially positive. On the day it was released, U.S. Secretary of State Shultz called the treaty an "important step forward" and commented favorably on its conditional acceptance by Honduras, El Salvador, and Costa Rica. He then went on to repeat U.S. accusations that "Nicaragua, on the other hand, has rejected key elements of the draft, including those dealing with binding obligations to internal democratization and to reductions in arms and troop levels."[28]

Just two weeks later, on September 21, Nicaragua unexpectedly announced that it was prepared to sign the Revised Act, but stipulated that no further changes be introduced and that the United States sign the agreement, as well as a protocol promising to halt support for the *contras*.[29] In accepting the Revised Act, Nicaragua conceded much of what the United States had demanded. Among the key concessions were agreements to expel all Soviet-bloc military advisors, halt all arms imports, reduce its 60,000-man army and eliminate part of its weapons inventory, end all assistance to the Salvadoran guerrillas, begin a dialogue with internal opposition groups, and permit onsite inspections by Contadora's verification commission. In return, the treaty required the United States to cease its support for the *contras* immediately, to end military maneuvers in the region within 30 days, to shut down all military installations in Central America within six months, and to suspend military aid programs in Honduras and El Salvador.[30]

STALEMATE

Caught completely off guard by the Nicaraguans' surprising decision, the Reagan administration was immediately forced on the defensive. It reacted quickly, declaring that the Revised Act was intended only as a draft document to be modified and rewritten in subsequent negotiations. U.S. spokesmen proceeded to detail specific criticisms of the treaty's verification procedures for failing to specify how the proposed commission on verification would be funded, how and to whom their reports on on-site inspections were to be submitted, how complaints of violations were to be written or disseminated, or how violators were to be punished. Reagan administration officials also objected to the provision that required a cutoff in foreign military aid to Central American countries thirty days after the pact was signed on the grounds that it would force a termination of U.S. military assistance to El Salvador and Honduras, pending the negotiation of arms-limitations agreements in Central America. "It would give the Nicaraguans veto power over future arms shipments to these countries."[31] Other criticisms were directed at the lack of a detailed timetable for the withdrawal of foreign troops and advisors. U.S. officials claimed that the proposed definitions would allow Nicaragua to keep "civilian" Cuban and Soviet personnel, while banning U.S. trainers in Honduras and El Salvador. Finally, the United States demanded tighter definitions of free, democratic elections, so that the Sandinistas' plans for elections on November 4, 1984, without the participation of key opposition leaders would not be allowed.[32]

Beyond these specific objections, off the record, senior Reagan administration officials expressed their conviction that the Sandinistas simply could not be trusted to comply with any diplomatic agreement. They concluded that long-term U.S. security interests in Central America would be threatened as long as the current Nicaraguan leadership remained in power.[33]

Nicaraguan junta leader Daniel Ortega denounced the U.S. objectives as a ploy designed "to slow the process" so that the United States would be in a better position to intervene militarily against Nicaragua. "The important thing is to sign the Act; in the implementation these details will be taken care of."[34] Reagan administration spokesmen counterattacked with accusations that the Sandinistas were merely adopting an old Soviet trick of accepting agreements for propaganda purposes without any intention of abiding by them.[35]

The Sandinistas clearly gained a substantial propaganda edge over the Reagan administration with their acceptance of the Revised Act. The U.S. Congress was scheduled to take up the administration's request for additional *contra* aid at the end of October; Nicaragua's good press and more accommodating image made justifying continued U.S. backing for military pressure on Managua considerably more difficult. It also helped shift international attention away from the democratic character of Nicaragua's upcoming elections and to refocus it on the Reagan administration's efforts to "block" a Contadora treaty. In addition, it provided a more positive climate for Nicaragua at the joint Contadora-European Economic Community meeting programmed for September 29 in San José, Costa Rica and enhanced pro-Sandinista sentiment in the United Nations prior to Daniel Ortega's speech before the organization in late 1984.[36]

Mexican officials let it be known that they were irritated with Washington's sudden discovery of major flaws in a treaty process it had previously endorsed.[37] In fact, diplomats from all four Latin American nations disputed the U.S. contention that the Revised Act was only a draft document, claiming that after eighteen months of intense negotiations, "Everyone had treated it as a final document from the beginning."

These diplomatic sources added that in contacts with Contadora negotiators, U.S. representatives had also treated it as final.[38]

To refurbish its image and regain the propaganda offensive, the Reagan administration hastily arranged a series of consultations with its closest allies in Central America in late September. In early October, Honduras, El Salvador, and Costa Rica all publicly agreed that, despite the previous year and a half of negotiations, changes along the lines suggested by the United States were needed. They then scheduled a meeting in Tegucigalpa, Honduras, for October 19, well after Contadora's formal deadline for the submission of final proposed changes, to draw up their proposed amendments.[39]

At the Tegucigalpa meeting, the foreign ministers of Costa Rica, Honduras and El Salvador endorsed a series of major changes (subsequently known as the Tegucigalpa Draft) that clearly reflected U.S. preferences over those of Nicaragua. Guatemala attended the meeting but refused to sign off on the new "counterdraft." Among the key amendments proposed were alterations in the provisions for limitations on armies and troop levels in the region from criteria based on the defensive requirements of each country to a formula of parity among all the countries of the region. Such changes were clearly unacceptable to the Sandinistas who claimed that Nicaragua, unlike its neighbors, had to be prepared to defend itself against the combined forces of the *contras*, Honduras, perhaps El Salvador, and, potentially, a U.S. invasive force.[40]

The Tegucigalpa Draft also deleted the provisions of the Revised Act that would have required the elimination of U.S. military bases in the region and the immediate cessation of U.S. military maneuvers, while altering the restrictions on foreign military advisors. It also struck out the final protocol that would have required the United States to agree in writing to observe the provisions of the treaty and immediately cease funding the *contras*.[41]

The proposed Tegucigalpa modifications constituted a major setback for the Contadora process, for they so unabashedly tilted the agreement against Nicaragua that they were unacceptable to the Sandinistas. The Reagan administration clearly put a good deal of pressure on the Tegucigalpa group to come up with these new demands, and, in light of the Central Americans' overwhelming dependence on U.S. economic and military assistance, there is no doubt that they were susceptible to such pressures. Indeed, one of the critical flaws of Contadora has been its inability to provide an economic alternative to U.S. support for the Central Americans and thereby free them to adopt foreign policies more independent of Washington. At the same time, it would be simplistic to conclude that these nations were merely acting as U.S. proxies in the negotiation process. Honduras, for example, was especially concerned with the maintenance of U.S. bases and joint military maneuvers, for it feared that without a visible U.S. military presence it would be vulnerable to Nicaragua's larger armed forces. El Salvador required continued U.S. arms shipments and advisors to conduct its ongoing war with the FMLN. For its part, Costa Rica was genuinely repelled by the Sandinistas' increasing authoritarianism and greatly feared the possibility of future cross-border subversion.[42]

The impression that Contadora was stalemated was reinforced when the United States announced in early January 1985 that it was unilaterally suspending the Manzanillo talks with Nicaragua (after nine sessions had been held) on the grounds that Nicaragua was attempting to use the bilateral negotiations to avoid and undermine the Contadora peace process.[43] The Reagan administration's January 1985 decision formally rejecting the jurisdiction of the World Court in the case of the CIA-backed mining operations of Nicaraguan harbors struck yet another blow against Contadora's hopes for a negotiated settlement of the Central American crisis.[44]

In spite of their obvious dismay with the Tegucigalpa group's last minute requests for fundamental changes in the act and the hardening of the U.S. position towards Nicaragua, in late 1984 and early 1985, the Contadora Group turned its attention to the task of integrating the two versions into a single, viable agreement. Over the next ten months, the Contadora negotiations incorporated modifications that temporarily allowed the continuance of U.S. military maneuvers in the region, that required deep cutbacks in the size of Nicaragua's armed forces and that severely limited the number and type of military equipment Nicaragua would be authorized to retain. It also dropped the requirement for a U.S. signing of the Contadora protocol.[45]

Even while these concessions to the United States and the Tegucigalpa group were being negotiated, additional signs of intensifying American hostility towards Nicaragua became evident. On May 1, 1985, the White House announced that it would apply an economic embargo against the Sandinista regime. On June 12, the U.S. House of Representatives voted to approve the Reagan administration's request for $27 million in "humanitarian" aid for the *contras*. On the same day it also voted against extending the Boland amendment that had prohibited the U.S. government from attempting to overthrow the Sandinistas militarily. On June 27, the House passed the so-called Foley amendment that authorized the president to order a direct military intervention against Nicaragua, without prior congressional approval, if that country were to endanger U.S. citizens, to directly attack its neighbors or indirectly support armed actions against them. On July 18, yet another House vote allowed the CIA to provide intelligence to the *contras*.[46]

In July 1985, as the Contadora negotiations crept slowly along, the Contadora nations took the novel step of endorsing the creation of a Contadora support group, in an effort to bolster the endangered peace process. Initially known as the Lima group because its first meeting was held in the Peruvian capital on the occasion of President Alan Garcia's inauguration, the Support Group included Peru and the recently installed democratic governments of Brazil, Argentina, and Uruguay. Its basic function was essentially symbolic, to demonstrate Latin American solidarity with the Contadora process. The support countries did not assume an active role in the negotiations, but rather remained on the sidelines as observers.[47]

In a meeting of U.S. ambassadors to Central America, with Assistant Secretary of State Elliot Abrams, held in Washington in early September, Abrams revealed U.S. concern with the potential impact of the Support Group. In a "secret document" that was subsequently leaked to the press, he stated that "it's necessary that we develop an active diplomacy in order to hinder the attempts at Latin American solidarity that could be directed against the U.S. and its allies, whether these efforts are initiated by the Support Group, Cuba, or Nicaragua."[48]

On September 12, 1985, the Contadora Group finally unveiled its revised version of the treaty. This version continued to call for the removal of foreign bases and advisors, an end to the arms race, the proscription of arms trafficking, and "democracy." But it backed away from outright prohibitions of military maneuvers and settled instead for their "regulation." It also eliminated the requirement for an immediate cessation of U.S. support for the *contras*. During the meeting in Panama City, it was agreed that a forty-five day permanent negotiation session would begin on October 7 and a deadline of November 22 was set to finalize an accord.[49]

On November 11, the Sandinista leadership informed the Contadora nations that the treaty was unacceptable and that Nicaragua would not sign. While emphasizing their acceptance of one hundred of the treaty's one hundred seventeen provisions, the Sandinistas indicated that the introduction of new amendments that permitted the continuance of U.S. military maneuvers in Honduras, the sharp cuts demanded in Nicaragua's troop and arms levels, and the failure to require the United States to agree to a nonaggression pact with Nicaragua or to halt its support for the *contras* were concessions they would not make.[50]

By late November, the negotiation process had reached a complete standstill. In early December, after repeating its accusations that the new treaty proposal completely ignored the U.S.-backed *contra* threat to Nicaragua, the Sandinista regime endorsed a recent Costa Rican proposal for a six-month suspension of the Contadora negotiations. They justified this request with the argument that upcoming changes in the governments of Guatemala, Costa Rica and Honduras were likely to help restore some balance within the region and thus increase the possibilities of achieving a workable treaty.[51]

Why did the Contadora Group agree to alterations in the treaty so obviously unacceptable to Nicaragua? In part, it is apparent that the Contadora countries were convinced that they had to make concessions to the Reagan administration and its allies in Central America just to keep the peace process alive.

The failure of the Sandinistas to reach an agreement with Arturo Cruz and other Nicaraguan opposition leaders that would have brought them into the country's November 4, 1984, elections was clearly a factor as well. The Venezuelans, in particular, became increasingly distrustful of the Sandinistas' democratic intentions in the wake of the elections. Indeed, Carlos Andrés Pérez, former president of Acción Democrática and current vice-president of the Socialist International, subsequently refused to attend Nicaraguan president Daniel Ortega's 1985 inauguration ceremony to show his disappointment with the Sandinista government. Under these circumstances, the administration of Venezuela's ADECO President Jaime Lusinchi proved more open to toughening up the treaty requirements than it had been previously.[52]

Colombia's Conservative president, Belisario Betancur, who had assumed an active role in the failed effort to bring about an agreement between the Sandinistas and the opposition in the 1984 electoral process, was also sorely disappointed with both the Sandinistas' and Arturo Cruz's inflexibility. Moreover, in April 1985, Colombia's deteriorating domestic economic situation had forced Betancur to seek support from the Reagan administration in his negotiations with the International Monetary Fund (IMF) for a special "enhanced surveillance" arrangement. As a result, Colombia was less inclined to confront Washington and its Central American allies on behalf of the Sandinistas.[53]

Similar factors also seemed to have been at work in Mexico. President Miguel de la Madrid and his government grew noticeably more disillusioned with the Sandinistas in 1984–1985; in part because of perceived Sandinista intransigence, and in part because of rising domestic opposition from conservatives and the military regarding Mexico's pro-Sandinista position within the Contadora process. Even more important, Mexico's severe debt crisis had weakened the Mexican government and forced President de la Madrid to adopt a more conciliatory approach to the Reagan administration in order to assure U.S. support in Mexico's painful and protracted negotiations with the IMF and the World Bank.[54]

Although Panama had never been a major player in the Contadora process on a par with the other three members, the fragile government of Nicolas Ardito Barletta was even less inclined than the previous de la Espriella administration to champion Nicaragua's cause in the face of the Reagan administration's adamant criticisms. Barletta himself was moderately conservative and pro-American in his outlook. Moreover, his administration desperately needed strong U.S. backing simply to stay in power.[55]

While none of the Contadora countries was interested in abandoning Contadora, neither were they willing, either individually or collectively, to defy Washington by siding with Nicaragua. Reflecting the disarray and uncertainty within the Contadora Group, in early December, Colombia, Venezuela, and Panama withdrew the revised Contadora act from the United Nations (where it had been submitted for signature) without informing Mexico. They then proceeded to hold meetings with the Tegucigalpa group (during which U.S. Ambassador to the United Nations Vernon Walters was consulted by telephone) in order to refine the proposal to accommodate U.S. objections to it. Thus, when in December 1985, Nicaragua petitioned for a temporary suspension of negotiations, many observers concluded that if Contadora was not already dead, it was clearly suffering from a terminal illness and that its days were numbered.

THE REVIVAL OF CONTADORA

Once again contradicting predictions of its imminent collapse, however, Contadora exhibited renewed life when the member nations and the Support Group met jointly on January 11–12, 1986, in Caraballeda, Venezuela, and issued the "Caraballeda Message on Central America's Peace, Security, and Democracy."[56] In this declaration, the Contadora and Support Groups reaffirmed their commitment to peace negotiations, called for renewed efforts to resolve the relatively few outstanding issues, and, most significantly, appealed to the Reagan administration to halt its aid to the *contras* and to renew the bilateral Manzanillo discussions. Peru and Argentina, the leading members of the Support Group, played key roles in orchestrating this revival.

Close on the heels of the Caraballeda message, Contadora received additional impetus when on January 15, 1985, Guatemala's Christian Democratic President Vinicio Cerezo seized upon the occasion of his inauguration to persuade the Central American governments in attendance to endorse the Caraballeda declaration.[57] Armed with this Central American endorsement, on February 10, 1986, the eight foreign ministers from the Contadora and Support Groups, visited Secretary Shultz to request that Washington cease further aid to the *contras* and that the bilateral discussions between the United States and Nicaragua in Manzanillo be reinitiated. Ignoring this appeal, just a few days later, the Reagan administration announced that it would seek renewed funding for the contras.[58]

Interpreting Caraballeda and the Central American endorsement of it as a vindication of its position and a direct criticism of the Reagan administration's support for the contras, Nicaragua dropped its request for a suspension of the negotiations and reentered the bargaining process. The Contadora Group and the five Central American participants renewed their negotiations on April 5–6, 1986, in Panama City. Mexico began the session with a proposal that all of the countries involved in the Contadora process join together to request that the United States halt all further assistance to the contras to give the Contadora nations enough time to complete negotiations and put a Contadora treaty into operation. The Tegucigalpa group—El Salvador, Honduras, and Costa Rica—refused and called for the negotiations to proceed without condemnations of U.S. aid to the contras. Meanwhile, Nicaragua demanded a declaration from Contadora along the lines suggested by Mexico and refused to resume negotiations until such an appeal was forthcoming.[59]

This stalemate lasted for the next three days and the meeting ended in disarray. In the final communique, the Contadora and Support Group countries, joined by all of the Central American nations except Nicaragua, agreed to set June 6, 1986, as the final deadline for approval of the treaty. Nicaragua remained adamant in its refusal, declaring that it would not agree to disarm unless the United States simultaneously committed itself to stop supporting the contras.[60] Hopes for a negotiated settlement appeared to be waning once again.

In comparison with Nicaragua's negative stance, the Central American governments appeared ready and willing to approve a Contadora treaty. To pressure Nicaragua, on April 14, Costa Rican Foreign Minster Carlos José Gutiérrez declared that his country "was willing to sign," adding, "we would like all the area countries to sign." The Guatemalan, Salvadoran, and Honduran foreign ministers all made similar statements.[61] Indeed, when it seemed in April that Nicaragua would not sign, Salvadoran Minister Rodolfo Antonio Castillo Claramount declared: "The Contadora Act is one of the most precise documents in history drafted to create conditions against war. Very few . . . have reached such a level of specificity, with so many details—creating organizations, mechanisms and methods to guarantee . . . peace in the region."[62]

In this context of deadlock, the public release of a letter, dated April 11, from Special Ambassador to Central America Philip Habib to Congressman James Slattery (D-Kansas), in which Habib stated that the Reagan administration interpreted the Contadora agreement to require an end to all assistance "from the date of signature," appeared to improve considerably the possibilities for a Contadora settlement.[63] "Ambassador Habib's letter seemed to bridge the gap between the Nicaraguan position, which was not to sign until the United States cut off the *contras*, and the U.S. position, which was not to cut off the *contras* until Nicaragua signed Contadora."[64] Liberals in Congress hailed Habib's letter as a significant shift on the part of the Reagan administration, for it committed the United States to a cessation of its aid to the *contras*, if a Contadora agreement was signed by all participants.[65]

Led by Congressman Jack Kemp (R-New York), conservative cries of alarm reverberated around Washington. In a letter of protest to President Reagan, Kemp charged that Habib's "confusing maneuvers and conflicting explanations potentially set the stage for a new Central American Yalta" and urged that Habib be fired.[66] Although the State Department had previously cleared the letter, the Reagan administration moved quickly to allay the conservatives' fears. Assistant Secretary of State for Inter-American Affairs, Elliot Abrams, declared that Habib "was in error" and added that the word "signature" should be changed to "implementation."[67] With this statement, Abrams placated the conservatives and effectively resurrected the stalemate between the United States and Nicaragua that had left the April Contadora meeting deadlocked. Indeed, on a not-for-attribution basis, a high-ranking State Department official let it be known that the Reagan administration was "hoping for the overthrow of the Sandinistas" and that he "saw little benefit to be gained from talking about a negotiated accord."[68]

Further evidence of the serious divisions within the Reagan administration over how to deal with the Contadora peace talks surfaced in the midst of the furor over the Habib letter. A Defense Department study formally released on May 20 argued that, if Nicaragua signs a Contadora treaty and then systematically violates it over a three-year period, an "effective" containment program would require a protracted commitment of U.S. forces involving at least 100,000 men and up to $8.5 billion a year.[69]

In a highly unusual public criticism of another agency, Charles Redman, a State Department spokesman, declared that the Pentagon study "has no standing as a United States government document."[70] Fred Ikle, Undersecretary of Defense for Policy and the sponsor of the Pentagon report, responded that Redman was just "plain wrong."[71] Striving to defuse this interagency feud, the White House denied that there were any differences between Defense and State over the study.[72]

This heated exchange prompted Congressman Richard A. Gephardt (D-Missouri), a Contadora supporter, to comment that "there is a furious debate in the administration" over Contadora; "they don't know what they want to do."[73] Congressman Lee Hamilton (D-Indiana) concluded that the Pentagon study confirmed that the Reagan administration "does not genuinely support the Contadora efforts even though it professes to do so."[74]

Against this backdrop of internal divisions and confusion in Washington, the five Central American presidents met on May 25–26 in Esquípulas, Guatemala. At the meeting, Nicaraguan president Ortega came under intense pressure from the other presidents to sign the Contadora agreement. At the conclusion of this weekend conclave, the presidents of El Salvador, Honduras, Costa Rica, and Guatemala issued a document pledging to sign the treaty. They also acknowledged that they still had "some differences and discrepancies" over how to resolve the region's conflicts and agreed to request an extension of the June 6 deadline in order to allow time for further negotiations.[75]

In an effort to ease the mounting pressure on Managua to negotiate seriously, and with an eye towards taking advantage of the window of opportunity that the Habib letter opened for Nicaragua, on May 27 President Ortega announced that his country was prepared to seek "concrete agreements on arms control" in an effort to break the deadlock in the Contadora negotiations. Specifically, he stated that the Sandinista government was willing to discuss a list of possible offensive arms reductions, including aircraft, airfields, tanks, large mortars, artillery, and rocket launchers. He did not, however, offer to reduce the size of Nicaragua's armed forces. In many quarters, this new Nicaraguan offer was interpreted as an important conciliatory gesture that substantially altered Managua's past refusal to discuss disarmament as long as the United States continued to support the *contras*.[76]

Following a final two-day meeting in Panama City on May 27–28, convened to discuss arms limitations and Nicaragua's latest proposal, the Contadora Group submitted its "final" draft agreement on June 6, 1986.[77] This version adopted Nicaragua's formula of a "reasonable" balance of forces but combined it with an earlier Guatemalan-Costa Rican proposal for a weighted point system for calculating force-level equivalencies. The draft avoided the still unresolved problems concerning U.S. military maneuvers, army sizes and arms limitations by proposing that they be dealt with in negotiations to be held after the signing of the treaty. It did, however, include clear guidelines for negotiating these points. Inventories detailing existing weapons systems and troop levels were to be submitted to the verification commission according to a precise timetable. The commission was then to draw up recommendations for maximum limits based upon the point system included in the treaty. By tying the banning of American advisors, bases and exercises to a final accord on army sizes, the agreement built incentives for Nicaragua to cooperate into the treaty. Failure to achieve agreement according to the established schedule would have freed Honduras to renew joint maneuvers with the United States, to reintroduce American advisors and to reestablish U.S. bases. Nevertheless, the removal of foreign bases and military personnel and an end to *contra* support were required upon signing of the treaty.[78]

The June 6 draft also strengthened the verification and control commission and provided for the establishment of a new International Corps of Inspectors, with broad powers of on site inspection to ensure compliance with commitments on security questions. This corps was a direct response to a previous U.S. request for a "rapid reaction observation unit" in each country to guarantee prompt and effective verification of Nicaragua's fulfillment of its obligations under the Contadora treaty.[79]

In the accompanying Declaration of Panama, the Contadora and Support Groups put forward three minimal agreements they felt would be needed to permit the Contadora process to advance. First, they advocated that no national territory be used to attack another country and that no logistical or military support be given to irregular forces or subversive groups. Second, they proposed that no country enter into military or political alliances that threatened, directly or indirectly, the peace and security of the region, thus drawing it into the East-West conflict. Third, they recommended that no world power give military or logistical aid to irregular forces in the area or threaten to use force as a means of defeating a government of the region.[80]

Although the Contadora Group had sought to strike a balance between Nicaragua and the pro-U.S. Tegucigalpa group at the June 6 meeting, Costa Rica, Honduras, and El Salvador petitioned for a reopening of negotiations on the treaty provisions concerning national reconciliation and democratization. They argued that the requirements were not stringent enough to force Nicaragua to negotiate seriously with its internal opponents or the *contras*. On June 12, Costa Rica and El Salvador issued a joint communique denouncing the agreement's lack of adequate verification mechanisms. A day later, Honduras attacked the treaty for failing to establish reciprocal obligations sufficient to guarantee its security. In their declaration, the Hondurans claimed that all the Central American democracies agreed with the United States that the proposed Contadora agreement did not ". . . make possible the verification of the reduction of the arms buildups, troops, and foreign military advisors."[81] As early as June 4, diplomatic sources in El Salvador were reported to have predicted that Honduras, Costa Rica, and El Salvador would all reject the June 6 treaty as a result of U.S. envoy Habib's trip through the region in early June.[82]

On June 20, Nicaragua announced that it would accept the new treaty. On the same day, Assistant Secretary of State Abrams rejected it as "inadequate." According to Abrams, ". . . this draft says . . . 'sign now and negotiate later,' so that you are signing what is actually a sort of half-blank page, and I'm not surprised that the democracies have refused to do that."[84] On June 22, the Reagan administration dismissed Nicaragua's acceptance of the June 6 Contadora agreement as "propagandistic," simply a tactic to defeat the administration's pending request for aid to the *contras*. On June 24, President Reagan declared that the United States would only sign an agreement that brought "real democracy" to Nicaragua.[85] In view of the fact that the Sandinista government is labeled by Washington as a "totalitarian, Marxist-Leninist" regime, Reagan's statement can only be interpreted as a rejection of any agreement, including the June 6 Contadora treaty, that leaves the Sandinista regime in power in Managua.

Under these circumstances, no treaty was signed. Despite the failure to reach an agreement by the June 6 deadline, on June 7, the Contadora Four pledged once again to continue their efforts to promote a Central American peace treaty. Thus, it is likely that Contadora-sponsored peace negotiations will continue indefinitely. By proposing continued talks without setting any new deadlines for agreement, the Contadora Group made it possible to extend the negotiation process unhampered by the specter of failure on any specific date. In the face of the current impasse, however, more time for negotiations seems to promise very little.

AFTERMATH: THE WINDS OF WAR

On June 25, 1986, the U.S. House of Representatives voted by a slim margin (221 to 209) to approve the Reagan administration's request for $100 million in aid for the *contras*, including $70 million earmarked for direct military assistance. U.S. training for the *contras* was also part of the package. This vote was heavy with symbolism for, in effect, it officially declared limited, surrogate war against the Sandinista regime. As one Reagan official commented after the vote, "No one around here is talking about negotiations."[86]

The House action clearly dealt a severe, and very possibly fatal, blow to the Contadora's quest for a peaceful settlement in Central America. The Reagan administration appears singularly untroubled by the prospect of Contadora's failure. Indeed, it has repeatedly stated that it would prefer no treaty at all, rather than a "bad" agreement.[87] For Washington, a bad treaty is apparently any accord that would leave the Sandinista regime as presently structured in power in Managua. Speaking more bluntly than ever before, in August President Reagan declared that unless the Nicaraguan government seeks democracy, the "only alternative" for the *contras* would be "to have their way and take over."[88]

For Washington, Contadora's efforts to come up with a verifiable treaty that effectively neutralizes Nicaragua as a security threat via agreements on the withdrawal of foreign bases and advisors, limits on the size of military establishments, controls on arms buildups and mutual non-aggression pacts, have been both inadequate and irrelevant. They are inadequate because, according to the Reagan administration, "communists cannot be trusted"; hence, independent of its specific provisions, any such treaty would not be worth the paper on which it was written. Only a democratic government would be trustworthy. They are irrelevant because, despite rhetorical endorsements of national reconciliation and pluralistic democracy, Contadora cannot guarantee to the United States that the Sandinistas will be willing to allow democracy to flourish. In fact, for the Reagan administration, the only acceptable empirical proof of the democratic character of the Nicaraguan regime would appear to be the voluntary departure of the Sandinistas from power. If the Sandinistas were to hold, and win, elections in which the opposition participated, it is probable that such a victory would be attributed to Sandinista fraud and manipulation and rejected as nondemocratic.

Behind Washington's publicly voiced concerns about U.S. national security and democracy in Nicaragua lies the implicit issue of the restoration of U.S. hegemony in Central America. Even if Contadora were able to produce a verifiable and enforceable treaty that nullified potential security threats from Nicaragua, the consolidation of a radical Sandinista government is clearly incompatible with the goals of a "resurgent America" in the region and, therefore, would not be acceptable to the U.S. government.

Following this logic, the Reagan administration has opted for increasing "pressures" on the Sandinistas by means of the *contras*. Some Reagan advisors hope that these pressures will lead to an internal coup within the Sandinista army against their *Comandantes*, and thus bring to power a new government that would distance itself from the Cubans and the Soviets while engaging in a rapprochement with Washington; thereby avoiding the need for a prolonged conflict. There is very little reason to believe that such an outcome is likely.

In the absence of such an internal coup, many Reagan administration officials appear to believe that, with enough U.S. support and training, the *contras* will eventually be able to win the war against the Sandinistas. A few seem convinced that such a victory is attainable within a relatively short period—perhaps within a year or two.[89]

Most critics doubt that the *contras* will ever be able to defeat the Sandinista forces. They predict that Cuba and the Soviet Union will increase their military support in order to provide the Nicaraguan regime with the wherewithal to keep the *contras* at bay.[90] From this perspective, the most likely outcome of the U.S.-inspired *contra* strategy is protracted, low-intensity guerrilla warfare in Nicaragua with possible spillover effects in both Honduras and Costa Rica. Rather than eliminating the Soviet and Cuban presence in Nicaragua, the critics contend that this approach is more likely to expand Soviet-Cuban influence as the Sandinistas become progressively more dependent on their military, economic, and technical assistance.[91] Moreover, instead of promoting pluralist democracy in Nicaragua, they foresee that the *contra* strategy will drive the Sandinistas to become more authoritarian than ever as they seek to stamp out the last vestiges of internal opposition.[92]

Even if the U.S.-backed *contras* were to succeed, it is implausible in the extreme to believe that they would be able to create a stable democratic political system within any reasonable time frame. First, the *contras'* democratic credentials are by no means entirely in order. Whatever the claims of civilian opposition leaders like Arturo Cruz or Alfonso Robelo, power will almost inevitably rest with the military commanders—many of whom are ex-Somocistas—who actually win victory on the battlefield. Second, it is probable that the Sandinistas—if driven out of Managua—would launch a protracted guerrilla war against any U.S.-backed regime finally installed that would prevent the institutionalization of a democratic government in Nicaragua for the foreseeable future.

If, as now seems likely, the U.S.-assisted *contras* prove unable to triumph over the Soviet- and Cuban-backed Sandinistas, the choices available to the United States will be quite stark. On the one hand, Washington—most likely after the Reagan administration leaves office— could give up its avowed goal of democratizing the Sandinista regime and seek a Contadora-style accommodation that would establish security guarantees for the United States and other countries in the region in exchange for cessation of U.S. efforts to overthrow the Sandinistas; such a deal could, of course, be cut by Washington directly with Managua or via the OAS, and thus would not require the mediation of the Contadora Group. On the other hand, the U.S. government could escalate its involvement in the war against the Sandinistas, up to and including a direct U.S. intervention.

For the moment, the Reagan administration has opted to up the ante by pursuing the proxy war via the *contras*. It is likely that the *contras* will be encouraged to attempt to seize territory and a town, probably along Nicaragua's Atlantic coast. If successful, this would allow Washington to recognize a *contra* government in exile, step-up its logistical support, and perhaps even provide air cover to the *contras* within Nicaragua.[93] If unsuccessful, the Reagan administration could decide to intervene directly.

In the present context of escalation, the Contadora process has become essentially irrelevant. The Contadora countries are certainly aware of this fact. Their current options appear quite limited. One alternative would be to declare that they had done their best and then to retreat into their traditional passivity, abandoning any serious effort at continued mediation and any pretensions regarding collective leadership in the region. An elegant way of burying Contadora would be, as recently elected Colombian President Virgilio Barco Vargas has proposed, to turn future negotiation efforts over to the OAS. A second option would be to join with the United States and the Tegucigalpa group in focusing exclusively on attempts to convince the Sandinistas to undertake a democratization process along the lines sought by Washington. A final option would be to confront the Reagan administration by increasing their criticisms of the U.S. strategy in the region in an effort to revive negotiations on a Contadora peace treaty.[94]

None of these alternatives offer much hope for a negotiated settlement. The OAS has been paralyzed for years and is unlikely to be able to sponsor effective negotiations unless the United States agrees. Direct criticism of Nicaragua will almost certainly drive the Sandinistas further into the embrace of the Soviet Union and Cuba. Rhetorical attacks against the Reagan administration are unlikely to persuade it to abandon its present strategy of surrogate warfare. Moreover, this final option would carry great risks for the individual Contadora countries, for they could not expect much cooperation from Washington on bilateral trade issues, debt negotiations or other critical areas.

No member of Contadora is likely to withdraw formally, for none want to shoulder responsibility for the definitive demise of the group. Most likely, there will be a continuation of progressively feebler efforts to negotiate as conflict in the region intensifies over the next year.

A final balance sheet on Contadora cannot yet be drawn. Ultimately, only time will tell. As many Contadora diplomats claim, it does seem to have contributed to the prevention of a direct U.S. military intervention in the region during the 1983–1986 period, although such a counterfactual hypothesis is impossible to prove. At the same time, the Contadora countries have clearly been unable to prevent the Reagan administration from pursuing its strategy of intensifying pressures on Nicaragua or to inhibit the growth of Cuban and Soviet influence in that country. In that sense, it has failed to provide a Latin American solution to the Central American crisis or to generate a collective alternative to U.S. hegemonic leadership in the region.

NOTES

1. See the "Information Bulletin" issued at the initial Contadora meeting and reprinted in Bruce Michael Bagley, Roberto Alvarez, and Katherine J. Hagedorn

(eds.), *Contadora and the Central American Peace Process: Selected Documents* (Boulder: Westview Press and Foreign Policy Institute, School of Advanced International Studies, The Johns Hopkins University, 1985), pp. 164–166.

2. Peter H. Smith, "The Origins of Crisis," in Morris J. Blackman, William LeoGrande, and Kenneth Sharpe (eds.), *Confronting Revolution: Security Through Diplomacy in Central America* (New York: Pantheon Books, 1986), pp. 3–22.

3. Susan Kaufman Purcell, "Demystifying Contadora," *Foreign Affairs*, Vol. 64, No. 1 (Fall 1985), p. 3.

4. These differences in perspective are analyzed in Bruce Michael Bagley, "Mexico in Central America: The Limits of Regional Power," in Wolf Grabendorff and H. Krumwiede (eds.), *Political Change in Central America* (Boulder: Westview Press, 1984); also Viron Vaky, "Reagan's Central American Policy: An Isthmus Restored," in Robert S. Leiken (ed.), *Central America: Anatomy of Conflict* (New York: Pergamon Press, 1984), pp. 233–258; Luis Maira, "El pensamiento geopolítico norteamericano frente al de América Latina y el Caribe: Un choque de visiones antagónicas," *Cuadernos Semestrales: Estados Unidos Perspectiva Latinoamericana*, No. 17 (1985), pp. 31–50.

5. See Francisco Villagran Kramer, "The Background to the Current Political Crisis in Central America," in Richard E. Feinberg (ed.), *Central America: International Dimensions of the Crisis* (New York: Holmes and Meier Publishers, 1982), pp. 15–38; William M. LeoGrande, "U.S. Policy Options in Central America," in Richard Fagen and Olga Pellicer (eds.), *The Future of Central America* (Stanford, CA: Stanford University Press, 1983), pp. 99–118; Jose Miguel Insulza, "Centroamerica y Estados Unidos," *Cuadernos Semestrales: Estados Unidos Perspectiva Latinoamericana*, No. 17 (1985), pp. 113–135.

6. See Bruce Michael Bagley, "Regional Powers in the Caribbean Basin: Mexico, Venezuela, and Colombia" (Washington, DC: Latin American Studies Program, School of Advanced International Studies, The Johns Hopkins University, Occasional Paper No. 2, 1983), pp. 100–107; Gerhard Dreknoja, "Contenidos y metas de la nueva política exterior latinoamericana," in G. Drekonja and Juan G. Tokatlian, *Teoría y práctica de la política exterior latinoamericana* (Bogota: Fondo Editorial CEREC and Centro de Estudios Internacionales, Uniandes, 1983), pp. 1–24; Guadalupe González, "México," in *Ibid.*, pp. 299–354.

7. Personal Interview with Foreign Minister Lloreda Caicedo, January 12, 1983, Bogota, Colombia.

8. See Bagley, "Regional Powers . . . ," *op. cit.*, pp. 2–4, 53–79.

9. *Ibid.*, pp. i–iv.

10. For the texts of these documents, see Bagley et al., *Contadora . . .* , *op. cit.*, pp. 152–155 and 100–102.

11. Bagley, "Regional Powers . . . ," *op. cit.*, pp. 100–105; Purcell, *op. cit.*, pp. 75–76.

12. Bruce Michael Bagley, "Mexico in the 1980s: A New Regional Power," *Current History*, Vol. 80, No. 469 (Nov. 1981), pp. 353–356, 393–394; and Bagley, "Mexican Foreign Policy: The Decline of a Regional Power," *Current History*, Vol. 82, No. 488 (Dec. 1983), pp. 406–409, 437.

13. Bagley et al., *op. cit.*, p. 170. The technical group consisted of one representative from each of the nine countries involved in the Contadora negotiations. Its first meeting was scheduled for June 14, 1983, in Panama City.

14. For the text of the Cancun Declaration, see *Ibid.*, pp. 170–174.

15. For the text of the Document of Objectives, see *Ibid.*, pp. 177–186.

16. *Ibid.*, p. 180.

17. Robert S. Greenberger, "Latin Quandary: Distrusting Nicaragua, White House is Facing Dilemma Over Policy," *Wall Street Journal*, December 30, 1983, pp. 1, 4. While the Reagan administration maintained that it supported the 21 Points, it also expressed serious doubts that the "Sandinista tiger will ever change its stripes."

18. See George Shultz, "Comprehensive Strategy for Central America," (Washington, DC: U.S. Department of State, Bureau of Public Affairs, Current Policy No. 502, August 4, 1983), pp. 2–3.

19. Efforts to revive CONDECA involved the "northern tier" countries (Honduras, El Salvador, Guatemala) and actually began in early October, several weeks before the Grenadian invasion. See "Three Latin Nations Agree to Revive Defense Pact," *New York Times*, October 4, 1983. Negotiations intensified in the wake of the invasion but broke down in late November when the Guatemalans refused to cooperate unless the United States agreed to renew military and economic aid. The Reagan administration's requests for aid to Guatemala were, however, repeatedly rejected by the Democrat-controlled House of Representatives because of the ruling military junta's abusive human rights record. See Lydia Chavez, "Guatemala's Interest in Regional Pact Wanes," *New York Times*, November 23, 1983.

20. For the proposed "Norms for the Implementation of the Commitments of the Document of Objectives," see Bagley et al., *op. cit.*, pp. 180–183.

21. For the text of the Kissinger Commission Report, see *Report of the National Bipartisan Commission on Central America* (Washington, DC: U.S. Government Printing Office, 1984). For a critical analysis, see William LeoGrande, "Through the Looking Glass: The Report of the National Bipartisan Commission on Central America," *World Policy Journal*, Vol. I, No. 2 (Winter 1984), pp. 251–284.

22. "Report of the National . . . ," *op. cit.*, p. 119.

23. Don Oberdorfer, "U.S. Says Nicaragua Won't Back Up. Claimed Peaceful Intentions," *Washington Post*, May 1, 1984, p. A16.

24. *Ibid.*

25. Robert S. Greenberger, "Shultz Nicaragua Trip is Faulted by Some as Step to Quiet Critics, Not Spur Talks," *Wall Street Journal*, June 4, 1984, p. 2.

26. *Ibid.*; also Bernard Gwertzman, "Shultz Trip: A Serious Bid for Peace?" *New York Times*, June 4, 1984, p. A3.

27. The reference to final signing was contained in a letter from the Contadora Ministers to the Central American participants that accompanied the text of the Revised Act. See Bagley et al., *op. cit.*, p. 190. For the full text of the proposed treaty, see *Ibid.*, pp. 190–217.

28. Secretary of State George Shultz in a letter to the European Economic Community foreign ministers, September 7, 1984, cited by William Goodfellow, "Reagan vs. the Sandinistas: The Undeclared War on Nicaragua" (Washington, DC: Center for International Policy, 1986, unpublished manuscript), pp. 12–13.

29. Letter from Daniel Ortega to the Contadora foreign ministers, September 21, 1984. Also, "Nicaraguans Vow to Sign Latin Accord," *Washington Post*, September 23, 1984, p. A34.

30. Goodfellow, *op. cit.*, p. 14.

31. Phillip Taubman, "Latin Peace Plans: Why the U.S. Balks," *New York Times*, October 3, 1984, p. A3.

32. Robert S. Greenberger, "Reagan Administration Moves to Limit Treaty 'Ploy' by Nicaraguan Marxists," *Wall Street Journal*, September 26, 1984, p. 36.

33. Taubman, *op. cit.*, p. A3.

34. Joanne Omang, "U.S. Plays Contadora Catch-Up," *Washington Post*, October 15, 1984, p. A14.

35. Greenberger, *op. cit.*, "Reagan . . . ," p. 36.

36. Joanne Omang, "Nicaragua Acquiescence on Peace Plan Puts U.S. on Defensive," *Washington Post*, September 27, 1984, p. A7; Stephen Kinzer, "Nicaragua Says U.S. No Longer Backs Peace Plan," *New York Times*, September 25, 1984, p. A12.

37. Omang, *op. cit.*, "U.S. Plays . . . ," p. A14.

38. United Press International, "U.S. Version of Contadora Draft Disputed," *Washington Post*, October 3, 1984, p. A24.

39. Goodfellow, *op. cit.*, p. 15.

40. *Ibid.*, p. 16.

41. *Ibid.*, pp. 16–17; U.S. Department of State, "Resource Book: The Contadora Peace Process," (Washington, DC: U.S. Department of State, Office of Public Diplomacy for Latin America and the Caribbean, 1985), Annex 3, pp. 1–3.

42. Purcell, *op. cit.*, pp. 87–91.

43. Alan Riding, "U.S. Rules Out New Nicaragua Talks," *New York Times*, December 3, 1985.

44. As early as April 1984, the Reagan administration had said that it would reject the jurisdiction of the World Court in the U.S. dispute with Nicaragua. See Don Oberdorfer and Fred Hiatt, "U.S. to Bar Role for Court," *Washington Post*, April 9, 1984, pp. A1 and A14. The court rejected the U.S. argument that its competence did not extend to cases involving ongoing armed conflicts in November 1984. In January, the Reagan government said it would defy the court and ignore further proceedings. See Paul Lewis, "World Court Supports Nicaragua After U.S. Rejected Judge's Role," *New York Times*, June 28, 1986, pp. A1 and A4.

45. Goodfellow, *op. cit.*, p. 16; "Contadora Group Calls for Peace," *Central American Bulletin*, Vol. 5, No. 2 (Dec. 1985), pp. 1–2, 6–7.

46. "Congress: Going Reagan's Way," *Central American Bulletin*, Vol. 5, No. 2 (Dec. 1985), p. 3; also Don Oberdorfer, "Applying Pressure in Central America," *Washington Post*, November 23, 1985.

47. Although the Support Group did not become an active participant in the Contadora negotiations, during the initial July 27 meeting in Lima the possibility of creating an all-Latin American peace force to establish a "military security cordon" in Central America was raised. This suggestion was brought up again during the August 24-25, 1985, Contadora-Support Group meeting held in

Cartagena, Colombia. The proposal was, however, ultimately abandoned when Mexico refused to participate, invoking its tradition of nonintervention; and Brazil raised the specter of the outbreak of a shooting war that could catch the peacekeeping force in a crossfire between the Sandinistas and U.S. troops. See Roberto Russell and Juan G. Tokatlian, "Argentina y la crisis centroamericana" (Buenos Aires: FLACSO, Serie de Documentos e Informes de Investigación No. 36, Abril de 1986), pp. 27–29.

48. The document was entitled, "The View from Washington." See Charles R. Babcock, "Latin Aid Boost to be Bought," *Washington Post*, September 8, 1985, pp. A1 and A18.

49. "Contadora Group . . . ," *op. cit.*, p. 1.

50. Goodfellow, *op. cit.*, p. 16–17.

51. *Ibid.*, p. 17.

52. The Reagan administration pressured Cruz and the *contras'* political front, the Nicaraguan Democratic Force (Fuerza Democrática Nicaraguense—FDN), not to agree to participate in the November elections and thereby "legitimize" the Sandinista regime. On the evolution of Venezuela's stance within Contadora, see Terry Karl, "Mexico, Venezuela, and the Contadora Initiative," in Morris Blackman, William LeoGrande, and Kenneth Sharpe (eds.), *Confronting Revolution: Security Through Diplomacy in Central America* (New York: Pantheon Books, 1986), pp. 277–292; also, Purcell, *op. cit.*, pp. 82–83.

53. For an analysis of the Colombian role in Contadora, see Bruce Michael Bagley and Juan Gabriel Tokatlian, "Colombian Foreign Policy in the 1980s: The Search for Leverage," *Journal of Inter-American Studies and World Affairs*, Vol. 27, No. 3 (Fall 1985), pp. 47–48; and Fernando Cepeda Ullca, "Contadora: El Proceso de la Paz en Colombia y Centroamérica," *Revista Nacional de Agricultura*, No. 87 (Marzo 1985), pp. 80–102.

54. Mexico's change in policy was clearly evident in the cutoff of oil supplies to Nicaragua in 1985, in its decision to name an ambassador to El Salvador after the inauguration of President José Napoleón Duarte, and in the more subdued tone of President de la Madrid's rhetoric regarding Contadora and Central America during 1985. See Bruce Michael Bagley, "Mexico in Crisis: The Parameters of Accommodation" (Washington, DC: The Foreign Policy Institute, School of Advanced International Studies of The Johns Hopkins University, 1986), pp. 11–16; also Adolfo Aguilar Zinzer, "Mexico y Centroamerica," in Pablo González Casanova (ed.), *Ante la Crisis* (Mexico: Siglo XXI, 1985), pp. 100–111.

55. Thomas John Bossert, "Panama," in M. Blackman, et al. (eds.), *op. cit.*, pp. 202–204; Purcell *op. cit.*, pp. 85–87.

56. See "The Caraballeda Message," *Baltimore Sun*, February 26, 1986.

57. Robert J. McCartney, "Contadora Peace Efforts Revived," *Washington Post*, January 16, 1986, p. A30.

58. Despite their request, President Reagan would not see the Contadora and Support Group foreign ministers although a few days later he did meet with the *contra* leadership. See Joanne Omang, "Latins Urge U.S. to Halt Contra Aid," *Washington Post*, February 11, 1986, p. A9. Early in February, the State Department proposed that a gesture be made to Nicaragua to revive the Contadora

peace talks, but the idea was vetoed by the White House and the Defense Department. This rebuff led to a "stonewall" response from Secretary Shultz during his meeting with the Contadora and Support Group foreign ministers. See Joanne Omang, "Latin Peace Talks Move Vetoed," *Washington Post*, February 16, 1986, p. A25.

59. Goodfellow, *op. cit.*, p. 18.

60. *Ibid.*; Stephen Kinzer, "Nicaragua Shuns Area Peace Plan," *New York Times*, May 15, 1986, p. A8.

61. Center for International Policy, "Contadora Will Continue," (Washington, DC: CIP, June 27, 1986, mimeo), pp. 4–5.

62. *Ibid.*, p. 2.

63. Bernard Gwertzman, "Habib Finds Himself in Hotseat," *New York Times*, July 17, 1986, p. A20.

64. Goodfellow, *op. cit.*, p. 19.

65. *Ibid.*, pp. 19–20. Habib's formula of immediate cessation of U.S. support for the *contras* was warmly received in Latin America and contributed to the growing diplomatic isolation of Nicaragua, for it appeared to remove the principal Sandinista excuse for not signing the Contadora Act. On May 8, Vice President Bush reinforced Habib's interpretation when he told the Contadora and Support Group foreign ministers that Habib's letter reflected U.S. policy " . . . at the highest level of my government." Center for International Policy, *op. cit.*, pp. 3–4.

66. Joanne Omang, "Habib Called Wrong, Imprecise in Letter on U.S. Latin Policy," *Washington Post*, May 24, 1986, p. A21.

67. *Ibid.*

68. Gwertzman, "Habib Finds . . . ," *op. cit.*, p. A20.

69. Leslie H. Gelb, "Pentagon Predicts Big War If Latins Sign Peace Accord," *New York Times*, May 20, 1986, p. A4.

70. Bernard Gwertzman, "State Dept. Assails the Pentagon Over Study of Latin Peace Talks," *New York Times*, May 21, 1986, p. A1.

71. Joanne Omang, "Contadora Talks Split U.S. Agencies," *Washington Post*, May 21, 1986, p. A35.

72. *Ibid.*

73. Gwertzman, "State Dept. Assails . . . ," *op. cit.*, p. A5.

74. *Ibid.*

75. Edward Cody, "Contadora Deadline Imperiled," *Washington Post*, May 16, 1986, A1, A12; also Francisco Rojas Aravena, "Contadora ha muerto . . . , Viva Contadora," *Cono Sur*, Vol. V, No. 4 (September 1986), p. 10.

76. Goodfellow, *op. cit.*, p. 20. President Ortega's declared purpose was ". . . not to disarm Nicaragua but for all Central American nations to reach an agreement on what weapons we can reduce, limit, regulate and omit" ("Nicaraguan Leader in an Offer on Arms," *New York Times*, May 28, 1986, p. A3.)

77. For the text of the treaty, see "Contadora Act on Peace and Cooperation in Central America," (Washington, DC: Center for International Policy, June 27, 1986, unofficial translation). In the late May Contadora meeting, the unity of the Tegucigalpa Group broke down, at least temporarily, when the members

were faced with the need to set actual limits on their armed forces. Guatemala and El Salvador joined Nicaragua in opposing the inclusion of limits on militia forces. Honduras, in contrast, demanded that all militias be dismantled. Honduras wanted the right to continue international military maneuvers while Nicaragua, Costa Rica, and Guatemala sought to end them. Finally, Nicaragua was joined by Guatemala in arguing that arms limits should be adjusted to the security needs of individual countries and not based on absolute parity. See "Contadora: A Shift in Position?" *Central American Bulletin*, Vol 5, No. 11 (Sept. 1986), pp. 6-7. At the close of this final session, the Reagan administration expressed its satisfaction that the leaders of the Central American democracies were not being "forced into acting" on a treaty that fell short of democratizing Nicaragua. See Gerald M. Boyd, "Set Own Pace, U.S. Tells Latin Chiefs," *New York Times*, May 28, 1986, p. A3.

78. Center for International Policy, *op. cit.*, p. 2.

79. *Ibid.* A four-page State Department analysis of the Contadora Treaty entitled, "Essential Elements of Effective Verification," released in May, had estimated that it would cost $40 million annually and require 1,300 permanent observers to insure compliance. Start-up costs would be $9.2 million, including $8 million for vehicles. The annual $40 million bueget set aside $15 million for helicopters alone. As in the Sinai process, the report argued that the Central American system should have a civilian headquarters staff of approximately 25 in each national capital. This staff would, in turn, oversee teams of 25 that would carry out periodic random surveys and surprise inspections. It also called for "sector command posts" in each country and military personnel at key sites such as airports, posts, border crossings and military facilities. In all, the State Department claimed that effective verification of the treaty would require 270 individuals for each of the five countries. See Joanne Omang, "Policing a Latin American Peace Projected to Cost Millions," *Washington Post*, May 11, 1986, p. A4.

80. "Contadora: A Shift . . . ," *op. cit.*, p. 3.

81. Center for International Policy, *op. cit.*, p. 6.

82. *Ibid.*

83. Goodfellow, *op. cit.*, pp. 20-21.

84. Center for International Policy, *op. cit.*, p. 1.

85. *Ibid.*

86. Richard Meislin, "Contra Aid is Seen Hindering Accord," *New York Times*, September 18, 1986, p. A19; Edward Walsh, "House, in Reversal, Backs Reagan Plan for Aid to the Contras," *Washington Post*, June 26, 1986, p. A34. The House Aid Package provided $40 million to the *contras*, including military funds, that was to become available on September 1, 1986. An additional $20 million was authorized for October 15, and the final $40 million installment was due on February 15, 1987. The measure also lifted a congressional ban on covert activities by U.S. agencies against Nicaragua and provide $300 million in economic funds to the four Central American democracies. To get this agreement, the Reagan administration had to agree to delay delivery of "heavy weapons" to the *contras* until February 1987 and to provide the $3200 million to Nicaragua's

neighbors. It also had to bar U.S. personnel from coming within 20 miles of the Nicaraguan border to train or otherwise aid the *contras*. By making these concessions, President Reagan was able to defeat the "McCurdy Plan" that would have required a second congressional vote to authorize military assistance sometime after October 1.

87. This phrase comes from Assistant Secretary Elliot Abrams. See Babcock, *op. cit.*, p. A18.

88. Bernard Weinstraub, "Contra Takeover May Be Necessary, Reagan Declares," *New York Times*, August 20, 1986, pp. A1–A2.

89. This position has been forcefully articulated by the Reagan administration's former U.N. Ambassador, Jeane Kirkpatrick. See her "The Contadora Treaty? Communists Don't Comply," *Washington Post*, May 26, 1986; "Why Deal with Swindlers in Nicaragua," *Washington Post*, May 19, 1986, p. A15; and "And Now 'Proximity Talks,'" *Washington Post*, May 4, 1986, p. C7.

90. See Robert S. Leiken, "Who Says the Contras Cannot Succeed?" *Washington Post*, July 27, 1986, p. D2; Julia Preston, "Contras See Aid Bringing Victory in Year," *Washington Post*, August 9, 1986, p. A18; Joanne Omang, "Administration Mobilizes to Direct Aid to Rebels," *Washington Post*, July 13, 1986, p. A16.

91. Indeed, the tripling of Nicaragua's stock of Soviet-made transport helicopters during June and July 1986 indicated that this process was already underway. See Stephen Kinzer, "Sandinista Forces Are Said to Triple Stock of Copters," *New York Times*, July 10, 1986, p. A10.

92. Just a day after the House vote, the Sandinistas responded by closing down the only opposition newspaper—*La Prensa*—and by announcing new steps against opposition groups accused of supporting the Reagan administration and the *contras*. See Stephen Kinzer, "Anger of Sandinistas is Directed at Foes at Home," *New York Times*, June 27, 1986, p. A10; Joanne Omang, "A Surrogate War on Nicaragua," *Washington Post*, June 29, 1986, p. A28.

93. Stephen Kinzer, "Contras Likely Tactics Include Taking a Town," *New York Times*, August 11, 1986, p. A8.

94. For discussions of Contadora's limited options, see Juan Gabriel Tokatlian, "Las tres opciones de Contadora" (Washington, DC: SAIS, The Johns Hopkins University, Unpublished manuscript, 1986, 8 pp.); Rojas, *op. cit.*, pp. 8–10.

Appendix
Contadora Act on Peace and Cooperation in Central America

PREAMBLE

The Governments of the Republics of Costa Rica, El Salvador, Guatemala, Honduras and Nicaragua:

1. AWARE of the urgent need to strengthen peace, co-operation, confidence, democracy and economic and social development among the peoples of the region, through the observance of principles and measures that would facilitate a better understanding among the Central American Governments;

2. CONCERNED about the situation in Central America, which is characterized by a serious decline in political confidence; a profound economic and social crisis; a serious situation with refugees and displaced persons; frontier incidents; an arms build-up; arms traffic; the presence of foreign military advisers; the holding of international military manoeuvres in the territory of States of the region; the presence of military bases,

---

Note: Passages underlined represent changes from the September 12, 1985 draft. This is an unofficial translation by the Center for International Policy.

schools and installations; other forms of foreign military presence; and the use by irregular forces of the territories of certain States to carry out destabilizing operations against other States in the region;

CONVINCED:

3. That the tension and the present conflicts may worsen and lead to widespread hostilities;
4. That the restoration of peace and confidence in the region may be achieved only through unconditional respect for the principles of international law, particularly the principle which concerns the right of peoples to choose freely and without external interference in the form of political, economic and social organization that best serves their interests, and to do so through institutions which represent their freely-expressed will;
5. Of the importance of creating, promoting and strengthening democratic systems that are representative, participatory and pluralistic in all the countries of the region;
6. Of the need to create political conditions designed to guarantee the security, integrity and soverignty of the States of the region;
7. That the achievement of genuine regional stability hinges on the conclusion of agreements on security and disarmament;
8. That, in the adoption of measures aimed at halting the arms race in all its forms, account should be taken of the national security interests of the States of the region, with a view to the establishment of a reasonable balance of forces;
9. That, in order to establish the reasonable balance of forces, it is highly desirable to set maximum limits for military development and consequently reduce and control armaments, troops under arms and military installations, in accordance with the requirements of stability and security in the area;

10. That military superiority as an objective
of the States of the region, the presence of foreign military advisers, the holding of international military manoeuvres in the territory of States
of the region, the presence of military bases,
schools and installations, other forms of foreign
military presence, the presence of irregular forces
and traffic in arms endanger regional security and
constitute destabilizing factors in the region;

11. That the agreements on regional security
must be subject to an effective system of verification and control;

12. That the destabilization of the Governments
in the region, taking the form of encouragement or
support of the activities of irregular groups or
forces, acts of terrorism, subversion or sabotage
and the use of the territory of a State for operations affecting the security of another State, is
contrary to the fundamental norms of international
law and peaceful coexistence among States;

13. That the elaboration of instruments to permit the application of a policy of detente should
be based on the existence of trust among States
which would effectively reduce political and military tension among them;

14. RECALLING the provisions adopted by the
United Nations concerning the definition of aggression and other acts prohibited by international
law, in particular General Assembly resolutions
3314 (XXIX), 2625 (XXV) and 2131 (XX) and the relevant resolutions of the Organization of American
States;

15. TAKING INTO ACCOUNT the Declaration on the
Strengthening of International Security, adopted by
the United Nations General Assembly in resolution
2734 (XXV), and the corresponding legal instruments
of the inter-American system;

16. REAFFIRMING the need to promote national
reconciliation in those cases where deep divisions
have occurred within society, so as to permit the
people to participate, in accordance with the law,
in authentic political processes of a democratic

nature:

CONSIDERING:

17. That, on the basis of the United Nations Charter of 1945 and the Universal Declaration of Human Rights of 1948, various international organizations and conferences have elaborated and adopted declarations, covenants, protocols, conventions and statutes designed to provide effective protection of human rights in general, or of certain human rights in particular;

18. That not all Central American States have accepted the entirety of the existing international instruments on human rights, and that it would be desirable that they should do so in order to have a universal regime in the interests of promoting the observance and guarantee of human, political, civil, economic, social, religious and cultural rights;

19. That in many cases inadequate domestic legislation interferes with the effective enjoyment of human rights as defined in declarations and other international instruments;

20. That it should be the concern of each State to modernize its legislation with a view to making it capable of guaranteeing the effective enjoyment of human rights;

21. That one of the most effective ways of securing the enjoyment of human rights embodied in international instruments, political constitutions and the laws of individual States lies in ensuring that the judiciary enjoys sufficient authority and autonomy to put an end to violations of those rights;

22. That, to that end, the absolute independence of the judiciary must be guaranteed;

23. That that guarantee may be achieved only if judicial officials enjoy security of office and if the judiciary is ensured budgetary autonomy so that it may be absolutely and unquestionably independent of the other authorities;

CONVINCED ALSO:

24. Of the need to strengthen equitable economic and social structures in order to promote a
genuinely democratic system and permit full enjoyment by the people of the right to work, education,
health and culture;
25. Of the high level of interdependence of the
Central American countries and the prospects which
economic integration offers;
26. That the magnitude of the economic and social crisis affecting the region has highlighted
the need for changes in the economic and social
structures that would reduce the dependence and
promote the self-sufficiency of the Central American countries, enabling them to reaffirm their own
identity;
27. Of the need to co-operate with each country
in its efforts to accelerate its economic and social development, by actively providing assistance
in accordance with its development needs and objectives;
28. That Central American economic integration
should constitute an effective tool for economic
and social development based on justice, solidarity
and mutual benefit;
29. Of the need to reactivate, improve and restructure the process of Central American economic
integration with the active and institutional participation of all the States of the region;
30. That, in the reform of the existing economic and social structures and the strengthening
of regional integration, the Central American institutions and authorities are called upon to assume primary responsibility;
31. Of the necessity and appropriateness of un-
dertaking joint programmes of economic and social
development which would help to promote economic
integration in Central America in the context of
the development plans and priorities adopted by our
sovereign States;
32. That the basic investment needs for the de-

velopment and economic recovery of the Central
American countries and of the efforts undertaken
jointly by them to obtain financing for specific
priority projects make it imperative to expand and
strengthen the programmes of international, regional and subregional financial institutions intended
for Central America;

33. That the regional crisis has provoked massive flows of refugees and displaced persons, and
that the situation demands urgent attention;

34. CONCERNED about the constant worsening of
social conditions, including the situation with regard to employment, education, health and housing
in the Central American countries;

35. REAFFIRMING, without prejudice to the right
of recourse to other competent international for-
ums, the desire to settle their disputes within the
framework of this Act;

36. RECALLING the support given by the Contadora Group to United Nations Security Council resolutions 530 and 562 and General Assembly resolutions 38/10 and 39/4, as well as to resolutions AG/
RES 675 (XIII-0/83) and AG/RES (XIV-84) adopted by
the General Assembly of the Organization of
American States; and

37. BEING READY to implement fully the Document
of Objectives and the norms for the implementation
of the undertakings made therein, adopted by their
Ministers for Foreign Affairs in Panama on 9 September 1983 and 8 January 1984 respectively, under
the auspices of the Governments of Colombia, Mexico, Panama and Venezuela, which comprise the Contadora Group;

Have agreed as follows:

CONTADORA ACT ON PEACE AND CO-OPERATION
IN CENTRAL AMERICA

PART I: COMMITMENTS

Chapter I: General Commitments

Sole Section.   PRINCIPLES

THE PARTIES undertake, in accordance with their
obligations under international law:

1. To abide by the following principles:
    (a) The principle of refraining from the
    threat or use of force against the territori-
    al integrity or political independence of
    States;
    (b) The peaceful settlement of disputes;
    (c) Non-interference in the internal affairs
    of other States;
    (d) Co-operation between States in solving in-
    ternational problems;
    (e) Juridical equality of States, respect for
    sovereignty, self-determination of peoples and
    the promotion of respect for human rights;
    (f) The right to engage freely in internation-
    al trade;
    (g) The principle of refraining from discrim-
    inatory practices in economic relations between
    States by respecting their systems of politi-
    cal, economic and social organization;
    (h) The fulfillment in good faith of obliga-
    tions assumed under international law.

2. In pursuance of the foregoing principles:
    (a) They shall refrain from any action incon-
    sistent with the purposes and principles of the
    Charter of the United Nations and the Charter
    of the Organization of American States aimed
    against the territorial integrity, political

independence or unity of any State, and, in particular, from any such action involving the threat or use of force.

(b) They shall settle their disputes by peaceful means in accordance with the fundamental principles of international law embodied in the Charter of the United Nations and the Charter of the Organization of American States.

(c) They shall respect the norms embodied in treaties and other international agreements relating to diplomatic and territorial asylum.

(d) They shall respect the existing international boundaries between States.

(e) They shall refrain from militarily occupying territory of any other State in the region.

(f) They shall refrain from any act of military, political, economic or other form of coercion aimed at subordinating to their interests the exercise by other States of rights inherent in their sovereignty.

(g) They shall take such action as is necessary to secure their frontiers against irregular groups of forces operating from their territory with the aim of destabilizing the Governments of other States.

(h) They shall not permit their territory to be used for acts which violate the sovereign rights of other States, and shall see to it that the conditions obtaining in their territory do not pose a threat to international peace and security.

(i) They shall respect the principle that no State or group of States has the right to intervene either directly or indirectly through the use of arms or any other form of interference in the internal or external affairs of another State.

(j) They shall respect the right of all peoples to self-determination free from outside intervention or coercion by refraining from the threat or the direct or covert use of force to disrupt the national unity and territorial integrity of any other State.

Chapter II: Commitments with Regard to Political Matters

Section 1. COMMITMENTS WITH REGARD TO REGIONAL DETENTE AND CONFIDENCE-BUILDING

THE PARTIES undertake:

3. To promote mutual trust by every means at their disposal and to refrain from any action which might disturb peace and security in the Central American region;

4. To refrain from issuing or promoting propaganda in support of violence or war, and hostile propaganda against any Central American Government, and to abide by and foster the principles of peaceful coexistence and friendly co-operation;

5. Towards that end, their respective governmental authorities shall:
    (a) Avoid any oral or written statement which might aggravate the situation of conflict in the area;
    (b) Urge the mass media to help to promote understanding and co-operation between peoples of the region;
    (c) Promote increased contacts between their peoples and a better knowledge of each other's peoples through co-operation in all spheres relating to education, science, technology and culture;
    (d) Consider together future action and mechanisms for bringing about and solidifying a climate of stable and lasting peace;

6. Join together in seeking a regional settlement which will eliminate the causes of tension in Central America by safeguarding the inalienable rights

of its peoples from foreign pressure and
interests.

Section 2.   COMMITMENTS WITH REGARD TO NATIONAL
RECONCILIATION

Each Party recognizes vis-a-vis the other Central
American States the commitment assumed vis-a-vis
its own people to ensure the preservation of domestic peace as a contribution to peace in the region,
and they accordingly resolve:

7. To adopt measures for the establishment or, as
the case may be, the further development of representative and pluralistic democratic systems guaranteeing effective participation by the people,
through political organizations, in the decision-
making process, and ensuring the different currents
of opinion free access to honest and periodic elections based on the full observance of the rights of
citizens;

8. Where deep divisions have come about within
society, urgently to promote actions of national
reconciliation which will make it possible for the
people to participate, with full guarantees, in
genuine democratic political processes on the basis
of justice, liberty and democracy, and, towards
that end, to create mechanisms making possible, in
accordance with the law, dialogue with opposition
groups;

9. To adopt and, as the case may be, endorse,
broaden and improve legal measures for a genuine
amnesty which will enable their citizens, to resume
full participation in political, economic and social affairs, and similarly, to guarantee the in-
violability of life, the liberty and the security
of person of those to whom such amnesty is granted.

Section 3.   COMMITMENTS WITH REGARD TO HUMAN RIGHTS

THE PARTIES undertake, in accordance with their respective national laws and their obligations under international law:

10. To guarantee full respect for human rights and, towards that end, to comply with the obligations laid down in international legal instruments and constitutional provisions relating to human rights;

11. To set in motion the constitutional procedures necessary for them to become parties to the following international instruments:
(a) The 1966 International Covenant on Economic, Social and Cultural Rights;
(b) The 1966 International Covenant on Civil and Political Rights;
(c) The 1966 Optional Protocol to the International Covenant on Civil and Political Rights;
(d) The 1965 International Convention on the Elimination of All Forms of Racial Discrimination;
(e) The 1951 Convention relating to the Status of Refugees;
(f) The 1967 Protocol relating to the Status of Refugees;
(g) The 1952 Convention on the Political Rights of Women;
(h) The 1979 Convention on the Elimination of All Forms of Discrimination Against Women;
(i) The 1953 Protocol Amending the 1926 Slavery Convention;
(j) The 1956 Supplementary Convention on the Abolition of Slavery, the Slave Trade and Institutions and Practices Similar to Slavery;
(k) The 1953 Convention on the Civil and Political Rights of Women;
(l) The 1969 American Convention on Human Rights;
(m) The 1985 International Convention against Torture and Other Cruel, Inhuman or Degrading

Treatment or Punishment;

12. To prepare the necessary draft legislation and
submit it to their competent internal organs with a
view to accelerating the process of modernizing and
updating their legislation, so as to make it more
capable of promoting and guaranteeing due respect
for human rights;

13. To prepare and submit to their competent internal organs draft legislation necessary for:
   (a) Guaranteeing the independence and stability of the members of the judiciary, so
   that they can act without being subjected to
   political pressures, and themselves guarantee
   the stability of other judicial officials;
   (b) Guaranteeing the budgetary autonomy and
   self-sufficiency of the judiciary, so as to
   preserve its independence from the other
   authorities.

Section 4. COMMITMENTS WITH REGARD TO ELECTION
           PROCESSES AND PARLIAMENTARY
           CO-OPERATION

Each PARTY shall recognize vis-a-vis the other Central American States the commitment assumed vis-a-
vis its own people to guarantee the preservation of
internal peace as a contribution to peace in the
region and to that end shall resolve:

14. To adopt measures that guarantee the participation of political parties in electoral processes
on an equal footing, and ensure that they have access to the mass communication media and enjoy
freedom of assembly and freedom of expression;

15. They likewise commit themselves to:

   Take the following measures:
   (1) Promulgate or revise the electoral legislation with a view to the holding of elections

that guarantee effective participation by the people;

(2) Establish independent electoral organs that will prepare a reliable voting register and ensure the impartiality and democratic nature of the process;

(3) Formulate or, where appropriate, update the rules guaranteeing the existence and participation of political parties representing various currents of opinion;

(4) Establish an electoral timetable and adopt measures to ensure that the political parties participate on an equal footing;

Propose to their respective legislative organs that they should:

(1) Hold regular meetings at alternating sites that would enable them to exchange experience, contribute to detente and foster better communication with a view to rapprochement among the countries of the area;

(2) Take measures aimed at maintaining relations with the Latin American Parliament and its respective Working Commissions;

(3) Exchange information and experience on the matters within their competence and collect with a view to comparative study, the electoral legislation in force in each country, together with related provisions;

(4) Follow, as observers, the various stages in the electoral processes taking place in the region. To that end, the express invitation of the State in which the electoral process is taking place shall be essential;

(5) Hold periodic technical meetings in the place and with the agenda determined by consensus at each preceding meeting.

Chapter III: Commitments With Regard to Security Matters

In conformity with their obligations under international law and in accordance with the objective of laying the foundations for effective and lasting peace, the Parties assume commitments with regard to security matters relating to the prohibition of international military manoeuvres; the cessation of the arms build-up; the dismantling of military foreign bases, schools or other installations; the withdrawal of foreign military advisers and other foreign elements participating in military or security activities; the prohibition of the traffic in arms; the cessation of support for irregular forces; the denial of encouragement or support for acts of terrorism, subversion or sabotage; and lastly, the establishment of a regional system of direct communication.

To that end, the Parties undertake to take specific action in accordance with the following:

Section 1. COMMITMENTS WITH REGARD TO MILITARY MANOEUVRES

16. To comply with the following provisions as regards the holding of national military manoeuvres, with effect from the entry into force of this Act:

(a) When national military manoeuvres are held in areas less than 30 kilometres from the territory of another State, the appropriate prior notification to the other States Parties and the Verification and Control Commission, mentioned in Part II of this Act, shall be made at least 30 days beforehand.

(b) The notification shall contain the following information:

(1) Name;

(2) Purpose;

(3) Participating troops, units, and forces;

(4) Area where the manoeuvre is scheduled;

(5) Programme and timetable;
(6) Equipment and weapons to be used.
(c) Invitations shall be issued to observers from neighbouring States Parties.

17. To comply with the following provisions as regards the holding of international military manoeuvres in their respective territories:
1. From the entry into force of this Act and for a period of 90 days, the holding of international military manoeuvres involving the presence on their respective territories of armed forces belonging to States outside the Central American region shall be suspended.

2. After 90 days, the Parties by mutual agreement, and taking into account the recommendations of the Verification and Control Commission, can continue the suspension of international military manoeuvres until the maximum limits for armaments and troop strength provided for in paragraph 19 of the Chapter are reached. If there is no agreement on continuing the suspension, international military manoeuvres shall be subject during this period to the following provisions:
(a) The Parties shall ensure that manoeuvres involve no form of intimidation against a Central American State or any other State;
(b) They shall give at least 30 days' notice of the holding of manoeuvres to the States Parties and the Verification and Control Commission referred to in Part II of this Act. The notification shall contain the following information:
(1) Name;
(2) Purpose;
(3) Participating States;
(4) Participating troops, units and forces;

(5)   Area where the manoeuvre is scheduled;
(6)   Programme and timetable;
(7)   Equipment and weapons to be used.

(c)   They shall not be held within a zone situated less than 50 kilometres from the territory of a State that is not participating, unless that State gives its express consent;

(d)   The Parties shall limit manoeuvres to one a year; it shall last not longer than 15 days;

(e)   They shall limit to 3,000 the total number of military troops participating in a manoeuvre. Under no circumstances shall the number of troops of other States exceed the number of nationals participating in a manoeuvre;

(f)   Observers from the States Parties shall be invited.

(g)   A State Party which believes that there has been a violation of the above provisions may resort to the Verification and Control Commission.

3.   International military manoeuvres involving the participation of States outside the Central American region shall be prohibited once the maximum limits for armaments and troops strength agreed by the Parties have been reached, in accordance with the provisions of paragraph 19 of this Chapter.

4.   The holding of international manoeuvres with the participation exclusively of Central American States in their respective territories shall be subject to the following provisions from the date of the entry into force of this Act:

(a)   The participating States shall give at least 45 days' notice of the holding of manoeuvres to the States Parties and to the Verification and Control Commission

229

referred to in Part II of this Act. The
notification shall contain the following
information:
    (1) Name;
    (2) Purpose;
    (3) Participating States;
    (4) Participating troops, units and
forces;
    (5) Area where the manoeuvre is
scheduled;
    (6) Program and timetable;
    (7) Equipment and weapons to be
used.
(b) The manoeuvres shall not be held
within a zone situated less than 40 kilo-
meters from the territory of a State that
is not participating, unless that State
gives its express consent;
(c) The Parties shall limit manoeuvres
to 30 days a year; if there is more than
one manoeuvre per year each one shall last
not longer than 15 days;
(d) They shall limit to 4,000 the total
number of military troops participating in
a manoeuvre;
(e) Observers from the States Parties
shall be invited;
(f) A State Party which believes that
there has been a violation of the above
provisions may resort to the Verification
and Control Commission.
5. The commitments regarding international
military manoeuvres shall be subject to those
established in paragraph 19 of this Chapter.

Section 2. COMMITMENTS WITH REGARD TO ARMAMENTS
AND TROOP STRENGTH

18. To halt the arms race in all its forms, and
begin immediately negotiations on the control and
reduction of the current inventory of weapons, as
well as on the number of troops under arms, with

the object of establishing a reasonable balance of forces in the area.

19. On the basis of the foregoing, the Parties agree on the following implementation stages:

FIRST STAGE:

(a) The Parties undertake not to acquire, after the date of the entry into force of the Act, any more military materiel, with the exception of replenishment supplies, ammunition and spare parts needed to keep existing materiel in operation, and not to increase their military forces, pending the establishment of the maximum limits for military development within the time-limit stipulated for the second stage.

(b) The Parties undertake to submit simultaneously to the Verification and Control Commission their respective current inventories of weapons, military installations and troops under arms within 15 days of the entry into force of this Act.

The inventories shall be prepared in accordance with the definitions and basic criteria contained in the Annex to this Act;

(c) Within 60 days of the entry into force of this Act, the Verification and Control Commission shall conclude the technical studies and shall suggest to the States Parties, without prejudice to any negotiations which they have agreed to initiate, the maximum limits for their military development, in accordance with the basic criteria laid down in paragraph 20 of this section and in accordance with the respective timetables for reduction and dismantling.

SECOND STAGE:

After a period of 60 days from the entry into force of this Act, the Parties shall establish within the following 30 days:

(a) Maximum limits for the types of weapons classified in the annex to this Act, as well as timetables for their reduction;

(b) Maximum limits for troops and military installations which each Party may have, as well as timetables for their reduction or dismantling.

(c) If the Parties do not reach agreement on the above-mentioned maximum limits and time-tables within such period, those suggested by the Verification and Control Commission in its technical studies shall apply provisionally, with the prior consent of the Parties. The Parties shall set by mutual agreement a new time-limit for the negotiation and establishment of the above-mentioned limits.

In case the Parties fail to reach agreement on maximum limits, they shall suspend implementation of the commitments with regard to international military manoeuvres, foreign military bases and installations, and foreign military advisers for which time-limits have been set in the Act, except in those cases where the Parties agree otherwise.

The maximum limits referred to in subparagraphs (a), (b), and (c) and the timetables shall be regarded as an integral part of this Act and shall have the same legally binding force from the day after the completion of the 30 days of the second stage, or on the day after they have been established by agreement among the Parties.

Unless the Parties agree otherwise, the maximum agreed limits set in subparagraph (c) shall be reached in 180 days from the entry into force of the Act or in a period established by the Parties.

20. In order to satisfy the requirements of peace, stability, security and economic and social development of the countries of the region, and in order to establish the maximum limits for the military development of the Central American countries and to regulate and reduce their military establishments, the Parties will agree on a table of values that will consider the following basic criteria, and in which all armaments will be subject to regulation and reduction:

(1) Security needs and defense capacity of every Central American State;

(2) Extent of the territory and population;

(3) Range and characteristics of its borders;

(4) Military expenditure in relation to gross domestic product (GDP);

(5) Military budget in relation to public expenditure and other social indicators;

(6) Military technology, relative combat capability, troops, quality and quantity of installations and military assets;

(7) Armament subject to control; armament subject to reduction;

(8) The foreign military presence and foreign military advisers in each Central American State.

21. Not to introduce new weapons systems that alter the quality or quantity of current inventories of war materiel.

22. Not to introduce, possess or use lethal chemical weapons or biological, radiological or other weapons which may be deemed to be excessively injurious or to have indiscriminate effects.

23. Not to permit the transit, stationing, mobilization or any other form of utilization of their territories by foreign armed forces whose actions could mean a threat to the independence, sovereign-

ty, and territorial integrity of any Central American State.

24. To initiate constitutional procedures so as to be in a position to sign, ratify or accede to treaties and other international agreements on disarmament, if they have not already done so.

Section 3. COMMITMENTS WITH REGARD TO FOREIGN MILITARY BASES

25. To close down any foreign military bases, schools or installations in their respective territories, as defined in paragraphs 11, 12 and 13 of the annex within 180 days of the signing of this Act. For that purpose, the parties undertake to submit simultaneously to the Verification and Control Commission, within 15 days of the signing of this Act, a list of such foreign military bases, schools or installations, which shall be prepared in accordance with the criteria set forth in the above-mentioned paragraphs of the annex.

26. Not to authorize in their respective territories the establishment of foreign bases, schools or other installations of a military nature.

Section 4. COMMITMENTS WITH REGARD TO FOREIGN MILITARY ADVISERS

27. To submit to the Verification and Control Commission a list of any foreign military advisers or other foreign elements participating in military, paramilitary and security activities in their territory, within 15 days of the signing of this Act. In the preparation of the list, account shall be taken of the definitions set forth in paragraph 14 of the annex.

28. To withdraw, within a period of not more than 180 days from the signing of this Act and in accordance with the studies and recommendations of the

Verification and Control Commission, any foreign
military advisers and other foreign elements likely
to participate in military, paramilitary and security activities.

29. As for advisers performing technical functions
related to the installation and maintenance of
military equipment, a control register shall be
maintained in accordance with the terms laid down
in the respective contracts or agreements. On the
basis of that register, the Verification and Control Commission shall propose to the Parties reasonable limits on the number of such advisers,
within the time-limit established in paragraph 27
above. The agreed limits shall form an integral
part of the Act.

Section 5. COMMITMENTS WITH REGARD TO THE TRAFFIC
           IN ARMS

30. To stop the illegal flow of arms, as defined
in paragraph 15 of the annex, towards persons, organizations, irregular forces or armed bands trying
to destabilize the Governments of the States
Parties.

31. To establish for that purpose control
mechanisms at airports, landing strips, harbours,
terminals and border crossings, on roads, air
routes, sea lanes and waterways, and at any other
point or in any other area likely to be used for
the traffic in arms.

32. On the basis of presumption or established
facts, to report any violations to the Verification
and Control Commission, with sufficient evidence to
enable it to carry out the necessary investigation
and submit such conclusions and recommendations as
it may consider useful.

Section 6. COMMITMENTS WITH REGARD TO THE
           PROHIBITION OF SUPPORT FOR IRREGULAR

FORCES

33. To refrain from giving any political, military, financial or other support to individuals, groups, irregular forces or armed bands advocating the overthrow or destabilization of other Governments, and to prevent, by all means at their disposal, the use of their territory for attacks on another State or for the organization of attacks, acts of sabotage, kidnappings or criminal activities in the territory of another State.

34. To exercise strict control over their respective borders, with a view to preventing their own territory from being used to carry out any military action against a neighbouring State.

35. To deny the use of and dismantle installations, equipment and facilities providing logistical support or serving operational functions in their territory, if the latter is used for acts against neighbouring Governments.

36. To disarm and remove from the border area any group or irregular force identified as being responsible for acts against a neighbouring State. Once the irregular forces have been disbanded, to proceed, with the financial and logistical support of international organizations and Governments interested in bringing peace to Central America, to relocate them or return them to their respective countries, in accordance with the conditions laid laid down by the Governments concerned.

37. On the basis of presumption or established facts, to report any violations to the Verification and Control Commission, with sufficient evidence to enable it to carry out the necessary investigation and submit such conclusions and recommendations as it may consider useful.

Section 7. COMMITMENTS WITH REGARD TO TERRORISM,

SUBVERSION OR SABOTAGE

38. To refrain from giving political, military, financial or any other support for acts of subversion, terrorism or sabotage intended to destabilize or overthrow Governments of the region.

39. To refrain from organizing, instigating or participating in acts of terrorism, subversion or sabotage in another State, or acquiescing in organized activities within their territory directed towards the commission of such criminal acts.

40. To abide by the following treaties and international agreements:
    (a) The Convention for the Suppression of Unlawful Seizure of Aircraft, 1970;
    (b) The Convention to prevent and punish the acts of terrorism taking the form of crimes against persons and related extortion that are of international significance, 1971;
    (c) The Convention for the Suppression of Unlawful Acts against the Safety of Civil Aviation, 1971;
    (d) The Convention on the Prevention and Punishment of Crimes against Internationally Protected Persons, including Diplomatic Agents, 1973;
    (e) The International Convention against the Taking of Hostages, 1979.

41. To initiate constitutional procedures so as to be in a position to sign, ratify or accede to the treaties and international agreements referred to in the preceding paragraph, if they have not already done so.

42. To prevent in their respective territories the planning or commission of criminal acts against other States or the nationals of such States by terrorist groups or organizations. To that end, they shall strengthen co-operation between the

competent migration offices and police departments
and between the corresponding civilian authorities.

43. On the basis of presumption or established
facts, to report any violations to the Verification
and Control Commission, with sufficient evidence to
enable it to carry out the necessary investigation
and submit such conclusions and recommendations as
it may consider useful.

Section 8. COMMITMENTS WITH REGARD TO DIRECT
COMMUNICATIONS SYSTEMS

44. To establish a regional communications system
which guarantees timely liaison between the competent government, civilian and military authorities,
and with the Verification and Control Commission,
with a view to preventing incidents.

45. To establish joint security commissions in
order to prevent incidents and settle disputes
between neighbouring States.

Chapter IV: Commitments with Regard to Economic
and Social Affairs

Section 1. COMMITMENTS WITH REGARD TO ECONOMIC AND
AND SOCIAL MATTERS

With a view to strengthening the process of
Central American economic integration and the
institutions representing and supporting it, the
Parties undertake:

46. To reactivate, perfect and restructure the
process of Central American economic integration,
harmonizing it with the various forms of political,
economic and social organization of the countries
of the region.

47. To endorse resolution 1/84, adopted at the

thirtieth Meeting of Ministers responsible for
Central American Economic Integration held on 27
July 1984, which is designed to re-establish the
institutional basis of the Central American
economic integration process.

48. To support and promote the conclusion of
agreements designed to intensify trade between
Central American countries within the legal framework and in the spirit of integration.

49. Not to adopt or support any coercive or dis-
criminatory measures detrimental to the economy of
any of the Central American countries.

50. To adopt measures designed to strengthen the
financial agencies in the area, including the Central American Bank for Economic Integration, supporting their efforts to obtain resources and di-
versify their operations, while safeguarding their
decision-making powers and the interests of all the
Central American countries.

51. To strengthen the multilateral payments
machinery within the Central American Common Market
Fund and to reactivate the machinery already in
operation through the Central American Clearing
House. In order to attain these objectives, recourse may be had to available international financial assistance.

52. To undertake sectoral co-operation projects in
the area, such as those pertaining to the power
production and distribution system, the regional
food security system, the Plan for Priority Health
Needs in Central America and Panama and others
which would contribute to Central American economic
integration.

53. To examine jointly the problem of the Central
American external debt through an evaluation taking
into account the domestic circumstances of each

country, its payments capacity, the critical economic situation in the area and the flow of additional resources necessary for its economic and social
development.

54. To support the elaboration and subsequent
application of a new Central American tariff and
customs regime.

55. To adopt joint measures to protect and promote
their exports, integrating as far as possible the
processing, marketing and transport of their
products.

56. To adopt the necessary measures to confer
legal status on the Central American Monetary
Council.

57. To support the efforts CADESCA is making, in
co-ordination with subregional agencies, to obtain
from the international community the additional financial resources needed to revitalize the Central
American economy.

58. To implement the international norms governing
labour and, with the co-operation of ILO, to adapt
their domestic laws to these norms, particularly
those which are conducive to the reconstruction of
Central American societies and economies. In addition, to carry out, with the co-operation of the
aforesaid agency, programmes to create jobs and
provide vocational training and instruction and
also for the application of appropriate technolo-
gies designed to make greater use of the manpower
and natural resources of each country.

59. To request the support of the Pan-American
Health Organization and UNICEF, and of other devel-
opment agencies and the international financial
community, to finance the Plan for Priority Health
Needs in Central America and Panama, adopted by the
Ministers of Health of the Central American Isthmus

at San Jose on 16 March 1984.

Section 2. COMMITMENTS WITH REGARD TO REFUGEES

THE PARTIES undertake to make the necessary efforts:

60. To carry out, if they have not yet done so, the constitutional procedures for accession to the 1951 Convention relating to the Status of Refugees and the 1967 Protocol relating to the Status of Refugees.

61. To adopt the terminology established in the Convention and Protocol referred to in the foregoing paragraph with a view to distinguishing refugees from other categories of migrants.

62. To establish the internal machinery necessary for the implementation, upon accession, of the provisions of the Convention and Protocol referred to in paragraph 57.

63. To establish machinery for consultation between the Central American countries and representatives of the government offices responsible for dealing with the problem of refugees in each State.

64. To support the work performed by the United Nations High Commissioner for Refugees (UNHCR) in Central America and to establish direct co-ordination machinery to facilitate the fulfillment of his mandate.

65. To ensure that any repatriation of refugees is voluntary, and is declared to be so on an individual basis, and is carried out with the co-operation of UNHCR.

66. To ensure the establishment of tripartite commissions, composed of representatives of the State of origin, of the receiving State and of UNHCR,

with a view to facilitating the repatriation of refugees.

67. To reinforce programmes for protection of and assistance to refugees, particularly in the areas of health, education, labour and safety.

68. To ensure that programmes and projects are set up with a view to ensuring the self-sufficiency of refugees.

69. To train the officials responsible in each State for protection of and assistance to refugees, with the co-operation of UNHCR and other international agencies.

70. To request immediate assistance from the international community for Central American refugees, to be provided either directly, through bilateral or multilateral agreements, or through UNHCR and other organizations and agencies.

71. To identify, with the co-operation of UNHCR, other countries which might receive Central American refugees. In no case shall a refugee be transferred to a third country against his will.

72. To ensure that the Governments of the area make the necessary efforts to eradicate the causes of the refugee problem.

73. To ensure that, once agreement has been reached on the bases for voluntary and individual repatriation, with full guarantees for the refugees, the receiving countries permit official delegations of the country of origin, accompanied by representatives of UNHCR and the receiving country, to visit the refugee camps.

74. To ensure that the receiving countries facilitate, in co-ordination with UNHCR, the departure procedure for refugees in instances of voluntary

and individual repatriation.

75. To institute appropriate measures in the receiving countries to prevent the participation of refugees in activities directed against the country of origin, while at all times respecting the human rights of the refugees.

76. To regard as displaced those persons who have been forced to leave their customary residence, their property and their means of employment as a result of the prevailing conflicts, and have moved to another area of their own country in search of protection and personal safety and assistance in meeting their basis needs.

77. At the request of the party concerned, to act in co-ordination with the international community for the purpose of obtaining the necessary co-operation in programmes being developed by each Central American country with regard to displaced persons.

PART II: COMMITMENTS WITH REGARD TO EXECUTION AND FOLLOW-UP

1. The Ministers for Foreign Affairs of the Central American States shall receive the opinions, reports and recommendations presented by the execution and follow-up mechanisms provided for in this part II and shall take unanimously and without delay the appropriate decisions to ensure full compliance with the commitments contracted in the Act. For the purposes of the present Act, "unanimously" is understood as the absence of any express opposition that would constitute an obstacle to the adoption of a decision under study and in which all the States Parties participate.

2. In order to ensure the execution and follow-up of the commitments contained in this Act, the Par-

ties decide to establish the following mechanisms:
A. Ad Hoc Committee for Evaluation and
Follow-up of Commitments concerning Political
and Refugee Matters;
B. Verification and Control Commission for
Security Matters; and
C. Ad Hoc Committee for Evaluation and
Follow-up of Commitments concerning Economic
and Social Matters.

3. The mechanisms established in the Act shall
have the following composition, structure and
functions:
A. Ad Hoc Committee for Evaluation and
Follow-up of Commitments concerning Political
and Refugee Matters.
(a) Composition

The Committee shall be composed of five
(5) persons of recognized competence and
impartiality, proposed by the Contadora
Group and accepted by common agreement by
the Parties. The members of the Committee
must be of a nationality different from
those of the Parties. The Committee shall
have a Technical and Administrative Secretariat responsible for its on-going
operation.
(b) Functions

The Committee shall consider the reports
which the Parties undertake to submit
annually on the ways in which they have
proceeded to implement the commitments
with regard to national reconciliation,
human rights, electoral processes and
refugees.

In addition, the Committee shall receive
the communications on these subjects
transmitted for its information by organizations or individuals which might contri-

bute data useful for the fulfillment of
its mandate.

The Committee shall elicit the information which it deems relevant; to that end,
the Party to which the communication refers refers shall permit the members of
the Committee to enter its territory and
shall accord them the necessary
facilities.

The Committee shall prepare an annual report and such special reports as it deems
necessary on compliance with the commitments, which may include conclusions and
recommendations.

The Committee shall send its reports to
the Parties and to the Governments of the
Contadora Group. When the period established by the rules for the submission of
observations by the States Parties has ex-
pired, the Committee shall prepare final
reports, which shall be public unless the
Committee itself decides otherwise.
(c) Rules of procedure

The Committee shall draw up its own rules
of procedure, which it shall make known to
the Parties.
(d)   The Committee shall be established at
the time when the Act enters into force.
B.   Verification and Control Commission for
Security Matters
(a) Composition

      - The Commission shall be composed of
      Four Commissioners, representing four
      States of recognized impartiality
      having a genuine interest in contri-
      ibuting to the solution of the Central
      American crisis, proposed by the

Contadora Group and accepted by the
Parties.
- A Latin American Executive
Secretary, with technical and
administrative duties, proposed by the
Contadora Group and accepted by common
agreement by the Parties, who shall be
responsible for the ongoing operation
of the Commission.
(b) Functions

For the performance of its functions,
the the Commission shall have an
International Corps of Inspectors,
provided by the member States of the
Commission and co-ordinated by a
Director of Operations.

The International Corps of Inspectors
shall carry out the functions assigned
to it by the Commission, with the ways
and means that the Commission deter-
mines or establishes in its rules of
procedure.

The International Corps of Inspectors
shall have at its disposal all the resources in personnel and finances, as
decided by the Commission, necessary
to ensure the strict observance of the
commitments on security matters. Its
proceedings shall be prompt and
thorough.

The Parties obligate themselves to
give the Commission all necessary co-
cooperation in facilitating and dis-
charging its responsibilities.

For the purpose of collaborating in
the performance of the functions of
the Commission, the latter shall have

an Advisory Body consisting of one
representative of each Central American State and having the following
duties:
1. To serve as a liaison between the
Verification and Control Commission
and the Parties.
2. To help in the fulfillment of the
duties assigned to the Verification
and Control Commission.
3. To cooperate, at the request of
the Commission, in the swift resolution of incidents or controversies.
    The Commission may invite a repre-
sentative of the Secretary—General of
the United Nations and a representative of the Secretary General of the
Organization of American States to
participate in its meetings as
observers.
    The Commission may establish
auxiliary bodies and seek the assistance and collaboration of any Mixed
Commissions that may exist.
(c) Functions of the Commission

    The function of the Commission shall
be to ensure compliance with the commitments assumed concerning to security
matters. To that end it shall:
    - Verify that the commitments con-
cerning military manoeuvres provided
for in this Act are complied with.
    - Ascertain that no more military
materiel is acquired and that military
forces are not increased, in accordance with the provisions of paragraph
19 (a) of chapter III of this Act.
    - Receive simultaneously from the
Parties their respective current inventories of armaments and military
installations and their census of

troops under arms in accordance with
the provisions of subparagraph (b) of
the FIRST STAGE in paragraph 19 of
Part I, chapter III of this Act.
- Carry out the technical studies
provided for in subparagraph (c) of
the FIRST STAGE in paragraph 19 of
Part I, chapter III of this Act.
- Ascertain that the Parties comply
fully with the maximum limits that
were previously established or are
provisionally in effect for the
various categories of armaments,
military installations and troops
under arms and with the reduction
timetables agreed upon or provisionally in effect.
- Ascertain that the munitions, spare
parts, and replacement equipment acquired are compatible with the
inventories and registers submitted
previously by the Parties and with the
limits and schedules agreed upon or
provisionally in effect.
- Verify that no new weapons are introduced which qualitatively or quan-
titatively alter current inventories,
and that weapons prohibited in this
Act are not introduced, possessed, or
used.
- Establish a register of all transfers of weapons carried out by the
Parties, including donations and any
other transfers of war materiel.
- Verify the fulfillment of the commitment by the States Parties to initiate and complete constitutional
procedures for signing, ratifying or
acceding to the treaties and other
international agreements on
disarmament and to proceed with the
actions directed to that end.

248

- Receive simultaneously from the Parties the list of foreign military bases, schools and installations and verify their dismantlement, in accordance with the provisions of this Act.
- Receive the census of foreign military advisers and other foreign elements participating in military and security activities and verify their withdrawal in accordance with the recommendations of the Verification and Control Commission.
- Verify compliance with this Act in respect of traffic in arms and consider any reports of non-compliance. For that purpose the following criteria shall be taken into account:

(1) Origin of the arms traffic: port or airport of embarkation of the weapons, munitions, equipment or other military supplies intended for the Central American region.

(2) Personnel involved: persons, groups or organizations participating in the organization and conduct of the traffic in arms, including the participation of Governments or their representatives.

(3) Type of weapon, munitions, equipment or other military supplies; category and calibre of weapons; country in which they were manufactured; country of origin; and the quantities of each type of weapon, munitions, equipment or other military supplies.

(4) Extraregional means of transport; land, maritime or air transport, including nationality.

(5) Extraregional transport routes: indicating the traffic routes used, including stops or

intermediate destinations.
(6) Places where weapons, munitions, equipment and other military
supplies are stored.
(7) Intraregional traffic areas
and routes: description of the
areas and routes, participation of
governmental or other sectors in
the conduct of the traffic in arms;
frequency of use of these areas and
routes.
(8) Intraregional means of
transport: determination of the
means of transport used; ownership
of these means; facilities means;
facilities provided by Governments,
governmental and other sectors; and
other means of delivery.
(9) Receiving unit or unit for
which the arms are destined:
determination of the persons,
groups or organizations to whom the
arms traffic is destined.
─ Verify compliance with this Act
with regard to irregular forces and
the non-use of their own territory in
destabilizing actions against another
State, and consider any report in that
connection.

To that purpose, the following
criteria should be taken into account:
     (1) Installations, means, bases,
     camps or logistic and operational
     support facilities for irregular
     forces, inclu- ding command
     centres, radiocommunications
     centres and radio transmitters.
     (2) Determination of propaganda
     activities or political, material,
     economic or military support for
     actions directed against any State

of the region.

(3) Identification of persons, groups and governmental sectors involved in such actions.

- Verify compliance with the commitments concerning terrorism. subversion and sabo- tage contained in this Act.

- The Commission and the States Parties may request as they deem convenient the assistance of the International Committee of the Red Cross to help solve humanitarian problems that affect the Central American countries.

(d) Norms and procedures

- The Commission shall receive any duly substantiated report concerning violations of the security commitments assumed under this Act, shall communicate it to the Parties involved and shall initiate such investigations as it deems appropriate.

- It shall also be empowered to carry out, on its own initiative the investigations it deems appropriate. The Commission shall carry out its investigations by making on-site inspections, gathering testimony and using any other procedure which it deems necessary for the performance of its functions.

- Above and beyond its quarterly and special reports, the Commission shall, in the event of any reports of violations or of non-compliance with the security commitments of this Act, prepare a report containing recommendations addressed to the Parties involved.

- The Commission shall be accorded every facility and prompt and full cooperation by the Parties for the

appropriate performance of its
functions. It shall also ensure the
confidentiality of all information
elicited or received in the course of
its investigations.
- The Commission shall transmit its
reports and recommendations to the
States Parties and to the Governments
of the Contadora Group on a confiden-
tial basis. It may make them public
when it considers that that would
contribute to full compliance with
the commitments contained in the Act.
(e) Rules of procedure
- After the Commission is established, it shall draw up its own rules
of procedure in consultation with the
States Parties.
(f) Duration of the mandate of the Com-
missioners
- The representatives of the member
States of the Commission shall have an
initial mandate of two years, extenda-
ble by common agreement among the
Parties, and the States particpating
in the Commission.
(g) Establishment
- The Commission shall be established
at the time when the Act is signed.
C. Ad Hoc Committee for Evaluation and Fol-
low-up of Commitments concerning Economic and
Social Matters
(a) Composition
- For the purposes of this Act, the
Meeting of Ministers for Economic
Affairs of Central America shall
constitute the Ad Hoc Committee for
Evaluation and Follow-up of
Commitments concerning Economic and
Social Matters.
- The Committee shall have a Techni-
cal and Administrative Secretariat

252

that will assure its permanent
functioning; this duty shall be
assumed by the Secretariat of
Central American Economic Integration (SIECA).
(b) Functions
- The committee shall receive annual
annual reports of the Parties con-
concerning progress in complying with
the commitments concerning economic
and social matters.
- The Committee shall make periodic
evaluations of the progress made in
complying with the commitments concerning economic and social matters,
using for that purpose the information produced by the Parties and by
the competent international and
regional organizations.
- The Committee shall present, in
its periodic reports, proposals for
strenghtening regional co-operation
and promoting development plans, with
particular emphasis on the aspects
mentioned in the commitments
contained in this Act.

4. Financing of the Execution and Follow-Up
Mechanisms
(a) The Execution and Follow-up Mechanisms
referred to in part II of the Act shall be
financed through a Fund for Peace in Central
America.
(b) The resources for that Fund shall be
obtained in the form of equal contributions by
the States Parties and additional contributions obtained from other States, international organizations or other sources, which may
be managed by the Central American States with
the collaboration of the Contadora Group.

PART III: FINAL PROVISIONS

1. The commitments made by the Parties in this Act and in the annex(es) thereto are of a legal nature and are therefore binding.

2. This Act shall be ratified in accordance with the constitutional procedures established in each of the Central American States. Each signatory State shall deposit its instrument of ratification with the Ministry of Foreign Affairs of the Republic of Panama.

3. This Act shall enter into force eight days after the date on which the fifth instrument of ratification is deposited.

4. The Parties, as from the date of signature and until the Act enters into force, shall refrain from any acts which would serve to frustrate the object and purpose of this Act, and shall seek in good faith and in accordance with their internal legislation to take the relevant individual measures necessary to assure the functioning of the mechanisms referred to in Part II of this Act.

5. Any dispute concerning the interpretation or application of this Act which cannot be settled through the machinery provided for in Part II of this Act, shall be referred to the Ministers for Foreign Affairs of the Parties for consideration and a unanimous decision.

6. Should the dispute continue, the Ministers for Foreign Affairs of the States comprising the Contadora Group shall, at the request of any of the Parties use their good offices so as to enable the Parties concerned to settle the respective dispute. After this venue has been tried, the Ministers for Foreign Affairs of the Contadora Group may suggest another peaceful means of settlement of disputes, in accordance with Article 33 of the Charter of the

United Nations, and article 24 of the Charter of the Organization of American States.

7. This Act shall not be subject to reservations.

8. The Annex(es) and Additional Protocols I to IV shall form an integral part of this Act.

9. The present Act shall be in force for five years, renewable for equal periods unless any of the Parties announces its decision to the contrary six months before the expiration of the five-year period. Six months before the expiration of each period the States Parties and the Contadora Group shall meet, at the request of any of the Parties, to evaluate the Act and take whatever steps they deem necessary.

10. This Act shall be registered by the Parties with the Secretariat of the United Nations in accordance with Article 102 ofthe Charter of the United Nations.

In witness whereof, the Ministers of Foreign Affairs of the respective governments of the Central American countries have signed the present Act, in six originals, in the Spanish language, one of which shall be deposited in the Ministry of Foreign Affairs of the Republic of Panama.

Done in Panama City, on the sixth of June of the year nineteen eighty-six.

The Government of the Republic of Costa Rica, the Government of the Republic of Guatemala, the Government of the Republic of El Salvador, the Government of the Republic of Honduras and the Government of the Republic of Nicaragua.

ANNEX

THE PARTIES hereby agree on the following
definitions of military terms:

1. Register: Numerical or graphical data on
military, paramilitary and security forces and
military installations.

2. Inventory: Detailed account of nationally- and
foreign-owned arms and military equipment, with as
many specifications as possible.

3. Census: Numerical data on foreign military or
civilian personnel acting in an advisory capacity
on matters of defence and/or security.

4. Military installation: Establishment or
infrastructure including airfields, barracks,
forts, camps, air and sea or similar installations
under military jurisdiction, and their geographical
location.

5. Organization and equipment chart (OEC):
document describing the mission, organization,
equipment, capabilities and limitations of a
standard military unit at its various levels.

6. Military equipment: Individual and collective,
nationally- or foreign-owned material, not
including weapons, used by a military force for its
day-to-day living and operations.

7. Classification of weapons:

    (a) By nature:
        (i)   Conventional.
        (ii) Chemical.
        (iii) Biological.
        (iv) Radiological.
    (b) By range:
        (i)   Short: individual and collective
             portable weapons.
        (ii) Medium: non-portable support

weapons (mortars, howitzers and cannons).

(iii) Long: rockets and guided missiles, subdivided into:
(a) Short-range rockets, with a maximum range of less than twenty (20) kilometres.
(b) Long-range rockets, with a range of twenty (20) kilometres or more;
(c) Short-range guided missiles, with a maximum range of one hundred (100) kilometres;
(d) Medium-range guided missiles, with a range of between one hundred (100) and five hundred (500) kilometres;
(e) Long-range guided missiles, with a range of five hundred (500) kilometres or more;

(c) By calibre and weight:
1. Light: one hundred and twenty 120 millimetres or less;
2. Medium: more than one hundred and twenty (120) and less than one hundred and sixty (160) millimetres;
3. Heavy: more than one hundred and sixty (160) and less than two hundred and ten (210) millimetres;
4. Very heavy: more than two hundred and ten (210) millimetres;

(d) By trajectory:

(i) Weapons with a flat trajectory.
(ii) Weapons with a curved trajectory.
(a) Mortars;
(b) Howitzers;
(c) Cannons;
(d) Rockets;

(e) By means of transportation:
1. On foot;
2. On horseback;

3. Towed or drawn;
4. Self-propelled;
5. All weapons can be transported by road, rail, sea or air;
6. Those transported by air are classified as follows:
    (a) Transported by helicopter;
    (b) Transported by aeroplane.

8. Characteristics to be considered in different types of aeroplanes and helicopters:
  (a) Model;
  (b) Quantity;
  (c) Crew;
  (d) Manufacture;
  (e) Speed;
  (f) Capacity;
  (g) System of propulsion;
  (h) Whether or not fitted with guns;
  (i) Type of weapons;
  (j) Radius of action;
  (k) Navigation system;
  (l) Communications system;
  (m) Type of mission performed.

9. Characteristics to be considered in different ships or vessels:
  (a) Type of ship;
  (b) Shipyard and year of manufacture;
  (c) Tonnage;
  (d) Displacement;
  (e) Draught;
  (f) Length;
  (g) System of propulsion;
  (h) Type of weapons and firing system;
  (i) Crew.

10. Services: logistical and administrative bodies providing general support for military, paramilitary and security forces.

11. Military training centres: establishments

for the teaching, instruction and training of
military personnel at the various levels and in the
various areas of specialization.

12. Military base: land, sea or air space which
includes military installations, personnel and
equipment under a military command. In defining a
foreign military base, the following elements
should be taken into account:
- Administration and control;
- Sources of financing;
- Percentage ratio of local and foreign
  personnel;
- Bilateral agreements;
- Geographical location and area;
- Transfer of part of the territory to
  another State;
  Number of personnel.

13. Foreign military installations: those built
for use by foreign units for the purposes of
manoeuvres, training or other military objectives,
in accordance with bilateral treaties or
agreements; these installations may be temporary or
permanent.

14. Foreign military advisers: military and
security advisers means foreign military or
civilian personnel performing technical, training
or advisory functions in the following operational
areas: tactics, logistics, strategy, organization
and security, in the land, sea, air or security
forces of Central American States, under agreements
concluded with one or more Governments.

15. Arms traffic: arms traffic means any kind of
transfer by Governments, individuals or regional
or extra-regional groups of weapons intended for
groups, irregular forces or armed bands that are
seeking to destabilize Governments in the region.
It also includes the passage of such traffic
through the territory of a third State, with or

without its consent, destined for the above-
mentioned groups in another State.

16. National military manoeuvres: these are
exercises or simulated combat or warfare carried
out by troops in peacetime for training purposes.
The armed forces of the country participate on
their own territory and may include land, sea and
air units, the object being to increase their
operational capability.

17. International military manoeuvres: these are
all operations carried out by the armed forces--
including land, sea and air units--of two or more
countries on the territory of one of their
countries or in an international area, with the
object of increasing their operational capability
and developing joint co-ordination measures.

18. The inventories drawn up in each State, a
separate one being made for each of their armed
forces, shall cover the personnel, weapons and
munitions, equipment and installations of the
forces mentioned below, in accordance with their
own organizational procedures:
    (a) Security Forces:
        1. Frontier guards;
        2. Urban and rural guards;
        3. Military forces assigned to other
           posts;
        4. Public security force;
        5. Training and instruction centre;
        6. Other.
    (b) Naval Forces:
        1. Location;
        2. Type of base;
        3. Number of vessels and
           characteristics of the naval
           fleet. Type of weapons;
        4. Defence system. Type of weapons;
        5. Communication systems;
        6. War materiel services;

260

```
            7.  Air or land transport services;
            8.  Health services;
            9.  Maintenance services;
           10.  Administrative services;
           11.  Recruitment and length of service;
           12.  Training and instruction centres;
           13.  Other.
      (c)  Air Forces:
            1.  Location;
            2.  Runway capacity;
            3.  Number of aircraft and
                characteristics of the fleet.  Type
                of weapons;
            4.  Defence system.  Type of weapons;
            5.  Communications system;
            6.  War materiel services;
            7.  Health services;
            8.  Land transport services;
            9.  Training and instruction centres;
           10.  Maintenance services;
           11.  Administrative services;
           12.  Recruitment and length of service;
           13.  Other.
      (d)  Army Forces:
            1.  Infantry;
            2.  Motorized infantry;
            3.  Airborne infantry;
            4.  Cavalry;
            5.  Artillery;
            6.  Armoured vehicles;
            7.  Signals;
            8.  Engineers;
            9.  Special troops;
           10.  Reconnaissance troops;
           11.  Health services;
           12.  Transport services;
           13.  War materiel services;
           14.  Maintenance services;
           15.  Administrative services;
           16.  Military police;
           17.  Training and instruction centre;
           18.  Precise information on system of
```

induction, recruitment and length of
service must be given in this
document.
19. Other.
(e) Paramilitary forces.
(f) Information required for airports:
existing airfields:
1. Detailed location and category:
2. Location of installations;
3. Dimensions of take-off runways, taxi
ways and maintenance strips;
4. Facilities: buildings, maintenance
installations, fuel supplies, navaga-
tional aids, communications systems.
(g) Information required for terminals and
ports:
1. Location and general characteristics;
2. Entry and approach lanes;
3. Piers;
4. Capacity of the terminal.
(h) Personnel: Numerical data must be given
for troops in active service, in the reserves,
in the security forces and in paramilitary
organizations. In addition, data on advisory
personnel must include their number, immigra-
tion status, specialty, nationality and
duration of stay in the country, and any
relevant agreements or contracts.
(i) Weapons: Munitions of all types,
explosives, ammunition for portable weapons,
artillery, bombs and torpedoes, rockets, hand
grenades and rifle grenades, depth charges,
land and sea mines, fuses, mortar and howitzer
shells, etc., must be included.
(j) Domestic and foreign military installations: Military hospitals and first-aid
posts, naval bases, airfields and landing
strips must be included.

19. Reasonable balance of forces: A reasonable
balance of forces is the equilibrium resulting from
a computation of the military forces needed by each

of the States to safeguard its sovereignty, political independence, security and territorial integrity.

ANNEX I: ADDITIONAL PROTOCOL I TO THE CONTADORA ACT ON PEACE AND CO-OPERATION IN CENTRAL AMERICA

THE GOVERNMENTS OF Colombia, Mexico, Panama and Venezuela, desiring to continue contributing to the achievement of peace and co-operation in Central America, which are the aims set forth in the Contadora Act on Peace and Co-operation in Central America.

Have agreed:

1. To co-operate with the Central American States in achieving the object and purpose of the Act;

2. To support in every way possible the establishment and functioning of the implementation and follow-up mechanisms provided for in the Act;

3. To contribute to the peaceful settlement of any dispute that may arise concerning the application and interpretation of the Act, in accordance with the provisions of part III thereof;

4. This Protocol shall not be subject to reservations;

5. This Protocol shall enter into force for each signatory State on the date on which its instrument of ratification has been deposited, which shall be done simultaneously with the Secretariats of the United Nations and of the Organization of American States;

6. This Protocol shall be registered with the United Nations Secretariat, in accordance with Article 102 of the United Nations Charter.

In witness whereof, the undersigned Plenipotentiaries, duly authorized by their respective
Governments, have signed the present Protocol, for
the Government of the Republic of Colombia, the
Government of the Republic of Panama, the Government of the United Mexican States, and the Government of the Republic of Venezuela.

This English, French, Portuguese and Spanish
Protocol, the texts of which are equally authentic,
shall be opened for signature at the United Nations
Secretariat.

ANNEX II: ADDITIONAL PROTOCOL II TO THE CONTADORA
ACT ON PEACE AND CO-OPERATION IN CENTRAL AMERICA

THE UNDERSIGNED PLENTIPOTENTIARIES, representatives
of States of the American continent, invested with
full powers by their respective Governments,

CONVINCED that the effective co-operation of the
States of the continent is necessary to guarantee
the validity, effectiveness and viability of the
Contadora Act on Peace and Co-operation in Central
America,

Have agreed:

1. To refrain from any act which would serve to
frustrate the object and purpose of the Act;

2. To co-operate with the Central American States
in order to achieve the object and purpose of the
Act;

3. To support in every way possible the fulfillment of the functions of the implementation and
follow-up mechanisms provided for in the Act, when
the Parties so require;

4. This Protocol shall not be subject to

reservations;

5. This Protocol shall be open to signature by all States of the American continent;

6. This Protocol shall enter into force for each signatory State on the date on which its instrument of ratification has been deposited with the Secretariat of the United Nations or of the Organization of American States;

7. This Protocol shall be registered with the United Nations Secretariat, in accordance with Article 102 of the United Nations Charter.

This English, French, Portuguese and Spanish Protocol, the texts of which are equally authentic, shall be opened for signature at the United Nations Secretariat.

ANNEX III: ADDITIONAL PROTOCOL III TO THE CONTADORA ACT ON PEACE AND CO-OPERATION IN CENTRAL AMERICA

THE UNDERSIGNED PLENIPOTENTIARIES, invested with full powers by their respective Governments,

CONVINCED that the effective co-operation of the international community is necessary to guarantee the validity, effectiveness and viability of the Contadora Act on Peace and Co-operation in Central America,

Have agreed:

1. To respect the commitments entered into by the Central American Governments;

2. To refrain from any act which would serve to frustrate the object and purpose of the Act;

3. To co-operate as far as possible with the Central American States for the economic and social development of the region;

4. This Protocol shall not be subject to reservations;

5. This Protocol shall be open to signature by any State desiring to contribute to peace and co-operation in Central America;

6. This Protocol shall enter into force for each signatory State on the date on which its instrument of ratification has been deposited with the United Nations Secretariat;

7. This Protocol shall be registered with the United Nations Secretariat, in accordance with Article 102 of the United Nations Charter.

This Protocol, the texts of which in the official languages of the United Nations are equally authentic, shall be opened for signature at the Headquarters of the United Nations Secretariat, at New York City.

For the Government of   For the Government of

For the Government of

ANNEX IV: ADDITIONAL PROTOCOL IV TO THE CONTADORA ACT ON PEACE AND CO-OPERATION IN CENTRAL AMERICA

THE UNDERSIGNED PLENIPOTENTIARIES, invested with full powers by their respective Governments,

CONVINCED of the need to help guarantee compliance

with the commitments entered into under the
Contadora Act on Peace and Co-operation in Central
America,

Have agreed:

1. To accept the invitation to participate and co-
operate in the establishment and functioning of the
implementation and follow-up mechanisms envisaged
in the Act, on the terms arranged by the PARTIES in
agreements to be annexed to this Protocol;

2. To act with complete impartiality in carrying
out the implementation and follow-up functions in
which they are involved;

3. This Protocol shall be open to signature by the
States proposed by the Contadora Group and accepted
by the PARTIES by mutual consent.

4. This Protocol shall enter into force for each
signatory State on the date on which its instrument
of ratification has been deposited with the United
Nations Secretariat;

5. This Protocol shall not be subject to
reservations;

6. This Protocol shall be registered with the
United Nations Secretariat, in accordance with
Article 102 of the United Nations Charter.

This Protocol, the texts of which in the
official languages of the United Nations are
equally authentic, shall be opened for signature at
the Headquarters of the United Nations Secretariat,
at New York City.

_____   _____
For the Government of   For the Government of

_____
For the Government of

Index